T0347763

"Jason can take a daunting amount of difficult information and transform it into something that's enlightening, educational, and thoroughly fascinating. As is so with his blogs, workshops, and other books, Jason is an effervescent and gifted teacher, storyteller, and scholar, and one hell of a writer too! What a delightful read!"

—Debra DeAngelo, author of *The Elements of Horse Spirit:*
The Magical Bond Between Humans and Horses

"*The Horned God of the Witches* is a remarkably well researched, thoughtful, and most importantly personal look at the Horned God. In many ways this book felt like a portrait of the author and their practices, as their passion for the Horned God shrines through in every passage. Comprehensive and approachable, it's a must have for the modern Witch's library."

—Mortellus, author of *Do I Have to Wear Black?*
Rituals, Customs & Funerary Etiquette for Modern Pagans

"Through reliable and fact-checked history, moving rituals, personal anecdotes, and well-informed speculation, Jason Mankey offers the ultimate exploration of this very nuanced and often misunderstood divine figure. Mankey's work is an essential read for anyone wishing to have an informed and well-rounded conversation about every European Witch's darling, the Horned God."

—Katrina Rasbold, author of *Crossroads of Conjure*
and *The Sacred Art of Brujeria*

"*The Horned God of the Witches* takes us on a tour through ancient times and up to the present, casting a fresh light upon many antlered and horned deities that have remained shrouded in mystery through the ages. Mankey offers simple yet meaningful rituals along the way while sharing valuable personal anecdotes from his own practice. This book is a solid must for new and seasoned practitioners who are looking to deepen their rapport with the horned gods."

—Kate Freuler, author of *Of Blood and Bones:*
Working with Shadow Magick & the Dark Moon

"Jason Mankey has given the craft a thorough, in-depth, and enjoyable analysis of the horned god of the witches!"

—Christopher Orapello, artist, cohost of the *Down at the Crossroads* podcast,
and coauthor of *Besom, Stang & Sword*

The
HORNED GOD
of the Witches

© Tymn Urban

ABOUT THE AUTHOR

Jason Mankey is a third-degree Gardnerian High Priest and helps run two Witchcraft covens in the San Francisco Bay Area with his wife, Ari. He is a popular speaker at Pagan and Witchcraft events across North America and Great Britain and has been recognized by his peers as an authority on the Horned God, Wiccan history, and occult influences in rock and roll. Jason writes online at *Raise the Horns* on Patheos Pagan and for the print magazine *Witches & Pagans*. You can follow him on Instagram and Twitter at @panmankey.

the
HORNED GOD
of the WITCHES

JASON MANKEY

Llewellyn Publications
Woodbury, Minnesota

FIRST EDITION
Third Printing, 2023

Cover design by Kevin R. Brown
Cover illustration by Laura Tempest Zakroff

For a list of interior art credits, please see page 275

Llewellyn Publications is a registered trademark of Llewellyn Worldwide Ltd.

Library of Congress Cataloging-in-Publication Data

Names: Mankey, Jason, author.
Title: The horned god of the witches / by Jason Mankey.
Description: First edition. | Woodbury, Minnesota : Llewellyn Worldwide,
    [2021] | Includes bibliographical references and index. | Summary: "This
    book is an in-depth look at the horned god as honored by today's
    witches"—Provided by publisher.
Identifiers: LCCN 2021005678 (print) | LCCN 2021005679 (ebook) | ISBN
    9780738763088 (paperback) | ISBN 9780738763156 (ebook)
Subjects: LCSH: horned god. | Witchcraft. | Paganism.
Classification: LCC BL460 .M26 2021 (print) | LCC BL460 (ebook) | DDC
    299/.942211—dc23
LC record available at https://lccn.loc.gov/2021005678
LC ebook record available at https://lccn.loc.gov/2021005679

Llewellyn Publications
A Division of Llewellyn Worldwide Ltd.
2143 Wooddale Drive
Woodbury, MN 55125-2989
www.llewellyn.com

Printed in the United States of America

OTHER BOOKS BY JASON MANKEY

Llewellyn's Little Book of Yule
(Llewellyn, 2020)

Witch's Wheel of the Year
(Llewellyn, 2019)

Transformative Witchcraft
(Llewellyn, 2019)

The Witch's Altar
(cowritten with Laura Tempest Zakroff, Llewellyn, 2019)

The Witch's Book of Shadows
(Llewellyn, 2017)

The Witch's Athame
(Llewellyn, 2016)

FORTHCOMING BOOKS BY JASON MANKEY

The Witch's Book of Spellcraft:
A Practical Guide to Connecting with the
Magick of Candles, Crystals, Plants & Herbs
(by Jason Mankey, with Matt Cavalli, Ari Mankey,
and Amanda Lynn, Llewellyn, 2022)

The Witch's Guide to the Greek Gods
(cowritten with Astrea Taylor, Llewellyn, 2022)

*This book is dedicated to the memory of
Dwayne Arthur Sortor (1968–2020).*

May your spirit run wild and free, my friend.

CONTENTS

FIGURES

Introduction

FINDING THE HORNED GOD

WITCHCRAFT PRACTICES ARE AS varied as the snowflakes that fall in winter. There are Witches who work in covens and Witches who prefer to work independently. Witchcraft practices can be thousands of years old or exceedingly contemporary. There are Witches who have learned from teachers in group settings and Witches who are self-taught, trusting their intuition and perhaps learning from books and other resources.

Many Witches build their practices around the use of magick, with little use for any other trappings. I know some Witches whose rites are focused almost exclusively on the dead, both those who have died during their lifetimes and also the souls of long-ago ancestors from thousands of years ago. There are Witches whose practices revolve around nature, the turn of the seasons, and the power of the natural world. And then there are Witches like me who work primarily with deities, the most prominent one in my life being the figure most people call the Horned God.

"The Horned God" is a god, a title, and a way of describing particular deities found in the various strains of Modern Witchcraft. The Horned God can even be a Horned Goddess or perhaps have no gender at all, and he's most certainly straight, gay, transgender, and everything in between. I have to assume that as a force greater than mere mortals, deity is complex and most likely appears in different forms to different people.

Over the last eighty years, most authors of Witchcraft books have written about the Horned God as a single, genuinely ancient deity. According to this line of thinking, every horned or antlered deity is simply a reflection of the original *one* Horned God, and all horned and antlered deities share a multitude of traits and characteristics. This is a lovely piece of mythology, but it's just not true. There was never just one horned god in pagan antiquity. Instead, there were a multitude of horned and antlered deities, all of them unique and different, with not all that much in common.

For the last hundred years, the Horned God has been pictured in a variety of ways, but his most important visual attribute is the set of horns or antlers atop his head. Yes, antlers and horns are very different things: horns are permanent structures, while antlers are shed and regrown annually. But pictures of the Horned God have included antlers for a very long time now, and "Antlered God" just doesn't roll off the tongue as easily.

DEFINING THE HORNED GOD

The term *Horned God* means different things to different people. For some, the Horned God is synonymous with nature and wild spaces. This is a Horned God whose journey through the Wheel of the Year mirrors the change of seasons, moving from youthful promise to young adulthood, middle age, and finally death. In my own practice, the Horned God is a figure who stands between two realms: this world and the lands of death.

In many modern myths of the Horned God, he has become a sacrificial deity, giving his own life so that the world may be renewed and made fertile once again. The Horned God's association with fertility has led many to think of him as a god of sex and lust, and as a provider of much that is good and pleasurable in our lives. But the Horned God is generally seen as being more than just a deity of passion and the wineskin; he's representative of a balanced life, a figure who embraces joy but also accepts responsibilities (and lives up to them).

The first modern, public, self-identifying Witch was an Englishman named Gerald Gardner (1884–1964). Today Gardner is hailed by many as the founder or architect of Wiccan-Witchcraft, but his writings on Witchcraft in general have been tremendously influential over the last eighty years. Gardner is quite explicit that the God of the Witches is a god with horns/antlers atop his head, which means the Horned God has been one of Modern Witchcraft's essential deities since Witchcraft became an ongoing, public concern.

In his 1959 book *The Meaning of Witchcraft*, Gardner writes about the Horned God of the Witches as embodying most of the traits he's associated with today. In one particularly striking passage, he calls the Horned One the "Opener of the Doorway of the Womb" and the "Lord of the Gates of Death." But to Gardner, the Horned God was more than just a figure residing in a faraway realm.

Gardner also placed the Horned God firmly in our world as "King of the Wood" and described him as the "renewer of life." More than a deity of the wild spaces, the Horned God was also the "God of Gardens" through his power as the "Phallic God." The Witch God written about by Gardner was nearly limitless, described as the "All Devourer, All-Begetter" and the "Beloved Saviour of the World."[1]

Gardner's Horned God was not just a being with an erect phallus and horns or antlers atop his head. He's the God of the Witches, and one who reigns over many of the currents that guide and shape our lives. Today most Witches see the Horned God in ways similar to that of Gardner (though they may individually emphasize one characteristic more than others). The Horned One is a god of nature, sex, fertility, sacrifice, death, and rebirth, and is also a figure to aspire to. Because these ideas are so important to understanding him, they are worth going over in a bit more detail.

NATURE AND THE NATURAL WORLD

Perhaps first and foremost, the Horned God is a figure that links us to the natural world. He's the god of the wilderness, of dark forests, majestic mountains, and sun-swept prairies. He's the Lord of the Wood and the magick that keeps us firmly rooted in nature, even if we are living in an apartment in a city of a million people.

---

1. Gardner, *The Meaning of Witchcraft*, 176.

Horns and antlers also link the Horned God to wild animals. The Horned God can be seen in the face of a stag or bull. Because many of the antlers and horns atop his head come from game animals, the Horned God is also a deity of responsible and ethical hunting practices.

The Horned God is the personification of nature, which means he can be both gentle and fierce. He is as pleasant as a warm spring day and as powerful as an autumn hurricane. Nature is sometimes scary; we should expect the same from a god who is a part of it.

As a deity who is a part of nature, the Horned God is also the protector of the earth's wild spaces. He's the deity to call on when the government turns its back on preserving the natural world. I'm not sure I'd call the Horned God vengeful, but polluters should probably be worried about him.

SEX, FERTILITY, AND SACRIFICE

As a god of nature, the Horned God is also a god of fertility. Fertility is about more than human babies; it's also about rich soil, blossoming flowers, and ripe fields. In some traditions, the Horned God annually sacrifices his essence in the autumn so that the natural world can be reborn in the spring.

The Horned God is also a god of sexual pleasure. Sex and sexuality are his gifts. They are something to be celebrated when engaged in consensually and not used to shame others. In many myths, the Horned God's sexual interests are strictly female, but history tells a different story. Horned gods like the Greek Pan were equal-opportunity sexual adventurers, loving men, women, their own hand, and everything in between. The Horned God embraces everyone who seeks him, regardless of sexual orientation. He is a life-affirming deity, and sex for pleasure is a life-affirming activity. He wants us to enjoy our time here on Earth, as fleeting as it may be.

In workshops I often describe the Horned God as "horned and horny," because deities that focus primarily on sex seem to be a major part of the Horned God mythos. If there's one identifying feature of the Horned God other than the horns (especially the many male versions), it's the erect phallus. Depictions of the Horned God are not required to include a raging boner, but it's become fairly common. Even gods who weren't pictured in antiquity with erect phalluses, like the Gaulish-Celtic Cernunnos, are sometimes now depicted with an excited member. How sexual the Horned God is probably depends on how horny we need him to be in our own lives.

DEATH AND RESURRECTION

It stands to reason that as a god of the natural world, the Horned God is also the Lord of Death. Without death, there is no life; both are necessary to keep the world going. A god of the hunt is also a deliverer of death, further linking the Horned God to the world beyond this one. The French phrase *la petite mort* translates as "the little death" and generally refers to orgasm, so there's that too!

But the Horned God does more than just usher souls into the realm of the dead; he also gives them safe passage back to the land of the living. For Witches who believe in reincarnation, it's often the Horned God who guards the portal between the Summerlands and this world.[2] It's this aspect of the Horned God who rules at the sabbat of Samhain and stands in wait for us when our mortal bodies die.

A MORE PERFECT MAN

One of my earliest memories of the Horned God did not come from personal experience or from a book, but rather from a cover image of *Green Egg* magazine, a periodical that was especially popular among Pagans in the 1990s. On that cover, the Horned God held up a young child in his hands above his head, with a giant smile on his face. It was an image filled with joy, of a figure who knew and understood his responsibilities.

In a world full of misogynists, racists, bigots, and other assholes, the Horned God is a figure to aspire to. He is a father, a lover, a nurturer, and a protector. He represents the best of what we can be. In a world where we

---

2. The term *Summerlands* is used by many Witches to indicate the land of the dead. The term comes from the practice of Spiritualism and the Theosophical Society, who use it for that purpose as well.

too often feel let down by those around us, the Horned God is a figure who always rises to the occasion.

Unlike some other deities, the Horned God is not a god of judgment. His disapproval is reserved for those who put themselves ahead of others and the natural world. He wants us to be happy, to live a life of joy and pleasure, but only if we can live that life without impeding the free will of others.

THE HORNED GOD, THE HORNED GODS, AND WITCHES

When I refer to the Horned God in this book, in my mind I'm referencing a very real god. To me, he is more than just a title or a type of energy; he's a distinct being most likely created from several different parts. In my mind, the Horned God is part Pan and part Cernunnos, and also contains just a little bit of the Christian Devil and several other small bits. In this book we'll be exploring all of those different angles. Sections of the book will also focus on specific *horned gods*, a general term that does not indicate a specific being.

I've also attempted to limit the focus of this book to the Horned God as worshipped by Modern Witches today. I believe that most cultures have a figure we might label as a "horned god," but I'm not sure they should be included in a book specifically for Witches. While Witches are free to work with whatever deities call to them, I think it's in poor taste to include extensive material on powers and deities who are still actively worked with and worshipped in cultures outside of Modern Witchcraft. This means I've decided not to write about figures such as the Hindu Shiva and the Navajo Kokopelli (more accurately known as Kookopölö). For those of you looking for more information on such gods, I hope you'll consult the bibliography for more information or visit with the people who actively work with those gods.

This book also has a very European slant, which I apologize for in advance, but the Horned God as experienced by most self-identified Modern Witches has its deepest roots in Europe. While I find both the use of horns in ancient China and the symbolism of the phallus in ancient India to be fascinating, they just didn't feel appropriate to include in this book. As stated above, there's a pretty long bibliography in the back for those interested in additional information on such things. (This book is already pretty long and includes over 280 footnotes. I think my editors would scream if I made it any longer.)

The Horned God as we know him today is both an ancient and a modern construct, and the way this book is laid out reflects that. After exploring the nature of deity, I chose to start this book by relating the Horned One's most prevalent myth in Modern Witchcraft circles and exploring the most ancient aspects of the Horned God: antler, horn, and phallus imagery. Then I examine two specific deities, Pan and Cernunnos. The story of the Horned God is the story of Cernunnos and Pan more so than any other two gods, both in the way they were worshipped in the ancient world and how they've been reinterpreted in ours.

From there, the book spends some time with a couple of more modern horned gods: Herne, Elen of the Ways, and the Green Man. I call these aspects of the Horned One "more modern" for reasons that will become apparent later in the text. While these figures are most likely not as ancient as Pan and Cernunnos, they are certainly very real and tangible deities, and are important to me as well. Most of the sections about specific deities include activities designed to help you, the reader, grow closer to them.

My original outline of this book included a ritual for every god mentioned in these pages. In the course of writing all of those rituals, I realized that many of them felt repetitive, and besides, there are a multitude of ways to grow closer to deity outside of ritual. Divination, altars, and magick, along with ritual, are all great ways to access the Horned God in his many guises. I find history interesting, but the most important thing in Witchcraft is to grow closer to the things you honor, which is why activities are important.

Over the last two hundred years, the Horned God has been influenced by a variety of literary sources. Most of that literature has focused on the Horned One in one of three aspects: nature deity, death god, and a being somehow associated with the Christian Devil. Most of the book's middle section focuses on these three aspects, along with a few side journeys into various things that didn't quite fit anywhere else in these pages.

That bit about the Horned One being associated with the Christian Devil can be a bit troubling to some, so let me expand upon it a bit. The Horned God of the Witches has never been the Christian Devil, but he has been influenced by how certain people have interpreted the Christian Devil over the centuries. Writings about the Devil have shown up in books about the Horned God and have contributed to our understanding of him, but that does not mean Pan or the Green Man is ruling over an Underworld full of fire and brimstone. I'll also add that some Witches really like to play up the links between the Horned God and the Devil not because they are especially wicked, but because it's fun to piss off uptight Christians.

The last part of the book looks at how the Horned God is viewed and has been reinterpreted over the past few decades in the traditions of Wiccan-Witchcraft and Traditional Witchcraft. The book ends with a ritual to the *Witchfather*, a version of the Horned God in Traditional Witchcraft, and one who is especially appealing to me. In many ways, the book's first ritual (Ritual to Meet the Horned God) and its last (Ritual to Meet the Witchfather) can be seen as mirror opposites. The first ritual serves as an introduction to the Horned God's mysteries, while the final ritual is a chance to receive the gifts he willingly gives to his Witches.

There are many individuals who choose to capitalize pronouns such as *his* and *he* when they refer to a specific deity. This is a practice I've never truly adopted, so I made the decision not to use it in this book. Some might find that choice disrespectful to the Horned One, but since he has allowed me to write this book, I feel like everything is fine in our relationship.

A book such as this one cries out for dozens of pictures, and in my travels over the last ten years, I've seen many of the things I write about in these pages. However, the copyright law when it comes to pictures is infuriatingly difficult to navigate. Just because you take a picture at a museum does not give you the right to use that picture in a book. However, we are lucky enough to live in an age where most of us have access to the internet, which is home to most everything mentioned in these pages. In other words, with a little work, you should be able to find the images I mention that were not included.

It's also truly my hope that no matter how you interpret the power of the Horned One, you will find something worthwhile in these pages. The hooves of the Horned God have been guiding my Witchcraft journey for over twenty years now. If you so choose, may they guide yours as well. Hail the Horned One!

Chapter One

THE NATURE OF DEITY

PERHAPS MY FAVORITE ANALOGY for describing the Horned God involves Play-Doh. For those of you who have blocked out parts of your childhood, Play-Doh is a soft, easily sculpted (and smooshed) putty-like material made primarily of flour and water. It's fun because you can build whatever you want out of it, and most of us have played with it at some point in our lives.

Now, the Horned God is most certainly not Play-Doh, but how we use that substance often reminds me of how various individuals see and interpret him. There are some people who like to build very precise sculptures with Play-Doh, and in our analogy, perhaps they build models of Pan and Cernunnos, with each figure being a solid color. During that play, they are very careful not to let the two gods come into contact with each other, because the different colors of Play-Doh can't really be separated after that happens. When they are done playing, they put the different colors of Play-Doh back in their own specific containers so the colors don't bleed together.

Then there are those people who like to use various colors of Play-Doh in the same sculpture, with the end result usually being streaks of blue or green running through a mostly red sculpture. This is how I used to create things when I was a kid. I didn't mind mixing my colors a little bit here and there, but I tried to keep them mostly separate. That was hard to do, and when I realized that there would be some mixing no matter what I did, I learned to live with it. When I was done playing, I'd try to put things away as neatly as I could, but my red Play-Doh sometimes ended up with a slight purple tint or perhaps a vein of yellow running through it.

Finally, there are always some people who are completely fine with letting all of their colors of Play-Doh mix together. The end result is usually a brown lump, with perhaps a few colored streaks running through it. For some people, having all the colors mix together is upsetting, but four cans of brown Play-Doh are still fun. You can still build whatever you want out of it and you don't have to worry about keeping the different colors of dough apart. Not having to worry about messing anything up often makes play more fun! Besides, if you want a specific color later, you can buy (or make) a new jar of it.

The Horned God is a lot like Play-Doh. There are some people who prefer to work only with individual models, and when they are done, everything goes back to where it started. Then there are some who are okay with a little bleed-through here and there but mostly keep things separate. And finally, there are those who let everything mix together. The Horned God has worshippers who honor only specific deities, others who see those individual gods as somewhat mergeable, and those who see all of the horned gods in history as part of one big Horned God, with very little separation.

There are many different ways to interpret deity, and no right or wrong way. I believe deity reveals itself to us in whatever way makes the most sense to our personal sensibilities. The various ways humans perceive deity is useful to go over in a book like this, but ultimately our interpretations are ours alone. Some of us put the Play-Doh back into separate cans, and some of us don't mind ending up with one big brown lump.

MANY IDEAS ABOUT DEITY

Witchcraft does not require a belief in gods, nor does it subscribe to any absolutes when it comes to religious or spiritual practice. For those of us who do believe in deity, there are a variety of cosmologies and explanations for that deity. Because the term Horned God means so many things to various Witches, it's worth spending some time contemplating the many ideas held by today's Witches when it comes to matters of deity.

Polytheism

There are many Witches today who are strict polytheists, which means they believe that individual deities are just that: individuals, and not a part of a greater whole. In other words, every deity who has ever been worshipped is unique unto themselves. Perhaps certain deities are related in some way, but they are related like you and I are related to our parents.

Polytheist Witches who use the term Horned God do so generally as a title, or as a way to describe certain specific gods. I have friends who use *Horned God* as a title, so when they call to "the Horned God," they are actually calling to specific deities such as Pan or Cernunnos but not using the names of those gods. Many polytheist Witches also use the term *horned god* (lowercase) as a way to categorize deities who are connected in some way to the natural world.

Soft Polytheism

Soft polytheism is a term reserved for those who look at deities as separate entities but still believe they might be related in some way. For example, we know that the gods Odin (Norse) and Woden (German) have a common ancestor, but a hard polytheist would say they are two different beings. A soft polytheist would argue the two are most likely the same god, just worshipped by two different names.

As a soft polytheist, I think gods like Pan and Cernunnos are distinct beings who don't have much in common, but I also believe they might be related in some abstract way. The end result is a "bigger" deity who shares attributes with several other gods. This all sounds rather confusing, but I have to assume that deity is more powerful than we are, and very different too! I think our modern Horned God is a combination of several figures that have come together so that we might better understand them. In my own practice, I honor those figures by their individual names, and sometimes collectively as the Horned God.

The Billionity, or All Gods Are One God

There are many who believe that all the deities that have ever been worshipped are related in some way. At the very beginning was an unknowable power that started by dividing itself into various ways of being: female, male, and all that lies between those two polarities. From there, those powers divided into more knowable forms, deities we know by generic names, such as Maiden, Mother, Crone, Horned God, Sun God, and so on.

In this sort of cosmology, all of the various horned (and antlered) gods that have ever been worshipped are aspects of one greater Horned God, who has chosen to reveal himself in various guises throughout the world. In India, he was Shiva; in Gaul, Cernunnos; in Rome, Faunus; and in Greece, Pan. The gods in this sort of construct are still somewhat distinct but can be traced back to an original source. When I was working with a college student group back in the early 2000s, someone described this theory as the *Billionity*, as opposed to the Christian *trinity*.

Duotheism

Many Wiccan-Witches are often accused of being *duotheists*. The idea is similar to the one above, the only difference being that there is one "Goddess" and one "God" who are each responsible for the various manifestations of male and female found throughout the world today. Much of the liturgy in Wicca sounds like duotheism, but I have yet to meet a Wiccan who actively self-identifies this way. It also limits sexuality to strict constructs of male and female, an idea no longer supported by science or the reality we live in.

Energies

There are some Witches who believe that deities are more akin to "energies" than to beings with a consciousness. When they invoke the Horned God, for example, they are invoking the wild energies of the earth for use in their magick or rituals. Gods as energies don't "think" like you or I do, but they can still affect our reality. For those who subscribe to this interpretation of deity, earth energies are natural things that exist around us, and to better understand them, we give them names and titles like the Horned God.

Though I'm not a believer in this theory, I do know that the energy of deities can transform us. When we call out to the Horned God and he chooses to show up, his energy has an impact on how we behave and act. Horned God energy might result, for example, in someone becoming sexually excited or feeling closer to the natural world.

The Gods Are Manifestations of Something Inside of Ourselves

I know several Witches who see figures like the Horned God as something from inside of ourselves. To them, the Horned God represents our relationship with the natural world, Witchcraft, and sex. He's a focus for rituals and rites, but his power comes from inside of us. According to this line of thinking, gods and goddesses are human constructs created to give us a sense of direction and purpose.

The Gods Are Not Real and Are Not Energies

There are very devout atheist Witches and Pagans in the world today. They don't believe in deities and don't even interpret those deities as the natural energies of the earth, yet they will often use terms such as the Horned God. In such instances, they are generally putting a poetic spin on references to the world's wild spaces and the mysteries of nature. To them, the Horned God is a term that represents the wonder of the natural world and the mysteries of love, lust, and union.

The Witch world is wide and diverse, and there are as many interpretations of just what deity is as there are Witches. When it comes to issues of theology, there are no absolutes. You might have found yourself nodding along with some of the ideas presented here, or perhaps your own beliefs are best represented by a combination of these ideas. There is no right or wrong, but just what works for you!

Chapter Two
MYTH AND ANCIENT HISTORY

THE 1990S WERE ONE OF THE most formative decades in the history of Modern Witchcraft. It was a decade that began with letter writing and print magazines and ended with email and blogs. It was a boom period for Witchcraft books written by actual Witches, and those books could be found just about everywhere. It was the era of the book superstore, which featured shelves overflowing with magickal and occult topics.

Despite all of those books (and the explosion in Witchcraft's popularity during the period), there wasn't much out there about the history of the Craft and figures like the Horned God, and the material that was available on those topics often wasn't very reliable. The history written about during this period was just as much hearsay as it was documented fact, and that hearsay was repeated online, in books, and around campfires at large Pagan gatherings.

The lack of quality information wasn't really anyone's fault; it simply didn't exist at the time. Scholars had yet to begin taking Modern Witchcraft and its deities seriously as an academic discipline, and the studies that were available were generally in difficult-to-access scholarly journals and books. We take the free flow of information for granted today, but research was far more difficult even just thirty years ago. "Histories" that make me laugh a bit today were simply the best most authors could do at the time.

In fairness, a lot of the bad information came from academic sources that had been popular in previous decades. Witches like Gerald Gardner took their history from books printed in the early twentieth century, then that particular version of history was shared again and again, with no one ever really bothering to check to see if it still held up. Many of the most popular Witch books ever published (and most of them are still bestsellers today) contain history that just doesn't hold up, but for many people, that history has been difficult to let go of.

The stories about the history of the Horned God that I heard growing up in the 1990s are what I've come to call *The Myth of the Horned God and Witchcraft*, and I call this body of work a *myth* for a very particular reason: because some of it is true. Not only true in the sense that there's a kernel of historicity there, but also true in a mythological sense. Our now-antiquated versions of the Horned God's history connect us with our ancient ancestors and to our more recent Craft ancestors who shared those stories.

The *myth* of the Horned God is worth telling because of the connections that arise from it. It's also worth retelling because it's still very present in the world of Witchcraft today. It's a tale that is still told around campfires, and often held onto as if it were holy writ, despite not holding up to academic scrutiny. It's a history that is also still present in a lot of Witchcraft books, and it's a history that speaks to a lot of people. No book on the Horned God would be complete without it.

THE MYTH OF THE HORNED GOD

Fifteen thousand years ago in the darkness of a massive system of caves located in modern-day France, some unknown person painted the first picture of the Horned God. Though he doesn't quite look like the Horned God many of us know today, he's still recognizable. His feet are those of a man and he stands upright, and he has a tail, perhaps so that all might see his animal nature. His body is covered in fur, but he clearly has hands instead of hooves or paws. His eyes are recognizable as human, though there's an odd owl-like appearance to his face. Most impressively of all, he has the antlers of a stag atop his head, and in that spot, they look completely natural. The antlers are no crown, but a part of his very being.

The animal attributes, so clearly visible on that cave wall, portray his connection to the earth and the natural world. This was no god of war or god of the sky; the Horned God was the deity of mountains, plains, and forests. His animal nature also revealed him to be a god of lust, sex, and physical desire. In addition to his horns, he was a god to whom the phallus was sacred. Over time, worship of this Horned God would spread from the cave where he was born throughout Europe and later the entire world.

The Greeks would come to know this deity as Pan, god of shepherds and the mountains of the Greek region known as Arcadia. Pan was a sexual god par excellence, and over time he would become one of the most popular gods of both Greece and later the Roman Empire. His praises would be sung (and snogged) from Britain to India.

Back in France (then known as Gaul), the Horned God came to be known as Cernunnos among the Celts who lived there. He, too, was a god of sexual desire and connection to the land, and was praised as the supreme deity of that land. Eventually the Celts of Gaul took his worship across the English Channel and into the land known as Great Britain.

In Britain, the Horned God adopted other names, though these were all clearly the same horned deity. In English folklore, he became known as Herne, god of the woods and of the Wild Hunt. In the area of Sherwood Forest, he was called Robin Hood, and in other places he was known as Puck or Jack in the Green. Wherever one went in the British Isles, one would find the Horned God.

Over time, the Horned God would end up everywhere, all because of that image on a cave wall first envisioned over ten thousand years ago. Every culture has their own version of him, but in all those places he's essentially the same: a god of nature and fertility. The images might change a little bit from place to place, but no matter the location, the figure is still essentially Pan/Cernunnos, the one Horned God.

By the end of the Middle Ages, Christians had had enough of the Horned God's influence on Europe's Witches and Pagans, and thus began the Burning

Times. Christians turned the Horned God of the Old Religion into the Devil of their new religion, forever polluting and corrupting how most people see him. In order to extinguish the Horned God's worship, they executed his followers, and upwards of nine million people, mostly women, died as a result.

With the *alleged* triumph of Christianity in Europe, the Horned God went underground, though he was still much loved by the common people. In order to keep his memory alive, they built his face into the temples and cathedrals of the new religion, which is why the Green Man greets so many Christians at their places of worship. Away from the cathedrals, Europe's Witches kept the Horned God alive, calling him Old Hornie (in honor of his horns and his lusty nature) and making him the center of their rites.

Over the centuries, the Horned God survived in secret through the rites and whispers of the Witches who kept his faith alive. Meeting in secret, these Witches would celebrate the fertility of the earth and sing the praises of Old Hornie and then eventually share their religion with younger family members. In this way, the secrets of Witchcraft and the Horned God survived to the present day.

By the start of the twentieth century, beliefs in things such as Witchcraft were no longer punishable by death, and both Witches and the Horned God reemerged in society. With the need for secrecy gone, Witches began writing about their beliefs and sharing their gods with the general public, bringing us to today and this book.

When I first found Witchcraft in the early 1990s, the story you just read (and/or something similar) was common in both books and conversations with other Witches. For many people, it was something akin to holy writ, absolutely unimpeachable and the stone-cold truth about the Horned God and the Craft. Unfortunately, except for a few points, most of what you just read is simply not true.

There are thousands of years separating Pan and the cave figure from France (generally known as "the Sorcerer"), with nothing in between connecting the two. In addition, the Sorcerer had antlers on top of his head and most certainly not the horns of a goat, which are two very different things. It's also likely that gods such as Pan and Cernunnos arose independently of one another, each one a product of the people who worshipped them and the lands that sustained those people.

Most spiritual pantheons, whether Greek, Norse, Native American, Yoruba, Sumerian, or Celtic, have some sort of nature deity or spirit and, more often than not, a figure related to sexual pleasure and/or fertility. It's possible that all of these figures are connected by some long-ago ancestor, but not very likely. Also, all of those figures have their own mythologies, stories, and modes of worship, which most often share only superficial attributes.

It is true that alleged Witches were persecuted and executed during the late Middle Ages and early modern period, and before that Pagan gods were often labeled as demons by overzealous Christians. But there is no evidence to suggest that the "witches" executed during that time were practicing an ancient pagan religion in secret.[3] The number of people estimated to have been executed during that time has been extensively revised too, with most scholars suggesting that the actual number of people executed for Witchcraft was 40,000 to 100,000 individuals.

The story of the Horned God outlined above comes primarily from the work of Dr. Margaret Alice Murray (1863–1963), and the most readable synthesis of it appears in her book *The God of the Witches*, first published in 1931. Murray was a brilliant Egyptologist and a true trailblazer for women in academia, but her work concerning the history of the Horned God and Witchcraft was often problematic. In fairness to Murray, her work on the history of Witches was more of a hobby than her life's calling, but in many circles (especially Witch ones), it's what she's most remembered for.

Though Murray's work involving the Horned God has not been taken seriously by most scholars since at least the 1970s (and in most instances even before that), her work has resonated strongly for nearly a hundred years now.[4] It would probably be best to think of Murray's story of the Horned God as mythology and not history. It's a powerful story and suggests how strongly people have needed figures like the Horned God over the centuries.

---

3. Hutton, *The Triumph of the Moon*, 376.

4. Hutton, *The Triumph of the Moon*, 375.

It also speaks to many of us today, even those of us who know that it's not literally true.

Margaret Murray is a name that will show up dozens of times in this book because her vision of the Horned God was so instrumental in how we perceive him today. I also believe that she was the first person to think of the Horned God (and horned gods) as a category of the divine. It's likely that you and I wouldn't be sharing these words right now if not for the work of Murray, and while I'm often critical of her, I'm also extremely appreciative.

And Murray didn't get everything wrong. The Myth of the Horned God does contain a grain of truth. There were horned gods in the ancient world, and people who practiced magick in the Middle Ages, and people who truly found solace in the natural world at the start of the modern era. Pieces of the story are true, and how we put them together in our hearts and minds helps to shape how we see the Horned One. There was also a very real horned figure on that cave wall all those thousands of years ago, and the real story of that figure is worth telling.

THE SORCERER AT TROIS-FRÈRES

Scattered throughout modern-day France, Spain, and Portugal are hundreds of caves featuring images of animals (both real and imaginary) painted and carved onto the rock walls. The art in some of these caves dates back over 30,000 years to a period of time known as the Upper Paleolithic, or Old Stone Age. The art in many of the caves is quite sophisticated, and there are images of animals in them that capture movement and facial expressions.

In a few of these caves are images of half-human, half-animal hybrids. The most common images feature bison with humanlike appendages, but there's also at least one bird-person. Many people assume that these images depict the first deities worshipped and/or honored by humans, but no one is quite sure. The exact culture of the people who painted these caves is unknown, but many of the caves were used for thousands upon thousands of years.

Whatever went on in the painted caves of Europe was an ongoing concern for longer than any modern religion has existed. Two or four thousand years feels like an eternity to us, but the people (or perhaps peoples) who used Europe's caves did so continually for over 25,000 years. If the caves were indeed used for religion, then the religion they were used for is the longest-lasting one in human history.

Europe's oldest figurative cave art depicting clearly identifiable animals comes from Chauvet Cave in Southern France and was probably created over 36,500 years ago.[5] Rediscovered in the 1990s, it was the subject of the 2010 documentary film *Cave of Forgotten Dreams*. (The oldest cave paintings of all from the island of Sulawesi, part of modern-day Indonesia, and are over 40,000 years old!) The most famous of Europe's painted caves is Lascaux (also in France), whose paintings are only 20,000 years old and include striking images of horses and bulls.

Most of the caves include handprints that might have been left by those who painted and carved the caves of the prehistoric world. Instead of tracing their hands, these ancient artists blew pigment around their hands and pressed them against the cave walls to create prints.[6] This gives the handprints an otherworldly quality. Judging by the prints, the artists who painted and carved these ancient caves were predominantly women, as three-quarters of the handprints discovered by archaeologists seem to be the hands of women.[7]

When it comes to the Horned God, the most interesting of these caves is the *Grotte des Trois-Frères*, the Cave of the Three Brothers, in modern-day France. This cave is a relative newcomer compared to Lascaux and Chauvet, with most of its images being only about 15,000 years old. Rediscovered in the early 1910s, Trois-Frères contains several unique elements missing from its cave brethren, and several figures that could be a horned god. Whatever was going on at Trois-Frères, it seems as if horned and antlered creatures were rather important.

Though I'm using the term *cave* to describe Trois-Frères, it's best to think of a cave such as this one as a series of interconnected rooms. The most interesting elements of Trois-Frères appear nearly three-quarters of a mile in,

5. Perkins, "An Early Start for Some of Europe's Oldest Cave Art."

6. Curtis, *The Cave Painters*, 172.

7. Hughes, "Were the First Artists Mostly Women?"

where visitors are greeted by two clay sculptures of bison. There's nothing comparable to those bison in the rest of Europe's caves. Deeper into the cave there is a room featuring a carving of a lion, and one passageway containing a carefully placed seashell, most likely used for some sort of devotional purpose.[8]

The most famous room at Trois-Frères is known as the "Sanctuary" and is located deep within the cave. The Sanctuary is famous for a couple of reasons, the first being a large wall featuring thousands of carvings of animals, both real and imaginary. The animals on this wall, which extends dozens of yards, are carved one on top of another, so that it almost looks like a jumbled mess. The animal carvings extend so far that they all probably have not been documented yet.

In the middle of the engravings found in the Sanctuary is an image unlike any of the others. The figure clearly has the head and horns of a bison, but his arms and legs appear human (figure 1). The figure's penis is clearly visible between his legs as well, and, most astonishingly, this "Bison-Man" seems to be carrying a tool of some sort. At first glance, that tool appears to be a hunting bow, but it would be thousands more years before bows and arrows were created.

It's much more likely that the tool is a nose flute, one of the earliest instruments known to human beings. This makes even more sense the more we look at Bison-Man's feet and legs, which appear to be engaged in some sort of movement, such as dancing. Unfortunately, the other carved figures around Bison-Man shed very little light on his activities. With the exception of one cowlike creature, most of the animals carved around him don't seem to note his presence.

Because the cave painters (and carvers) of Trois-Frères did their work long before alphabets were created, we have no idea what Bison-Man and the animals around him are meant to represent. It's possible that Bison-Man is a

---

8. The details of our journey of Trois-Frères come mostly from Gregory Curtis's 2006 book *The Cave Painters*. Curtis's adventure can be found on pages 172–186 of his book. Fewer than perhaps three thousand people have ever been in Trois-Frères, so I sort of have to rely on outside information.

person dressed in animal skins, wearing the head of a bison. It's possible that he's in the middle of hunting animals (even if he's not using a bow). Bison-Man is generally depicted as standing up, but he could also be crawling on the ground. (Flip this page and you'll see what I mean.) If he is crawling, it lends credence to the idea that he's a hunter. He also could be some sort of ancient shaman, dancing in order to ensure a successful hunt. Though we don't know if people 15,000 years ago worshipped deities, he could also be a god (or demigod), but there's no way to prove that. Whatever Bison-Man is, and whatever he's doing, it's unique.

Figure 1: Henri Breuil's drawing of the Bison-Man at Trois-Frères.
Is the figure walking, dancing, or crawling?

A second Bison-Man appears even deeper in the Sanctuary room and sports an even more noticeable phallus. This Bison-Man is surrounded almost entirely by bison and horses, and is missing the nose flute, which might make it more likely, or less likely (who knows), that he's hunting. We will probably never know for sure.

Also in the Sanctuary room is the image that Trois-Frères is most famous for: the Sorcerer. The most reproduced version of the image isn't a photograph, but a drawing by the first man to excavate Trois-Frères, Catholic monk and archaeologist Henri Breuil (1877–1961). Breuil's drawing of the figure is far more detailed than the image that appears in photographs, and more well-known too (figure 2). Breuil's Sorcerer (a name coined by the priest, since he originally believed the figure was a shaman or magician) has extremely large eyes and very detailed hands and feet. Breuil's drawing makes the Sorcerer look like a man in a suit being X-rayed. This image is so iconic that some people, upon seeing a photograph of the Sorcerer, are a bit disappointed.

Figure 2: The Sorcerer as drawn by Henri Breuil.
The image in the cave lacks the detail found in this drawing,
but this image of the Sorcerer has become the most famous.

But I would argue that there's no reason for disappointment. Even if the Sorcerer doesn't appear in his cave as vividly as we might like, he's still striking. Unlike the other images around him, the Sorcerer is both a painted and a carved figure. His outline is carved directly into the cave wall and outlined with black paint. His placement in the Sanctuary was chosen to make it seem like he is looking down at you when you're in the room, and surveying both you and the animals below.

The Sorcerer is not a huge image, but is larger than most others in the cave. He's about two and a half feet tall and eighteen inches across. His phallus is clearly visible, but there's also an easily seen tail and a body that almost looks like a horse. The horns can be hard to make out because they are carved and not painted over, but they are easy enough to see, as are the figure's eyes. Less noticeable are his beard and moustache.

If Bison-Man is an enigma, then the Sorcerer might be an even bigger one. It's possible that he is also dancing, but there's no nose flute to base that conjecture on. He seems separate from the carvings below him, and yet lords over them impressively. If he truly was a god, as Margaret Murray first suggested (something that Breuil would later come to believe as well), then he was a magnificent (and ancient) god.[9]

We will probably never know what went on in caves such as Trois-Frères. Some think that the caves served as a sort of sympathetic hunting magick (like attracts like: images of animals produce animals), while others think they served some sort of religious function. They might have also chronicled an individual group's history in a given area or served as a repository for dream images. It's even been proposed that they are all extensive outcroppings of ancient graffiti, and served no higher purpose than that. (This last theory especially seems absurd, given the care and work that went into the images.)

It's possible that figures like the Sorcerer had a variety of meanings. To some people, the figures might have been connected to hunting, while others might have used them as some sort of divine inspiration or way of connecting to higher powers. In my own ritual room, there's an image of the Sorcerer hanging on the wall, and he looks down upon my coven much like the original image might have looked down upon people 15,000 years ago. Whatever the Sorcerer was or might have been, he seems like an excellent place to begin our search for the Horned God.

---

9. Hutton, *Witches, Druids, and King Arthur,* 33 and 34.

Chapter Three
RITUAL TO MEET THE HORNED GOD

THERE IS NO RIGHT OR wrong way to "meet" the Horned God, and most of us who honor him in our rites and practices have our own individual meeting stories. Many who know the Horned God have specifically felt his "call," meaning they felt him reaching out and initiating a relationship. Others have introduced themselves to the Horned God after becoming acquainted with him in Witchcraft or mythology books. I'm sure there are some folks who have met him in their dreams or perhaps simply heard him whisper to them while out in nature.

This ritual is designed mostly for those who have yet to truly experience the Horned God. It serves as a way of introducing new Witches to the Horned One, and as a way for Old Hornie to reveal something of himself as well. If you are an experienced practitioner, this ritual might feel a bit simplistic or unnecessary, and I totally understand if you want to skip to some of the meatier rituals in this book. But everyone has to start somewhere, and this ritual is designed to fill that need, and also serves as a good reintroduction to the mysteries of the Horned God if it's been a while.

Ideally this ritual should be performed outdoors in a secluded spot. If that's not possible, I recommend doing it near a window so you can capture at least a little bit of sun or moonlight. Because this ritual attempts to capture all of the many varied attributes of the Horned God, enacting it at a liminal time such as the evening is ideal. (Sunrise would also work here if you are an early riser.) I've tried to keep this rite as simple as possible for those who might have to enact it in a public place such as a park or shared green space.

Like many of the rituals in this book, this rite is built around the idea of *reciprocity.* The gods are not simply an ATM machine for us to utilize when we have a problem or obstacle to overcome; our relationships with them require that we give as well as receive. If I'm going to ask a god for something, I should be prepared to give them something in return, and what I give them should mean something to me. If you see the gods as energies or powers without consciousness, then give your offerings to the power of the earth and the natural world instead.

Offerings should be meaningful, but they should not be a burden or put you in any sort of jeopardy. No god who has your best interest in mind is going to ask for all of your rent money or for you to sacrifice your cat. A "meaningful" offering is simply something within your means that you value. Giving the Horned God a bottle of cheap beer that you would never drink is not meaningful. Pouring half a glass of good wine onto the ground in honor of the Horned One is a meaningful offering!

For the rituals in this book, I've decided against including the "opening frame" in every rite, which means the quarter calls, cleansings, circle castings, etc., are not on these pages. For those looking for such things, they can be found in thousands of other books and online in various places. If you like my writing (and I hope you do!), you can find dozens of differing setups for your ritual space in my book *Witch's Wheel of the Year: Rituals for Circles, Solitaries & Covens.* This ritual is designed for the solitary Witch, but can easily be adapted for groups. Just be sure to buy enough supplies for everyone involved.

RITUAL SUPPLIES

For this ritual you will need:

- At least two acorns or other large seeds (You'll be placing these in the ground, so you might also need a garden trowel, though I find a large spoon usually works pretty well.)

- A small bowl of earth/soil (if you're doing this ritual indoors)
- A glass of wine or other beverage (What's important here is to pick a drink that you truly enjoy. That could be wine, cider, beer, whisky, or your favorite latte. What's most important is that it's a drink you value. It doesn't have to be alcoholic.)
- A skeleton or other ornamental key (If a key is not possible or you simply hate keys, a stone will work here as well.)
- A glass of water
- Cakes and ale (food and drink for grounding after the ritual)
- Whatever ritual tools you normally use

THE RITE

Set up your ritual space and then ask the Horned God to join you. If you are in a public (or semi-public) space, you don't have to say the words below out loud. Instead, you can simply read them silently while projecting their intentions outward. Say or read:

This day I seek the Horned One! I call to him as the god of the earth and the protector of the wild spaces. I reach out to him as the god of love, lust, and life; he who wants us to be happy and fulfilled. I seek the god of balance, of life and death, who holds us all in his hands.

Great Horned One, I wish to walk with you and experience your mysteries! Be a part of my life in this world and the next. Stand beside me so that I might know you and receive your blessings. I call to you of my own free will and ask you to be here with me if it pleases thee.

To the Horned God I say, "Hail and welcome!"

After calling the Horned God, close your eyes for a moment and tune in to the world around you. Does everything feel calm, or at least as it should? If, after calling the Horned God, it suddenly starts raining or a bunch of people come traipsing into your ritual space, that may be a sign that this is not the time to seek the Horned One. Gods don't always communicate through words like human beings do, so pay attention to your surroundings. Notice the breeze, the sun or moon, and everything that's around you. If all is as it should be, then proceed with the rite.

Begin by picking up your acorns (or seeds) and holding them in your dominant hand. Feel their energy pulse and flow in your hand, and think about how a tiny acorn grows to be a mighty oak. Once you've felt the power of the acorns in your hand, set them down and then, using your trowel or spoon, dig up a little bit of the earth near you. You don't have to dig very deep into the ground; just enough that your acorns will rest comfortably in the earth. Don't be worried about getting your hands dirty either. Take a moment to feel the dirt and soil you are digging up.

Now place your hands in the dirt and your acorns in the spot that you've dug up (or in the jar of soil, if you're indoors). Take a moment to notice the energy of the earth that comes from the ground. Feel the earth's power, its warmth and its pain. Draw that energy up into your body, through your hands, through your arms, and then into your body. Even if it's cold outside, that energy should feel warm and comforting. Once the earth's energy is inside of you, push some of your own energy into the ground and into the acorns nesting there. Say or read:

> *Guardian of the wild spaces, defender of the earth, Lord of nature's cycle, I have felt your power come to me in the earth. I have felt your power in the smallest seed and have touched your mysteries in the dust. As a follower of the Horned One, I am a part of this world, not separated from it. I have dominion only over myself and swear to be the best steward of this world that I can be. I give my energy to the earth and take energy from the earth. As a Witch, it has always been thus and always will be this way, for the heartbeat of the earth is the pulse of the Horned God!*

> *To you, Great One, I leave this acorn as a symbol and an offering. I am of the web! And I take this acorn with me as a reminder of who and what I am, and of my promise made this night. [Take your one remaining acorn out of the ground.] Horned Lord, bless this seed and may it pulse with your*

power! As we have shared our energies together this night, may I know you as
you now know me. So mote it be!

If your hands are especially dirty, take a moment to clean them off, then pick up your glass full of sacred beverage. Look upon the surface of your drink and then swirl it a bit. As you swirl the drink, let your mind drift a little, and envision all the things you want to do going forward as a Witch. Think of the magick you will work, but also think of the happiness that comes from the Craft.

Witchcraft is not a cosmic game of "good and bad." The gods, and especially the Horned God, want us to be happy as long as our happiness doesn't impede the free will and happiness of others. This means things such as consensual sex (or choosing not to have sex) are to be celebrated and not vilified. Imagine yourself laughing with others and simply enjoying life. The Horned God is not just a god of the earth; he's a god of the now, and derives pleasure from our pleasure.

As you swirl your drink and begin to let your mind wander, ask the Horned God for the gift of sight and look deeply into your glass. There you might catch glimpses of the future, or perhaps see an image of him so that you might know him better. Or you might see nothing at all, simply content to envision things within your mind's eye. When you are satisfied that you've seen all (or anything) that you were meant to see in the swirling liquid of your glass, address the Horned One once more:

I drink deeply from the cup of life. Life is a sacred gift, and I will make the
most of it. I will find pleasure when it is freely offered, and I will give pleasure
when the time is right. I will find the magickal in the mundane and the sacred
in the profane. Through the power of the Horned One, I will live a life that is
truly alive and embrace this body of flesh and bone!

Horned God, bless this drink that I hold in my hands. (Raise your glass in acknowledgment of the Horned God.) *Fill it with your power, energy,*
and lust for life! May its contents warm me and awaken me to all the joys and

*delights of this world. Let me live as you do, with respect and love for all. So
mote it be!*

Take a long drink from your cup and feel the liquid course through your
body. Don't just swallow; take a moment to feel your drink pass over your
tongue, down your throat, and into your stomach. Once it's in your belly,
let your drink's warmth radiate through you. It should feel warm and comforting, but it might also make you tingle and feel disoriented for a moment.
Slowly take several more sips of your drink, enjoying the sensations it brings.
When you have consumed about half of your drink, stop partaking and
address the Horned God once more:

> *As I receive the blessings of this world, I will also return those gifts. May
> my love be shared with all those who deserve it! When they arise, may mutual
> desires be satisfied together! To you, Horned One, I leave this drink, so that
> it might nourish you as it has nourished me, and so that we might grow
> together. So mote it be!*

Pour what remains in your glass upon the earth as an offering to the
Horned One. If you are indoors, you can pour it into the soil in which you
previously placed your acorn. Watch the liquid seep into the ground and
visualize it as being accepted by the Horned God as it does so. (If your beverage just pools on the ground, this could be a sign that your offering was not
accepted. Try asking him to accept your offering!)

Once your offering has gone into the ground, pick up your key (or stone)
and hold it in your dominant hand. As you hold it, look toward the sky, preferably at the setting sun or the rising moon. Clutch your key strongly and
think for a moment about what lies beyond this plane of existence. Though
this aspect of the deity is often overlooked, a god of life must also be a god of
death, because it's only through death that new life arises. Say or read:

> *Horned God, I wish to walk with you in this life and know that I will
> walk with you again in the next. Light the way that leads from the world of
> mortals to the realms of the Mighty Ones, and illuminate the path that leads
> to the cauldron of rebirth. When the time is right, bring my beloved dead*

back to me, and when my days here are at an end, let me go unafraid into your realm.

> *The realm of the dead, the blessed isle, our place of rest and renewal! Such a journey is not yet for me, but I acknowledge that journey as a part of this life and my existence. I pour this water onto the earth as a reminder of the Cauldron of Death and Rebirth, the cauldron stirred by the Horned One. May I honor all your mysteries and stand strong in the knowledge that you are both a god of the living and a god of the dead. Accept this offering for your cauldron!*

Hold your key, and while you pour the water upon the ground (or into your bowl of earth), let some splash over the key. As the waters touch your key, remember that it is the Horned God who stirs the Cauldron of Death and Rebirth and opens the portal that allows us to depart the world of shadows and reenter this realm. Say or read:

> *I take this key with me from this rite as a reminder that the Horned God is a god of two realms. Horned One, may this key serve as an entryway into the world of spirit. When I need to visit with my beloved dead or explore the mysteries of what lies beyond, may this key serve as a way to touch that power. Hail the Dread Lord of Shadows! Hail the Horned One!*

Now take your key and acorn and place them both in your hand. Feel the power of this world in the acorn and the power of the beyond in the key. Notice how their energies mix together while you hold both. As the energies of the key and the acorn enter your body, let them mix with the energy of the wine (or other drink) you consumed earlier. Feel all three of those powers mingle within you.

When you have felt the energies of the earth, of life, and of death all come together, you have truly felt the power of the Horned God, because he is the lord of all those things. To know him is to know life but also to know death. To know the Horned God is to embrace the world with joy and reverence and to embrace death with courage.

Once you are confident that you've felt all three of the powers you called mingle together, ground yourself by consuming your cakes and ale. Feel your consciousness return to this world, and let the energy coursing through your body seep out and down into the earth. When you are satisfied that you are nearly back to the mundane world, thank the Horned God for joining you in your rite:

> *Hail the Horned God! Horned One, thank you for joining me tonight in my rites and allowing me to feel your energy and power. May I walk forward with you and embrace your mysteries. Until we are next together in the circle, I bid you hail and farewell!*

When you've returned home, place your key and acorn on your altar or in some other secure space. When you have need of the Horned God and wish to access his power, you can utilize these tokens as a way of doing so. And when you need to feel all of his power, hold them while taking a drink of wine and feeling his many energies blend together.

Hail the Horned One!

Chapter Four

ANTLERS AND HORNS AND PHALLUSES IN THE ANCIENT WORLD

IT WAS A WARM NIGHT IN late July of 2005, and my wife and I were hosting a party. It was a lot like most of the parties we hosted back then, full of people drinking beer and singing along to the various songs that our community held dear. But it was also unlike any party I'd ever hosted or attended, because everyone there wanted to talk to me about a 28,000-year-old dildo that had recently been discovered in a cave located in Germany's Swabian Jura mountain range. (In my experience, when you are "the Horned God guy," you end up spending a lot of time talking about phalluses, horns, and antlers, whether you want to or not.)

There are two physical attributes that tend to come up more than any others when discussing the Horned God: antlers/horns and phalluses. Obviously, horns are a touchstone with the Horned God; that's where he gets his name. Phalluses are a bit harder to quantify, but the Horned God is often associated with sex and fertility, and gods like Pan are often depicted with an erect phallus, so it seems natural to connect the Horned God with penises.

My friends were excited by this particular dildo, and I couldn't blame them. *Anything* that is 28,000 years old is rare, let alone a sex toy that predates cities, agriculture, and alphabets! But there's one other thing I remember in particular about the conversations I had that night: most of my friends had some serious misconceptions about Germany's oldest dildo.

I think the biggest misconception most of my friends had about this phallus was its rarity. It's a rare item not just because it's genuinely ancient but also because there just aren't a whole lot of realistic representations of the phallus from 30,000 or even 20,000 years ago. When objects designed to look like a penis do show up in prehistory, they tend to be stylized, abstract, and most often painted.[10]

Most of my friends took it for granted that this particular stone phallus was a sex toy too, while the truth of the matter is probably more nuanced. We know, for instance, that ancient people used this stone phallus to knap (sharpen) flints, because there's scarring on it consistent with that practice. Could it be possible that this particular phallus was constructed as a humorous way to sharpen flints? We have no way of knowing for sure if it was used for physical pleasure, but we do know that it had a practical purpose aside from sexual gratification.

Even with the scarring on this particular stone phallus, it is likely that it was used as a sex toy. Someone spent a lot of time polishing it, which makes sense if you were going to place it inside a delicate personal area. It's also a pretty good size for a dildo, measuring about eight inches long and one and one-quarter inches around (20 cm x 3 cm), not monstrously big, nor all that small either.

There's one other misconception that seems to surround Germany's oldest sex-toy: that it was in some way a spiritual item. When we think of phalluses carved from bone, stone, antler, or wood, there's an assumption that they might have had some sort of religious significance. Curiously, most truly ancient representations of the phallus are quite abstract, with some even appearing winged. They are also painted with some frequency. The abstract nature of these objects suggests even more strongly that they probably have some sort of spiritual function, but there's no way of ever knowing for sure.

---

10. Hayden, *Shamans, Sorcerers, and Saints*, 154.

THE PHALLUS IN PREHISTORY

Even if we'll never know the exact meaning behind a 15,000-year-old phallus fashioned from antler, fertility will always be a pretty good guess. It's likely that male humans understood their role in the procreation process pretty well even 30,000 years ago. In addition, sex has always played a huge role in the behavior of people, so it makes sense that the phallus would take center stage now and again. But for whatever reason, phalluses, and the male gods attached to them, just didn't seem to mean much to our very distant ancestors (or at least they didn't feel the need to make representations of them with any frequency). Phallus imagery would become far more popular thousands of years later, after the start of agriculture and the development of cities.

We know that things suggesting fertility were somewhat common in prehistory. The famous Venus of Willendorf statue, for instance, is probably 30,000 years old,[11] and over two hundred other statues with similarly exaggerated breasts and other body parts related to child bearing have been found throughout Europe and into Siberia.[12] Most often it's suggested that these figures are goddesses, and even if that's not the case, they are stylized enough to suggest a spiritual purpose. I'm sure that men 25,000 years ago were obsessed with their penises, but that infatuation has resulted in a scant number of artifacts.

As someone who has researched and written about the Horned God for twenty years, I'd like to be able to tell you that there's a clear line running through history that shows how the veneration of horns and phalluses led directly to the Horned God of today, but history is rarely that straightforward. Instead, we are left with tantalizing clues that suggest some sort of spiritual significance with these items, but it's never exactly clear.

ANTLERS AND PREHISTORY

Most artifacts, especially ones dealing with what we assume is some sort of spirituality, could have a wide variety of meanings. One archaeologist commented on ancient history by saying, "We [archaeologists] have decided what

---

11. Amos, "Ancient Phallus Unearthed in Cave."
12. Hayden, *Shamans, Sorcerers, and Saints*, 153.

is male and female, or sacred and profane ... rather than knowing what the original inhabitants intended and in that sense it will always be *our* fiction."[13] In other words, there are multiple ways to interpret the past, and in nearly every case, what we find in books like this one are best guesses.

When I think of ancient people such as the ones who used the caves at Trois-Frères or lived and died in the Swabian Jura mountain range 28,000 years ago, I imagine them hunting; more specifically, I imagine them hunting animals with antlers or horns on top of their heads. Bison and deer were not just sources for a meat dinner, but also provided raw materials for clothing, shelter, and tools. It would be strange to me if horns weren't revered by ancient people, considering how important those sorts of animals were to preserving life.

Horns and antlers are also archetypal images. When people see a pair of horns or antlers on top of a human head, it immediately conjures up all sorts of visceral emotions. For Witches, those emotions are most likely positive, but in much of society, those feelings are extremely negative. The sight of horns implies devil worship, sinister actions, and at the very least that someone is a villain or at least worthy of mockery. In fantasy films, antagonists are often portrayed with a horned helm or sport a fancy pair of antlers on top of their head. None of this is by accident, as antlers and horns stir our emotions. Our most ancient ancestors were probably more like us, seeing horns and antlers as beneficial, but sadly, our world has changed a lot since then.

Modern human beings may not have even been the first people on this planet to revere antlers or horns. There's evidence to suggest that our Neanderthal ancestors might have done so first. Neanderthals could have (I say "could have" because there is a lot of disagreement on this issue) begun burying their dead over 400,000 years ago, and at least two of those burials have connections to horned and antlered animals. Discovered in 1938, the Neanderthal skeleton unearthed at Teshik-Tash Cave in Uzbekistan is that of an adolescent child, whose body was surrounded by a circle of goat horns, all

---

13. Lynn Meskell, quoted in Balter, *The Goddess and the Bull*, 321.

placed downward into the soil around the corpse.[14] What this means exactly is anyone's guess. A circle around a grave is a rather symbolic gesture, so I have to assume the placement of the horns had some spiritual meaning to those who chose that arrangement.

At Amud Cave in northern Israel, the body of a ten-month-old infant was placed in a difficult-to-access cave niche, most likely a deliberate burial. Over the child's pelvis was the jaw of a red deer.[15] Given the location of the discovery, it's hard to imagine the baby simply crawling away from its parents, grabbing a deer bone, and then crawling away to die. Again, there's no way of interpreting the meaning behind these remains with absolute certainty, but burial with an object suggests some sort of belief in an afterlife.

Northern Israel was also the home of the first human burials 92,000 years ago. So far, the remains of twenty-seven people have been found at Israel's Qafzeh cave, and in one of those burials a pair of antlers was interred with one of the dead. The individual buried with the antlers was most likely between the ages of twelve and thirteen and had apparently suffered some sort of head trauma eight years earlier.[16] What makes this discovery especially interesting is what can be inferred from the antlers. Perhaps they were left with the young person to suggest a rebirth, just as the antlers of deer are shed and regrown annually.

Over the millennia, more and more grave goods began to be interred with buried humans. Often those items were made of ivory, bone, antler, and amber, and served no practical purpose, meaning they were created primarily for their aesthetic or spiritual properties.[17] Grave goods suggest a belief in the afterlife, as items are often buried with the dead to assist them in their new state of existence.

---

14. Gargett et al., "Grave Shortcomings: The Evidence for Neandertal Burial [and Comments and Reply]." I should point out that Gargett doesn't share my enthusiasm for this burial being deliberate. You might have guessed as much from the title.

15. Riel-Salvatore and Clark, "Grave Markers."

16. Hirst, "Qafzeh Cave, Israel: Evidence for Middle Paleolithic Burials."

17. Hayden, *Shamans, Sorcerers, and Saints,* 130.

First turning up in the archaeological record 40,000 years ago and peaking between 15,0000 and 10,000 years ago were a series of wands, or *bâtons*, made out of reindeer antlers. Originally believed to be symbols of authority, these wands are now believed to be spear (and arrow) straighteners or instruments to throw spears.[18] What makes these tools so interesting is that many of them are decorated with animals and abstract symbols such as spirals. The symbols suggest the use of magick, and animals on them could represent the idea of "like attracts like," since spears were used for hunting.

A more elaborate use of antlers was discovered in the form of a headdress at Star Carr, a cave in England located near modern-day Yorkshire. Dating back 10,000 years, the headdresses from Star Carr were fashioned from red deer skulls with the antlers still attached. The skulls were modified in such a way that they could easily fit on the head of a person, with eye holes carved into the skulls. The antlers on the skulls were also trimmed down to make the headdresses lighter and more manageable for the wearer.[19]

Starr Car is not the only site in Europe where deer skull headwear was popular. Three sites in Germany (Bedburg-Königshoven, Berlin-Biesdorf, and Hohen Viecheln) have turned up similar findings. However, the headdresses discovered in Germany are not completely consistent with the ones discovered at Star Carr. The headdresses discovered at Bedburg-Königshoven, for example, utilize different parts of the skull, and the antlers on them have not been significantly altered.[20]

There's no way to know for sure what these headdresses were used for. They could have been used for some sort of hunting magick or perhaps as a way for hunters to sneak up on deer. It is interesting just how much these headdresses resemble the traditional dress of Asian shamans. Both Lapp and Siberian shamans have been pictured with antlers atop their head, and it's

---

18. Don's Maps, "Tools from the Stone Age."

19. This information comes from the placard of the Star Carr headdress at the British Museum in London.

20. Elliot, Knight, and Little, "Antler Frontlets."

most certainly possible that the headwear from Star Carr was used by individuals who served a similar purpose in society.[21]

THE BIRTH OF CITIES AND THE RISE OF DEITIES

The exact origins of deity are hard to pin down. Was the first goddess the Venus of Willendorf from 30,000 years ago? Was the first god the Sorcerer from Trois-Frères? What is not hard to imagine is a shaman wearing headwear like the kind from Star Carr inspiring worship of a horned god. Simply picturing such a figure dancing in the light of a campfire fills me with awe and wonder.

Five hundred years after the antlered headdresses of Star Carr, the first cities began to emerge. It's in cities where we really begin to see the development of spiritual concepts and deities. In some of those early cities, horned imagery played a major role in the lives of the people of who lived there. One of the more notable of these early cities is Çatalhöyük, located in modern-day Turkey and settled 9,500 years ago. Çatalhöyük was not the largest early settlement, but its imagery would eventually resonate throughout the Mediterranean.

Instead of antlers, the primary imagery at Çatalhöyük was centered on the horns of the bull. Çatalhöyük is home to hundreds of elaborate buildings, with many of them featuring enormous bull heads and horns on pedestals and walls.[22] In addition to the bull heads and horns, Çatalhöyük was also home to goddess statues, generally depicting a voluptuous woman sitting between two lions. For many years, the imagery found at Çatalhöyük was interpreted to mean that the people there worshipped a Mother Goddess and her son, who took the form of a bull.[23]

While the Mother Goddess hypothesis has held up over time, the idea that the bull imagery of Çatalhöyük suggests a bull god has changed. Many modern archaeologists now believe that the city's bull imagery either represents some

---

21. Hayden, *Shamans, Sorcerers, and Saints*, 49.

22. Balter, *The Goddess and the Bull*, 39.

23. Balter, *The Goddess and the Bull*, 39.

sort of ancestor worship or was used to commemorate certain events that the city's citizens wanted to remember.[24] That brings up the question, why use bulls to remember certain events or ancestors?

When we think about bulls today, we tend to think of bull fighting or perhaps the running of the bulls in Pamplona, Spain. What we tend not to dwell on is how powerful bulls are and how dangerous they were in the ancient world. Bulls were an important source of meat, but they also appealed to warriors because of their violence and strength.[25] Bulls were also seen as powerful examples of male virility. Eight thousand years ago, bulls were not yet domesticated and ran wild and free, their freedom perhaps making them even more worthy of idolization.

Bull imagery was so prevalent throughout the Mediterranean from 8800 to 6500 BCE that the period is sometimes referred to as the "Culture of the Bull."[26] Even today, it's impossible to escape just how important bulls were in early societies. The letter *A* actually represents the head of a bull![27] Various deities across the centuries have been depicted with the horns and face of a bull, and many more have taken the form of a bull while on Earth.

Contemporary with Çatalhöyük are the Sumerian cities of Eridu, Uruk, and Ur. Larger than even Çatalhöyük, they are often thought of as the world's first true cities. Located in Mesopotamia, these early cities are all considered Sumerian, and not surprisingly, Sumerian mythology also features several bull-related deities. The protective deity Lamassu was often pictured with a human head and the body of a bull. Lamassu's gender was variable, and appeared both female and male. The storm god Hadad, found among the Canaanites, was often depicted with four bull horns on top of his head and descended directly from the Sumerian storm god Iškur.

The most well-known piece of Sumerian mythology is the *Epic of Gilgamesh*, which contains even more bull energy. Gilgamesh's companion (and,

---

24. Balter, *The Goddess and the Bull*, 324.

25. Hayden, *Shamans, Sorcerers, and Saints*, 201.

26. Hayden, *Shamans, Sorcerers, and Saints*, 201.

27. Hayden, *Shamans, Sorcerers, and Saints*, 237.

most likely, lover) Enkidu is portrayed in the epic as a "wild man," and in my head I often picture him as looking like the European wild-man of lore, who was often depicted as something like the modern-day Sasquatch. Enkidu was not apelike at all, though, and was often pictured with the head and horns of a bull! Later in the story, Gilgamesh and Enkidu kill a bull sent by the gods to destroy them after Gilgamesh rejected the advances of the goddess Ishtar.

The Egyptian goddess Hathor (or *Athyr* to the Greeks) was often depicted as a cow or as a human with a cow's head. In human form, she was often crowned with the horns of a bull.[28] Hathor was not the only deity in ancient Egypt to utilize the symbolism of the bull. Gods such as Ra and Osiris were believed to visit the earth in the form of a bull. Solar deities such as Ra (who sometimes had the face of a ram, another horned animal) and Atum also had bulls in their mythology and worship. Ra's four-horned bull guarded the roads of heaven, and priests believed they could speak with Atum through a bull.[29] Worship of the bull god Apis arose from honors given to a sacred bull thought to be the son of Hathor.

The Palace at Knossos located on the Greek island of Crete is well known for its bull imagery. It's on Crete where we find beautiful frescoes where acrobats seem to perform amazing feats of agility over charging bulls. Crete was also home to striking *rhytons* (ceremonial chalices) in the shapes of bulls and bull heads. A rhyton appears to look more like a sculpture than a working tool, but on ancient Crete it was used for the pouring of libations after animal sacrifice.

Crete was also home to the fearsome Minotaur, who had the head of a bull. The Minotaur could have evolved from the images at Knossos and might be the remnant of a lost local deity. In later Greek mythology, the Minotaur was the son of the Cretan Queen Pasiphaë and a beautiful bull given to Pasiphaë and her husband, King Minos, by the sea god Poseidon.

Just as it did in Crete, the bull played a large role in the later religion of the Greeks. Gods such as Zeus, Dionysus, and Poseidon took the form of a

---

28. Barrett, *The Egyptian Gods & Goddesses*, 59.

29. Barrett, *The Egyptian Gods & Goddesses*, 144.

bull when visiting Earth, especially when coupling with human females. The Mysteries of Eleusis, sacred to Demeter and Persephone (and to some small extent Dionysus), ended with the sacrifice of a bull, both as a thank-you to the gods and as a main course for the feasting post-ritual.

Chapter Five

PAN AND THE OTHER HORNED GODS OF ANCIENT GREECE

I FIRST MET THE GREEK GOD Pan in the pages of *D'Aulaires' Book of Greek Myths* when I was in the first grade. Greek myth, which is full of incest, adultery, and rape, is hard to pull off in a children's book, but *D'Aulaires'* mostly succeeds (though as an adult I tend to laugh when Zeus's many adulterous lovers are introduced as his additional "wives"). The Pan introduced in *D'Aulaires'* is the god that most of us are familiar with today:

> He had goat's legs, pointed ears, a pair of small horns, and he was covered all over with dark, shaggy hair. He was so ugly that his mother, a nymph, ran away screaming when she first saw him. But his father, Hermes, was delighted with the strange looks of his son. He carried him up to Olympus to amuse the other gods and they all laughed and took him to their hearts. They called him Pan and sent him back to the dark woods and stony hills of Greece as the great god of nature. He was to be the protector of hunters, shepherds, and curly-fleeced sheep.[30]

For most of my adolescence and early adult life, I paid very little attention to Pan. My interest in Greek mythology generally revolved around heroes

---

30. Ingri D'Aulaire and Edgar Parin D'Aulaire, *D'Aulaires' Book of Greek Myths*, 90.

like Hercules, Perseus, and, not surprisingly, Jason and his Argonauts. When I did think about deities, it was usually about powerful gods such as Zeus and Apollo, or Aphrodite, who I hoped would bring my angsty teenage self a girlfriend. Pan seemed friendly enough, at least in the sanitized myths I was reading, but I didn't give him much thought.

Surprisingly, both Pan and the Horned God were absent from my early years as a Witch. Back then, my focus was almost entirely on the Goddess (and only the one "Goddess"), the moon, and magick. On the rare occasions that I called a male god into my circle, I called to the Lord of the Sun, and envisioned him as a young Apollo, and there were most certainly no horns on the top of his head. When reading books on Witchcraft, I tended to skip over the sections dealing with the Horned God out of fear. I wanted nothing to do with him.

But eventually I began to feel a yearning inside to honor the Greek Pan. He came up in nearly everything I read and was a frequent visitor in college mythology and literature classes. The bushes near the front door of my house also seemed to contain his energy. It sounds silly to write, but I swear there were days when I could see him grinning at me in those shrubby bushes, imploring me to acknowledge him.

He finally broke through my defenses at an Ostara (Spring Equinox) ritual after several years of trying to fend him off. In the middle of that ritual, I screamed "Pan!" and felt his energy wash over me. He had heard my call, and I his, and my life would never be the same again. He's primarily why you are currently holding this book in your hands (figure 3).

PAN AND ARCADIA

Most of us know Pan as a Greek god, but it's probably more accurate to say that he's an Arcadian-Greek god. Arcadia is a relatively isolated area of Greece, located east of Athens, on the central Peloponnese, a peninsula just south of mainland Greece. Arcadia is landlocked and mostly consists of rocky hills and mountains. It is not an agricultural area nor the home of great city-states like Thebes or Sparta.

(Ed.ᵗ Alinari) N° 11123 a. NAPOLI – R. Museo Nazionale. Pane e Olimpo. (Scultura Antica).

Figure 3: Pan.
A rather subdued and unaroused Pan teaches
the shepherd Daphnis how to play the panpipes.

The ancient Greeks and later the Romans both romanticized Arcadia. It was thought of as a primitive paradise, a land that was "older than Jupiter [the god] and the moon," and its first inhabitants were believed to have "preceded the moon."[31] Arcadia was the land of the first Greeks, the perfect place for a god who was unlike any other Olympian deity.

Pan's association with Arcadia was so strong in the ancient world that Arcadia was sometimes called *Pania* in his honor. In Arcadia, Pan was the most important of all the gods, save Zeus, and for several centuries was exclusively worshipped there.[32] In 490 BCE, Pan's worship spread to the city-state of Athens, and from there to the rest of the Greek-speaking world. Five hundred

31. Borgeaud, *The Cult of Pan in Ancient Greece*, 6.

32. Borgeaud, *The Cult of Pan in Ancient Greece*, 47–48.

years later, worship of Pan had spread throughout the Roman Empire, from India to Gaul (modern-day France).

Pan was never the most popular of Greek deities. There were no elaborate temples built for him outside of Arcadia, and his presence in myth is rather fleeting. However, Pan is a frequent motif in art, suggesting that he was popular in the ancient world, even if he wasn't everyone's favorite deity.

But what's not to love about Pan? In the ancient world, Pan was the god of music, dance, seduction, possession, panic, lustfulness, shepherds, flocks, and rough sexuality.[33] Pan's gifts were generally joyous ones, and as we shall see, panic was dealt only to those who dishonored the god. Music, dance, and lustfulness are not necessities in life, but they do make it worth living. Pan might not have been essential in the way Helios (god of the sun) and Demeter (goddess of the grain) were, but honoring him was still important.

Pan was a liminal god, existing on the edges of civilized society, which might be why he appeals to so many Witches today. Unlike most Greek deities, he chose to make his home on Earth, generally confining himself to Arcadia and nearby areas of Greece. In Arcadia, Pan was a shepherd of goats, a fitting role for someone who prefers solitude to the hustle and bustle of city life. Shepherds spend most of their time away from others, living in nature with only their goats or sheep for company. Pan's solitude is probably why he is sometimes credited with inventing masturbation.

In Arcadia, Pan was worshipped in temples, though his most holy places were entire mountains dedicated to him.[34] Urbanites who wished to worship Pan most often did so a few miles outside of town. Instead of being worshipped in conveniently located temples, Pan was worshipped primarily in caves that often required a substantial walk. Caves were perfect for the worship of Pan, because in Greece they were seen primarily as a temporary dwelling, uncivilized and unfit to live in.[35] They were also sometimes used by shepherds looking to escape an especially cold or harsh night before heading back into the woods.

---

33. Borgeaud, *The Cult of Pan in Ancient Greece*, 55.

34. Borgeaud, *The Cult of Pan in Ancient Greece*, 45.

35. Borgeaud, *The Cult of Pan in Ancient Greece*, 48.

PAN AND THE GODS OF OLYMPUS (AND BEYOND)

Though Pan's origins generally lie in Arcadian Greece, he has connections to other places and other deities. The name Pan derives from the Indo-European root word *peh*, which means to "guard or watch over."[36] (This is also the origin of the Latin word *pasture*, and the Greek root *pa(s)*, which translates as "shepherd," the origin of Pan's name. Pan literally means "shepherd."[37]) Pan shares the origin of his name with the ancient Hindu (Vedic) deity Pusan. Like Pan, Pusan had an affinity for goats, and both were gods of pastures. Pan was a shepherd, while Pusan watched over herds of cattle.[38]

Pan's father is generally given as Hermes in most Greek mythology, though that could vary depending on time and place. In Arcadia, Pan's father was said to be the Titan Cronus (Saturn in Roman myth, and often spelled Cronos or Kronos), which would make Pan the brother of Zeus. In other parts of Greece, his father was said to be Apollo, and even when they weren't linked as father/son, the two deities were still connected. Some myths tell of Pan teaching Apollo the art of prophecy, and Pan kept a cave at Delphi where it was said he divined using dice.[39] Both gods were also musical, with Pan's syrinx being the instrument of the common people and Apollo's lyre the instrument of sophisticated folks.

But it's with Hermes that Pan shares the most attributes. Both were pictured as and associated with shepherds. Hermes was also a phallic god, like Pan, and was sometimes depicted as just a penis.[40] Hermes is most famous for being the messenger of the gods and overseeing travelers, and in Egypt, Pan was the god of "good journeying."[41]

As a shepherd, Pan would have had to hunt for his own food while watching his flocks, and Pan was seen by many as a hunting god. As a hunter, Pan's style was rather primitive. Instead of using a bow, Pan was generally depicted

---

36. West, *Indo-European Poetry and Myth*, 282.

37. West, *Indo-European Poetry and Myth*, 282.

38. West, *Indo-European Poetry and Myth*, 282.

39. Borgeaud, *The Cult of Pan in Ancient Greece*, 180 and 109.

40. Borgeaud, *The Cult of Pan in Ancient Greece*, 66.

41. West, *Indo-European Poetry and Myth*, 282.

with a *lagobolon*, a slightly curved hunting stick used primarily to kill small game such as hares. In addition to killing animals for food, Pan was also considered a master of animals, both wild and domestic.[42]

In Greek myth, Pan was a frequent companion of the god Dionysus. Like Pan, Dionysus spent a great deal of time on Earth (though Dionysus eventually moved to Mount Olympus) and was fond of the wineskin. Dionysus and Pan were also both phallic deities, with sexual activity strongly encouraged in some of their rites. Both were also popular with female followers, with women often taking the lead when it came time to participate in a ritual in honor of those deities.[43]

Though Pan never married, he was associated with several goddesses in ancient mythology and art. His most successful courtship was with Selene, the goddess of the moon, whom he seduced by wearing a lambswool cloak that reflected her beauty. (Selene was so beautiful that she chose to fall in love with her reflection, only to find Pan instead.) Pan's courtship of Selene is more than a story of trickery; the two were worshipped together in Arcadia.[44] It was also thought that the moon was the preferred companion of Pan, because its light is useful to shepherds keeping watch over their flocks.[45]

Pan was also friendly with the goddess Artemis, but not because the two had any great love affair. Like Pan, Artemis was a deity of wild spaces and of hunting, though Pan wasn't quite as skilled as his Olympian relative.[46] Pan and Artemis also shared a dislike for the institution of marriage, Pan because he was very much against monogamy, and Artemis because she chose to guard her own virginity.

Though not frequent companions in mythology, Pan and Aphrodite were often depicted together in art. At the National Archaeological Museum in

---

42. Borgeaud, *The Cult of Pan in Ancient Greece*, 63.

43. Burkert, *Greek Religion*, 259. Depending on the deity being worshipped and the particular rite, participation was sometimes limited by biological sex in ancient Greece, but not so with Pan and Dionysus; Burkert, 258.

44. Borgeaud, *The Cult of Pan in Ancient Greece*, 7.

45. Borgeaud, *The Cult of Pan in Ancient Greece*, 3.

46. Borgeaud, *The Cult of Pan in Ancient Greece*, 64.

Athens, there's a striking sculpture of Aphrodite shooing away a horny Pan with her shoe while her son Eros (the Roman Cupid) looks on in delight. Some scholars believe that Aphrodite is actively fighting against the advances of Pan in the sculpture, but I find her posture and smile more playful than angry. That Eros, love, clutches one of Pan's horns in the sculpture suggests an eventual and consensual coupling.

Pan also has connections to far more ancient pieces of Greek myth. The ancient Greek lyric poet Pindar called him the "dog of the great goddess," a power older and stronger than that of Zeus or the Titans.[47] An early version of the Mysteries of Demeter (most associated today with Eleusis) celebrated in Arcadia may have featured Pan in a significant role.[48] What that role entailed exactly is hard to say, but a cave sacred to him was found near a spot where people were initiated into Demeter's mysteries.

Demeter is most well known for being the goddess of the grain and having her daughter Persephone abducted by Hades. As Demeter searched for her daughter on earth, she gave up her role as a fertility goddess, and the earth suffered. In many versions of that myth, it's the goddess Hekate who convinces Demeter to return life to the world, but in other versions it's Pan. As a god of liminal spaces, existing between humanity and the gods, the goat-footed one is well suited to the role, again suggesting a strong link between Pan and the natural world.

Perhaps the most familiar myths featuring Pan are those that involve the god in pursuit of a nymph. Pan does not come across well in these tales, and to call him a rapist in them would not be an exaggeration. Pan's pursuit of the nymphs Echo, Pitys, and Syrinx pit Pan against virginity, a state of being that angers the god.[49] In the stories of Pitys and Syrinx, the gods of Olympus turn Pitys into a pine tree to save her from the ravages of Pan, while the nymph sisters of Syrinx transform her into reeds to save her from Pan's pursuit, which the god then fashions into his famous pan flute, the syrinx. The most awful end comes to Echo, who upon rejecting the god was torn

---

47. Borgeaud, *The Cult of Pan in Ancient Greece*, 173.

48. Borgeaud, *The Cult of Pan in Ancient Greece*, 173.

49. Borgeaud, *The Cult of Pan in Ancient Greece*, 83.

to pieces by a group of shepherds driven to madness by the goat-foot god. Though her body was destroyed, Echo continued to live on as a disembodied voice.

These stories can be interpreted a number of ways. Some see them as cautionary tales, highlighting how important it is for young women to remain virgins.[50] Others see them as examples of what can arise from a sexuality divorced from marriage. Pursuit of a lover can have beneficial consequences, such as pine trees and pan flutes. (The benefits of these transformations don't seem to help Pitys or Syrinx all that much, though.)

PAN AND PANIC

One of the most difficult of Pan's attributes is his connection to the idea of panic. (The word *panic* actually derives from his name.) Pan could have a terrible temper, such as when being unexpectedly awoken from a midafternoon nap, and his wrath could be both violent and terrifying. Although sometimes connected to violence, Pan was not a god of war, and never appears on the battlefield in Greek art.[51]

In 490 BCE, the Greek runner Philippides (sometimes also spelled Pheidippides) was sent from Athens to Sparta to request the military aid of the Spartans against the Persians. On his way back to Athens, Philippides was met by Pan, and the god promised to aid the Athenians if they would begin worshipping him. The Athenians won their subsequent battle against the Persians, the Battle of Marathon, but just *what* sort of help Pan gave the Greeks is an open question. It's generally assumed that his assistance occurred not during battle but before or after, and that he threw the invading Persians into a panic-terror.

Panic was known to overtake ancient armies and cause them to turn on themselves. A soldier would hear the sound of what they thought to be an invading army in the night and call their comrades to arms. The fear and confusion from such shouts would lead to men on the same side killing one

---

50. Borgeaud, *The Cult of Pan in Ancient Greece*, 78.

51. Borgeaud, *The Cult of Pan in Ancient Greece*, 95–96.

another. Pan is said to have perfected this technique using echo.[52] After the war, the Athenians kept their word and built Pan a sanctuary at the mouth of a cave near the bottom of the Acropolis, where it still stands today. (When my wife and I visited Athens, the first ancient site we got to see up close was Pan's sanctuary at the bottom of the Acropolis. I saw it as a sign.)

There's another reason Pan helped the Athenians at Marathon: he simply did not like armies in his space. A large army moving through the countryside brings both civilization and order to what just moments before were wild spaces. Armies were the type of intrusion into his domain that Pan could not stand. In other, later battles, Pan was also given credit for inflicting panic upon armies.

Panic is more than a fear capable of gripping an army; I believe it's a way to commune with Pan himself. Panic is not a normal state of being; it's a liminal space where our imagination runs wild with speculation while our rational brain tries to process exactly what is happening to us. Panic can be fun, such as getting scared at a haunted house, or it can be an absolutely crippling and terrifying circumstance. A panicked state, with its rush of adrenaline, can put us in an alternate state of consciousness—the kind sometimes used to confer with gods and spirits.

PAN AND SEXUALITY

With the exception of his horns, Pan's most well-known physical attribute was his erect penis. The earliest images of Pan show a god who is more animal than man, resembling a goat on its hind legs. Over time, he would become more humanlike, but always retaining his horns and (usually) his erect phallus.

The phallus of Pan symbolized many things. Pan was a god of lust and sex for fun instead of procreation, but he was also the fertilizer of flocks and was held responsible when hunting was especially good (or bad).[53] Pan's sexuality was about taking advantage of what was available, whether that was

---

52. Borgeaud, *The Cult of Pan in Ancient Greece*, 90–91.

53. Borgeaud, *The Cult of Pan in Ancient Greece*, 78 and 63.

a lover, a hand, or a sheep.[54] Sex between males was especially important to Pan, and engaging in it was a way to honor the god.[55]

Pan's sexuality was straight, gay, bi, and other things that I don't have words for. This might have been the case partly because he wasn't completely a male god. Beginning at the end of the fifth century BCE, Pan began to sometimes be depicted as female.[56] This version of Pan featured the deity with an alluring feminine shape, along with horns and a tail. Pan was also sometimes depicted as a child, or as "many Pans," with each version of the god representing one of his many aspects.[57] In ancient Greek art, I've seen Pan depicted with the face of a philosopher-poet, as a mischievous child, and as an extremely lecherous man. Perhaps much of Pan's appeal both today and in the past comes from just how many different personas he has.

THE DEATH OF PAN

While Greek mythology is littered with stories chronicling the deaths of various demigods, Pan is the only Greek god who was believed to have "died" during pagan antiquity. In Plutarch's (c. 46–c. 120 CE) *Moralia*, he shares a strange story set during the reign of the Roman Emperor Tiberius (42 BCE–37 CE), who ruled from 14–37 CE. Much of Plutarch's information came to him secondhand, but the source of this story was someone well known to him, the son of his grammar teacher. According to that source, during a voyage from Western Greece to Italy, a strange voice called out from the island of Paxi to the boat's captain, an Egyptian by the name of Thamus. Everyone aboard the ship was amazed by this, as most of the travelers even on the boat were unaware of the captain's name.

Not recognizing the voice, Thamus ignored it initially, but after the third call, Thamus responded and the voice said, "When you come opposite to

---

54. Borgeaud, *The Cult of Pan in Ancient Greece*, 77.

55. Borgeaud, *The Cult of Pan in Ancient Greece*, 75.

56. Boardman, *The Great God Pan*, 33.

57. Boardman, *The Great God Pan*, 32.

Palodes, announce that Great Pan is dead."[58] All aboard the ship debated whether to share the news when they reached Palodes, and Thamus decided he would only share the information he was given if the seas were calm and the breeze quiet. As they neared Palodes, everything did grow still, so Thamus shared his message. Plutarch says the message was greeted with sadness and amazement, and as the passengers debarked in Italy from Thamus's boat, they shared their story with anyone who would listen.

One of those who ended up listening was Emperor Tiberius, who consulted his scholars about the strange message and dispatched people to investigate. Whatever became of Tiberius's investigation is unknown, but the fact that the emperor took such a message seriously suggests that there might be more to the story than what comes from Plutarch. For something that happened two thousand years ago, we have a surprising amount of detail, including several names and a couple of locations. Whatever happened on that riverboat was something that stayed with people.[59]

Over the centuries, several explanations have been offered for Plutarch's tale. One suggests that Thamus and his passengers simply misheard the voice calling to them from the island of Paxi. According to this theory, it was not Pan who died, but perhaps the deity Tammuz (also known as Dumuzid), who in Mesopotamian mythology was murdered by demons. The Greek Adonis, who was gored to death by either Artemis or Ares in the form of a bull, has also been suggested as the dead god. This theory does not explain how the voice from the shore knew the name of Thamus, or why the sea and the winds were calm when the boat reached Palodes, but it does seem more likely than a random voice suggesting that the Greek Pan was dead.

The most commonly shared explanation of Pan's death comes from Christians who argue that Pan must have died when Jesus was either crucified or resurrected from the dead. Why Jesus and his dad would have had to wait until such a moment to off Pan has never been explained, most likely

---

58. You may be wondering where Palodes is. I share this wonder. No one is really sure what Plutarch was referencing here.

59. Merivale, *Pan the Goat-God*, 11–12. This footnote is in reference to the entire tale as told by Plutarch.

because it's completely nonsensical. Whatever happened on that riverboat will always remain a mystery, though I should point out that worship of Pan continued over the next few centuries, at least until Christianity was made the official religion of the Roman Empire around 381 CE.

It's impossible to keep a good god down, though, and Pan would rise again. In fact, Pan would become even more popular in his second go-round. However, that tale won't be told in this book until chapter 11.

A PAN RITUAL IN ANCIENT GREECE

We don't really know very much about how Pan was worshipped in the ancient world. There are no surviving documents outlining a ritual for the god, and not much in the way of contemporary accounts either. However, we can piece together a reasonable approximation of a Pan ritual utilizing archaeological artifacts (including the caves where the god was worshipped), letters, plays, and what we know about Greek religion in general. The most useful account of a Pan ritual comes from the play *Dyskolos* (*The Grouch*), written by the playwright Menander (c. 342/41–c. 290 BCE). Using this play as a starting point, it's possible to reconstruct what a Pan ritual might have looked like in the year 300 BCE.

Unlike other gods, Pan had no major feast days on the calendars of most Greeks. In Athens, the god was honored yearly with a torchlight race, an honor he shared with the god Prometheus.[60] The race most likely commemorated Pan's introduction to the Athenian runner Philippides, who met Pan while running back to Athens from Sparta, but we don't know much else about it. Worship of Pan, as it generally occurred outside of city centers, happened when someone felt the need for it, either due to some deep longing or perhaps at the urging of the god himself.

Rituals for Pan most likely began before noon, when a procession of people would start to make their way to one of Pan's grottoes, usually a journey of at least a couple of miles. Flute music often accompanied the journey, and perhaps the sound of tambourines. Startling the god was considered foolhardy, so his worship spaces were always approached with music.

---

60. Borgeaud, *The Cult of Pan in Ancient Greece*, 153–154.

Upon arriving at Pan's grotto, always shared with nymphs, a sacrifice was made and/or given to the god (figure 4). If the problem being presented to the god was especially vexing, a large sacrifice would be made, such as a goat or lamb with its genitalia intact. The sacrifice was always presented with noise, in marked contrast to the sacrifices performed to other gods, which were generally done in silence.[61] Once the sacrifice was performed, the best cuts of meat were boiled and eaten by the ritual's participants, and the left-overs were given as a burnt offering to Pan and the nymphs of the grotto.

Figure 4: A sacrifice for Pan.
While far from accurate, this image does capture the
joy felt by those who celebrated the rites of Pan.

Most often, though, offerings to Pan did not involve animal sacrifice. He was far more likely to receive gifts such as grain, bread, figs, wine, grapes, olives, and milk.[62] These offerings would have been shared with those in attendance before being burned as an offering. While milk and foodstuffs

61. Borgeaud, *The Cult of Pan in Ancient Greece*, 166.

62. Burkert, *Greek Religion*, 67.

were actively shared by Pan and the nymphs, the wine was thought to be all for the god.

Once the sacrifice was completed, the men and women present at the ritual would separate. One group would conduct a vigil and wait for a sign from the god, while the other group would retreat to their wineskins and begin partying. Greek religion was extremely patriarchal, but when Pan was worshipped, women were generally on equal footing with their male counterparts. The women were just as likely to go and drink and make the men wait for a sign from the god. Once a sign had been observed, the two groups would reunite for the rest of the ritual.

In some Greek rites, religious activities included men and women hurling coarse insults at one another.[63] Scholars generally think such diversions were meant to incite laughter, but if they were used in Pan's rites, I think they may have had a different purpose: as a form of flirtation. When I was boy, I often teased the girls I liked in school, and even now, flirting between potential lovers sometimes involves a bit of teasing. I think a bit of mostly good-natured ribbing might have helped inflame desire before honoring the god.

Just what happened during the rest of the ritual is a rather open question. There are a couple of things we can say, though, with absolute certainty. Rituals to Pan involved dancing. Pan was a god of dance and of losing yourself (and your inhibitions) in that dance. The Greeks saw dance as an expression of joy, an emotion often felt by Pan, and one he liked to share with his followers.[64]

To accompany the dance, there would have been plenty of flute music. The flute was thought to bring about possession, in the best sense of the word.[65] Music can change how we feel, and, perhaps most importantly, the syrinx (Pan's flute) was thought to unite the energies of mortal and god and cause a feeling not much different from that of intoxication through alcohol.[66] The music of the syrinx would have been a part of the ritual until its end at dawn.

---

63. Borgeaud, *The Cult of Pan in Ancient Greece*, 169.

64. Borgeaud, *The Cult of Pan in Ancient Greece*, 169.

65. Burkert, *Greek Religion*, 172.

66. Borgeaud, *The Cult of Pan in Ancient Greece*, 120.

Sexual activity was likely a part of Pan's rites too. If you were looking for an orgy in the year 300 BCE, a ritual in honor of Pan was a likely place to find one. I'm doubtful that everyone at Pan's rites participated in the more amorous parts of his rituals, but at the very least there would have been plenty of flirting. In addition to the sexual activity, wine drinking would have continued long into the night, ending at daybreak. (It was considered an insult to the god to end the ritual before sunrise.)

In addition to the music being played in the grotto, the women at the ritual would have made a terrible sound called a *kragué*. The kragué is an anguished sound, like the sobs of a family finding out that a loved one had been killed in war, or the bleating of a goat. The cry would have been panicked, fearful, and unpleasant.[67] Its sound would have echoed off the walls of the grotto, mixing with the drunken revelry and the sounds of the flute.

This brings up a reasonable question: what's the point of making a terrible sound in a ritual that is dedicated mostly to joy? I'm of the belief that panic and fear were ways to feel the presence of the god. When experiencing emotions like panic and fear, our consciousness shifts and we perceive things in different ways; the boundaries between the mundane and the more magickal are stripped away. A sense of the unexpected brings about heightened anticipation and plays into Pan's role as a god of possession. (In Witchcraft, this type of activity plays out most vividly during initiation rituals into specific traditions.[68] There, prospective initiates are often left to wonder what exactly is going to happen. This heightened sense of anticipation makes every initiation unique to the individual who has experienced it. Fear of the unknown makes us more aware of our surroundings and a bit disoriented at the same time.

Imagine for a moment a dimly lit cave dedicated to Pan and the nymphs of the local countryside. Feel yourself in the middle of that cave while the sounds of the syrinx, sex, and the kragué echo off its walls. Imagine yourself tipsy from drink and the erotic energy pulsating all around you. All of that

---

67. Borgeaud, *The Cult of Pan in Ancient Greece*, 171.

68. I spend a lot of time and over 20,000 words writing about initiations in my 2018 book *Transformative Witchcraft: The Greater Mysteries*, also published by Llewellyn.

power would weigh heavily on your shoulders, almost like a cloak. Witch rituals are built on raising energy, and the techniques used in Pan's rituals would have raised a lot of it! A Pan ritual was a laboratory in which to mix joy and just a little bit of fear, creating an atmosphere unlike any other.

As the music and noise echoed off the walls of the cave, those celebrating would have believed Pan was present. Gods weren't just invited to rituals; it was assumed by the Greeks that they actually showed up. Pan would have danced until dawn with his worshippers, his voice that of the syrinx and the cries of anguish from the women honoring him.

DIONYSUS

Pan is not the only horned god of the Greeks, and was far from being the most popular horned deity in the ancient world. Though not often thought of as a horned god, Dionysus most certainly (probably) is one. Not only did Dionysus take the form of a bull on numerous occasions, but he was also sometimes depicted with the horns of that animal. In addition, phallic worship was incredibly important in his cult. Away from the pomp and circumstance of temples and state celebrations, the worship of Dionysus required only "a wine jar, a vine, a goat, a basket of figs, and then the phallus."[69]

During the time of the ancient Greeks and then later the Roman Empire, worship of Dionysus was widespread. Statues honoring the god of the grape can be found from India to Great Britain and all stops in between. His worship took place in public temple ceremonies and figured prominently in the initiation-only mysteries of both the classical Greeks and later those of the Roman Empire. Dionysus was honored in the Mysteries at Eleusis[70] and in the Orphic Mysteries, where he was thought to be the "king of the world."[71]

Dionysus remains a popular god, but today his popularity and familiarity are dwarfed by that of Pan, who traditionally was depicted as a *follower* of

---

69. Otto, *Dionysus*, 164.

70. The Eleusinian Mysteries are best known for the myth of Demeter and Persephone (Kore) at their heart and their relationship to the change of seasons. I write about them in *Transformative Witchcraft*.

71. Kerenyi, *Dionysos*, 265.

Dionysus. Some of that is most likely because of Pan's popularity in poetry (see chapter 11), but much of it may come down to Dionysus's complicated nature. With the exception of Hercules, there are more tales of Dionysus from the ancient world than any other Greek deity, and with widespread worship and immense popularity come conflicting understandings of the god.

Today Dionysus is most well known as the god of the (grape) vine and its resulting wine. In mythology, it is Dionysus who introduces viniculture to the world, mostly as a gift to human beings. Not only is wine generally safe to drink (the alcohol in it killing bacteria), but its inebriating effects are seen by many as pleasant. Of course, wine also has some formidable downsides: not only the morning-after hangover, but also the ability to produce drunkenness—madness-adjacent drunkenness.

For many of us, a few extra drinks might only result in a few embarrassing stories the next day. But being touched by the drunken madness of Dionysus often had much more far-reaching consequences. It could result in loss of life and the destruction of family ties. To abuse the gifts of Dionysus is to dishonor the god, who, while a fan of intoxication, is not a fan of bad behavior and inebriation to the point of incoherence.

Figure 5: Detail of a Grecian urn showing Dionysus flanked by satyrs and maenads. Dionysus was depicted in art as both bearded and clean-shaven.

When Dionysus chose to punish humans, he did so by driving them mad. The most well-known example of this appears in Euripides's play *The Bacchae*, a story that is not for the faint of heart. There the punishment for insulting the god is death through madness, most notably when the Theban King Pentheus dies at the hands of his mother, who has been driven violently mad by Dionysus (figure 5).

But madness does not always have to be negative; that is the result only when Dionysus's gifts are abused. When his gifts are honored through moderation and offerings, he's been known to gift his followers with "divine madness." Divine madness tears apart the veil that separates us from the divine. When this madness comes down upon us, we exist in a space shared with Dionysus. It opens up a portal to the artistic and magickal sides of ourselves that we often suppress. Madness in its best form brings us closer to the gods, while at its worst it separates us from the divine and those we love.

It's easy to picture Dionysus as a god of life and abundance, and I know that in my own practice I often honor him during the harvest. However, Dionysus is also intimately associated with death and the spirits of the dead. According to the Greek philosopher Heraclitus, "Hades and Dionysus, for whom they go mad and rage, are one and the same."[72] Many Dionysian festivals explicitly honored the spirits of the dead, and in some traditions it was Dionysus who helped escort souls to the Underworld. This association with death also links Dionysus even more firmly to the greater Horned God, with whom he shares this association.

The myths of Dionysus are peppered with death. Not only do many of his followers and adversaries die, but he himself dies more than once. In some myths, Dionysus is the son of Zeus and Persephone but is ripped apart by Titans shortly after his birth. His essence is later implanted into Semele, the Theban princess who would become his mortal mother as well as the lover of Zeus. Semele meets her mortal death after being tricked by the jealous Hera into asking Zeus to reveal his true form to her. Unfortunately for Semele, the true form of Zeus was a lightning bolt, and his taking of that form kills his mortal mistress. Dionysus is saved by being sewn into the thigh of Zeus, who later "gives birth" to his son. The story of Zeus giving birth to Dionysus highlights the patriarchal nature of ancient Greek culture, but also serves to illustrate the power of Dionysus to overcome death.

---

72. Otto, *Dionysus*, 116.

Dionysus is the patron deity of my home, primarily because of the close relationship he shares with both my wife and me. Ari often laments that she's "not liked" by Pan, but the affinity and affection she feels for Dionysus is quite real, and probably shouldn't be all that surprising. Women have always been influential in the worship and story of Dionysus, and it's not a stretch to say that in ancient Greece he was "the god of women."[73] Dionysus was raised by women. He turned the most important mortal women in his life into genuine deities, and everywhere he went he was accompanied by women.[74] During the Roman period, public worship of Dionysus was suppressed in many places primarily because women were the ones who led his cults!

The most well-known of Dionysus's followers are the *maenads,* whose very name is linked to the madness given to them by Dionysus.[75] The maenads are the female followers of Dionysus who feel and see the god in ritual and in wine but also experience him in moments of absolute silence. A maenad is a follower of the god who is capable of getting lost in his divine madness and will let nothing stand in her way of that.

For a god associated with both wine and the phallus, Dionysus was remarkably loyal to his wife, Ariadne. Once a mortal and the lover of the hero Theseus, Ariadne became a goddess upon marrying the god of the vine, who was captivated by her beauty. Deities such as Zeus and Poseidon have dozens of lovers (both male and female) in Greek myth, yet there are few tales of infidelity involving Dionysus. Did he have male lovers? Absolutely. Did he have lovers before Ariadne? Of course. But his myth makes him pretty comfortable with Ariadne (when he's not married to Persephone, as is implied in the Mysteries of Orpheus).

Like Pan, Dionysus was something of a gender bender. He was thought by some to be effeminate and was known to dress in drag. In the ancient world, many of Dionysus's most devoted followers were gay men, a trend that has continued into the modern age. In ritual, I once heard Dionysus referred to as "they," and the pronoun is an apt one for the wine god. Dionysus was and is

---

73. Kerenyi, *Dionysos,* 52.

74. Otto, *Dionysus,* 142.

75. Otto, *Dionysus,* 94.

capable of appearing in a multitude of roles, which is not surprising for a god who is said to have invented theater.

Apart from Dionysus and Pan there are other figures that might be considered horned (or horny) gods. Often confused with Pan, Greek satyrs very much resemble the god of Arcadia. Many a satyr statue (also half-goat and half-man) has been mistaken for an image of Pan. In myth, however, satyrs lack the refinement of Pan and are far closer to the wild animals of the forest than to a rational and thinking deity.

Priapus, most frequently said to be the son of Dionysus and Aphrodite, was far more phallus than person, with his erect member often depicted as being comically large. Worship of Priapus differed wildly in ancient Greece. According to some accounts, Priapus was cursed by a jealous Hera while in Aphrodite's womb, and with that constantly huge erection (even in the womb), it feels like Aphrodite was a victim of this curse, too. Priapus's problem was payback from Hera for Prince Paris of Troy finding Aphrodite more beautiful than her. Aside from this story, Priapus seems to have been worshipped as a fertility and harvest deity. Interestingly, in some places he and Dionysus were worshipped as one and the same, further cementing Dionysus's status as a truly phallic deity.[76]

---

76. Otto, *Dionysus*, 165.

Chapter Six

IGNITING THE FIRE:
A PAN RITUAL FOR TWO (OR MORE)

IN THE ANCIENT WORLD people performed rituals for Pan when they felt like they needed to tap into his energies. Not surprisingly, the energy most people were interested in tapping into involved his voracious appetite for sex. Couples and groups would visit Pan's grottoes in order to ramp up their sex lives, or perhaps reignite a spark lost to time and mundane circumstances.

In my own practice, I perform this ritual when trying to spice things up, and on certain occasions to add a little extra gravitas to my wife and I's lovemaking. This ritual is also an opportunity to thank Pan for his many blessings in our lives, and perhaps to serve as a reminder that he still likes us, even if we've embraced monogamy. Because the "panic sexuality" of Pan is especially charged, I recommend performing this ritual only if you have an established relationship with the god and are performing this ritual with an established partner (or partners).

It also goes without saying that any sexual activity and/or spiritual activity should have the consent of all parties involved. Safe sex practices should also be followed. Pan is cool with condoms in the twenty-first century. Every aspect of this ritual should be enacted by all parties involved.

I've written this ritual for two people, but it can easily be adapted for as many people as want to participate. This ritual can also be enacted by one person. Pan is just as cool with masturbation as he is with coupling or three-somes or whatever else you and your loved ones might choose to do.

This ritual can be performed indoors or out, or some combination of the two. My preference is to place Pan's offerings outside at the beginning of the ritual and then proceed indoors. What's most important is picking a space where you won't be disturbed or run into any problems.

RITUAL SUPPLIES

For this ritual you will need:

- Offerings for Pan (I suggest wine or some other form of alcohol. Whatever you offer Pan—and it doesn't have to be alcoholic—should be something you would enjoy drinking yourself. Pan also enjoys sweet pastries, so a piece of cake or a cupcake would be appropriate.)
- A chalice to hold the liquid offering for Pan
- A plate or bowl to carry the food offering for Pan
- A libation bowl (if your offerings are not left directly on the earth)
- A (preferably) red taper candle and holder
- Materials for safe sex
- A comfortable spot for sexual activity (Though if you're cool with the hard ground, more power to you.)
- A poem or devotional piece for Pan
- Background music (In my experience, Pan likes heavy metal, electronic dance music, reels and jigs, and traditional Greek pipes.)

THE RITUAL

My preference is to prepare my offerings indoors, pouring Pan a generous glass of wine (or beer or cider) and then placing his food offering on a ritual plate. As the offerings are being prepared for Pan, verbalize the intent behind them by saying, "For the great god Pan!" The sooner his name is invoked, the sooner he will seek out your ritual activity.

Once the offerings have been prepared, take them outdoors to a space where you can safely leave them and where you feel Pan would be comfortable receiving them. Across the street from my house there is a small park with a large oak tree. I like to leave my Pan offerings there because of the Arcadians' reverence for the oak. If you cannot leave your offerings outside, place them in a libation bowl to be given to Pan later. If the only place to leave an offering is far from where you live, it is acceptable to drive to a remote spot at the start or end of the ritual to leave your offerings.

If possible, you and your lover should walk together to the location where you plan to leave Pan's offerings. Even if you are headed to a spot nearby, such as in your backyard or at a nearby park, it's best to turn your walk into something a little extra. This means taking the long way to wherever you're going, providing you with a little bit of extra time to focus on the god as the ritual begins. If you can add a flute player to your walk, that's great, but if you are like me, a quiet chant is probably all that can be done without scaring the neighbors. When my wife and I proceed to our offering spot, we quietly chant this to Pan:

> *Pan, we honor you this day.*
> *Come and join us in our play!*

Once the offering spot has been reached, place the cake on the ground and pour your wine/beverage around it.[77] Then say:

> *We give this offering to the great god Pan! O bringer of lust and life, we ask today for your gifts. Charge our passions, fill us with your lust, let us experience the pleasures of the flesh anew and find solace, sensuality, and spirit in our lovemaking! Bless our coupling so that we might grow closer to both you and each other! So mote it be!*

Once the offering has been left, proceed back to your secluded place, preferably holding hands with your partner (or partners). When you arrive at your destination, put your red candle into a candleholder and place it on

---

77. Once, while pouring the wine on top of the cake, my wife asked me, "Do you want people pouring wine on your slice of cake?" I replied no and got the hint. If we don't like our food mixed like that, why do we think the gods would?

a safe spot, such as an altar or the top of a dresser. As you light your candle, invoke Pan into your space:

> *Be with us tonight, son of Hermes! Lend your energies to our intimacy!*
> *Let us feel you working through us, embracing your wild, untamed passions.*
> *May our union draw us closer to each other and to your mysteries. Enfold us*
> *in the joys and delights of the carnal world, allowing us to become as one. Let*
> *us find new delights in one another through the pleasures of the flesh! Great*
> *Pan, hail and welcome!*

Embrace your lover (or lovers) and begin exploring their body, slowly and sensuously removing each other's clothing (or quickly and ravenously, depending on the circumstances—Pan is fine with both ways). As skin and nakedness are revealed, take delight in the shape of your lover. All bodies are holy and sacred and are deserving of physical pleasure. Kiss each other and compliment each another, finding delight in the body of your lovemate. (If you are performing this ritual alone, say good things about yourself—you deserve it!)

As soon as everyone is as naked as they wish to be, say a devotional piece to Pan. My favorite pieces to read for him are not the ones I've written myself, but my favorite poems that feature the goat-legged one. Romantic eighteenth-century poetry is a good place to start (there's a lot of that in this book in chapter 11), but other options include excerpts from Tom Robbins' *Jitterbug Perfume* or perhaps Aleister Crowley's "Hymn to Pan" (also in chapter 11). While the devotional piece is being read, there's nothing that says you have to keep your hands to yourself. While your partner is reading whatever appeals to them, you are free to caress, kiss, stroke, or whatever else appeals to the two of you.

Letting every participant in the ritual read a small piece to Pan can be fun, too. My wife and I enjoy trying to "out-devotion" the other; she puts her acting skills to work, while I try my best to enunciate like my life depends on it. A little competition between lovers is a great way to stoke the flames of passion.

If you can't find a piece of poetry or literature that appeals to you, it's completely acceptable to just say whatever is in your heart directly to the god. Just remember that like us, the gods like to be flattered and complimented. If the words just aren't there, you could say something like this:

> *Great god Pan, inexhaustible lover, my heart and loins call to thee. Horned One of yesterday and today, I honor you this night. You are wanting and wanted. You are lust and the erotic longings within us all. You are the joy of sexual union, pleasure, and passion. Your words are poetry, your form the beauty of the natural world. O sacred goat-footed one, know that I adore and love thee! So mote it be!*

Once your devotional piece has been read (or simply said), play some sort of music representing how you and your partner are currently feeling. Will your lovemaking be soft and sensual? Will it be a bit more animalistic? You might find yourself wanting to dance very close together to a romantic love song, or maybe it's a night that calls for something a little heavier, like Black Sabbath. Whatever you choose, let it be freeing. Lose yourself in the music and the touch, feel, and look of your partner. Let all of your inhibitions slip away and simply live in the music...

By this point of the ritual, it's possible that all organized activities might begin to slip away from the participants. If you find yourself moving directly from dancing to lovemaking without any words, that's perfectly acceptable. In fact, it's a sign that the ritual has done exactly what it's supposed to do. If you want to prolong things a bit, take turns kissing an eight-pointed star on the body of your partner.

KISS OF THE EIGHT-POINTED STAR

The kiss of the eight-pointed star is designed to titillate various erogenous zones on the body. The kiss can be adapted depending on the needs of groups or couples. This version of the eight-pointed star involves kisses on the genitals, breasts, both sides of the neck, both ears, and the mouth. If you like feet, add feet! If elbows are an erogenous zone for a play-partner, add elbows. As long as its consensual, everything is fair game. The example here is simply what's comfortable in my home.

The person who is the first to be "adored" should lie on their back, with their partner sitting between their legs or perhaps lying (comfortably) on top of them. Once everyone is in position, invoke Pan once more:

Great Pan, in your name I taunt and tease. Bless our union and play. So mote it be.

Look down upon your partner and meet their gaze. Stare at each other and appreciate how beautiful and sensual they are. Slowly lean down and kiss them on the lips. The kiss can last as long as the two of you wish. At the end of the kiss say:

With moans and sighs, we worship the god of Arcadia and one another.

Kiss down your partner's body to their left breast, taking your time, adoring every inch of their body. When you reach their breast, tease and kiss it. If you've come this far, there's no need to rush things. Before moving up to the right side of their neck, say:

Passion's fire we ignite this night.

Trace your mouth slowly up their body until you reach the right side of their neck. Kiss that area and feel your partner's warmth. Enjoy the taste and feel of their body against yours. Say:

There is no me this night, only us.

Move toward your partner's left ear, and kiss and nuzzle it. Whisper into their ear how much you love them, or how attractive you think they are, or perhaps what you will be doing to each other shortly. Be erotic, get lost in the moment, and feel the energy of Pan around you and the energy being raised by you and your partner. Say:

I adore you. Know that you are beautiful.

Move from the left ear to the right, perhaps getting lost on your partner's lips as you move to the other side of their body. Again, share your feelings with them. People love to be complimented, and we do not flatter others nearly enough in our society. Say:

My body belongs to you.

Look into your partner's eyes once more, perhaps kissing their mouth again as you move to nuzzle and touch the right side of their neck. Feel the flushed energy moving about you both as your bodies touch. Say:

The delights of heaven are here upon the earth through our Lord Pan.

From the neck, move to the right breast, again taking your time. Use your hands to explore the body of your partner as you kiss the eight-pointed star upon their body. Share the excitement of your body with them as you kiss their right breast. Say:

Lust and desire we share this night.

And finally move to your partner's genitals. Tease and taunt those erogenous zones! Do whatever it is that brings your partner pleasure with your hands, mouth, or other parts of your body. Linger in that space. Feel the power of their sex, the energy of their being, become one with your own energies. Say:

I honor you.

If you aren't already making love by this point, this process can be repeated, with the giver becoming the adored on the second go-round. Again, if desire overtakes all the partners involved, great! There's no need to do this again, but if you want to draw things out a little longer, feel free!

In Witchcraft we have a saying, "What happens in the circle stays in the circle," so do whatever it is now that all involved wish to do. However you do it, though, be free and be unselfconscious! Sex is supposed to be pleasurable and fun! Grunt, groan, and even laugh if the energy takes you there. Make love until all involved are spent.

ENDING THE RITE

When everyone is satiated, you'll want to end the rite. Start by thanking your partner and telling them once more how you feel about them and how beautiful they are. Perhaps do some cuddling and a little bit more kissing if it feels right. Once you have honored each other, thank the god Pan for lending his energies to your rites:

> *Great Pan, god of longing and lost, thank you for being with us in our rites! May we continue to honor you and each other in the days, weeks, and months to come with our bodies and the pleasure they bring. We thank you for your gifts and the energy you have brought to our ritual this night. Continue to remind us that the sensual is also sacred, and that as Witches we honor both the body and the spirit. Hail and farewell!*

Blow out the candle you've lit for the god, and take down any sacred space you've created (thank the quarters, release the circle, etc.). Embrace your partner once more, and together let out a hearty "Io Pan!" as a final thank you to the god.[78]

Hail the power of Pan!

---

78. *Io* is a Latin exclamation of joy, originally from the Greek.

Chapter Seven
CERNUNNOS

WHEN PEOPLE PICTURE THE Horned God today, they generally envision a stylized version of the Gallic-Celtic deity Cernunnos. A google image search for "The Horned God" reveals hundreds of images of this book's subject, most of them featuring an adult, bearded male in Celtic-style dress, with antlers on the top of his head. Sure, there are a few images of Pan here and there, but generally what one sees are stylized images of Cernunnos.

In some of those images, the Horned God resembles Cernunnos as he appears on the famous Gundestrup cauldron (see image later in this chapter). In other pictures he looks less like he did traditionally two thousand years ago, perhaps with a skull for a face or cloven hooves for his feet. Even in such cases, it's clear that Cernunnos was the fundamental inspiration for the image, even if the work's author might be unaware of that truth.

Cernunnos, through his image, is nearly everywhere in Modern Witch-craft, but despite the popularity of his image, most people know very little about him. Much of the material alleging to be about Cernunnos over the decades applies more to Pan than to him. As Cernunnos is the most domi-nant *image* of the Horned God, it's easy to assume that any attribute of the Horned God can be found in him, but that's not really the case.

When it comes to Cernunnos, one of the biggest issues is that he's a god lacking any concrete mythology. While there are books today full of "Celtic mythology," generally originating from modern-day Ireland and Wales, most of that mythology is believed to have been written by Christian chroniclers during the Middle Ages, long after the pagan peoples in those areas had been Christianized.[79] That body of work also lacks any references to Cernunnos, or a god that even resembles him.

Over the last fifty years, there have been valiant attempts to link Cernunnos to specific deities from the Celtic myths originating in Great Britain. The most common analogue is probably the Welsh Gwyn ap Nudd, a figure who shows up in some tales of King Arthur and is generally linked to the realms of Faery and the dead. In a lot of Pagan art, Gwyn ap Nudd looks much like Cernunnos. Writer R. J. Stewart has linked Cernunnos in his role as "Lord of the Animals" to the Arthurian wizard Merlin.[80] Could Cernunnos be linked to these other figures? Absolutely, though I personally am rather skeptical.

The name Cernunnos appears only once in the ancient world, where it's inscribed on an altar known as the Pillar of the Boatmen, which dates back to the first century of the Common Era. Discovered in modern-day Paris (at the site of Notre Dame cathedral no less), the Pillar of the Boatmen is made up of four large blocks, one of which contains an image of Cernunnos. Above his head lies the word *CERNVNNOS*, or at least most of it anyway. The *C* is missing today, though drawings from the nineteenth century suggest it was once there.[81] The word *CERNVNNOS* most likely means something like "god with antlers (or horns)," from *kornu/kern,* Celtic for horns or antlers, and *nos,* indicating a deity. Though Cernunnos is a Gaulish name, on the Pillar of the Boatmen his name is written in Latin.

There are two other instances of a name *like* Cernunnos appearing in the ancient world. The most notable one comes from Southern France and features a dedication to the god from a worshipper: "Alletînos [son] of Alisontea, to Carnonos."[82] Most scholars accept *Carnonos* here as a variant of *Cernunnos,* with the exact translation from Gallic to English perhaps meaning "horned (or antlered) god." More contentious is a third inscription which reads: "To

---

79. Hutton, *Pagan Britain,* 362.

80. Stewart, *Celtic Gods, Celtic Goddesses,* 113.

81. Bober, "Cernunnos: Origin and Transformation of a Celtic Divinity," 14.

82. Deo Mercurio. "Kapnonoy: to Carnonos."

the god Cerunincus, Soltrius Pruscus fulfilled his vow freely and willingly."
It's possible here that the similarities between *Cerunincus* and *Cernunnos* or *Carnonos* are simply coincidence, though the bronze plaque (found in present-day Luxembourg) on which the inscription was found was buried next to an image that might be Cernunnos.[83]

Because the name Cernunnos seems to be referencing a title and not an actual name, some people have argued that Cernunnos is not the name of a god at all. I think such arguments are silly since gods in the ancient world were often known by titles. In addition, the Pillar of the Boatmen contains the names of other deities, so why would the block on which the image and name of Cernunnos appears simply feature a title he was known by?

I think we can safely say that Cernunnos was (and is) a deity; it's just that the area he was worshipped in was rather limited. To date, at least forty images of Cernunnos have been found, with most of them appearing in France, more specifically, in France near modern-day Paris.[84] Further afield, at least one probable image of the god has been found in England, while the famous Gundestrup cauldron was found in Denmark. Just how many images of Cernunnos have been found is a matter of debate, with some people arguing for a number much higher than forty. (For instance, the North Cross at Clonmacnoise monastery in Ireland has what many believe to be an imagine of Cernunnos, while others doubt the image has anything to do with the god. I'm in the latter camp; your individual interpretation may vary.)

I feel comfortable writing that at least forty images of Cernunnos have been discovered, because most of those images are remarkably consistent. Cernunnos nearly always has the antlers of a stag, appears to be sitting, wears and/or carries a torc, and appears with a ram-headed serpent or coins. If Cernunnos wasn't a god, it's unlikely he'd be represented in such a consistent manner. Images of Cernunnos have been found in a variety of settings, and the god has been found on bowls, cups, altars, and columns. There are also several small statues of the god that have survived to the present day.

---

83. Deo Mercurio. "Kapnonoy: to Carnonos."
84. Deo Mercurio. "Kapnonoy: to Carnonos."

The surviving images of Cernunnos are important because they provide insights into how he was possibly worshipped in the ancient world. We'll never know with absolute certainty what role Cernunnos filled for the Celts of Gaul, but we can make some pretty educated guesses. In this section of the book, we'll take a close look at some of the more famous images of Cernunnos and use them to shed some light on his worship two thousand years ago.

Figure 6: Val Camonica rock drawing (artist's rendition).
One of the oldest depictions of Cernunnos
is also one of the most unique.

The oldest surviving image of Cernunnos is a rock carving from Val Camonica, a valley in northern Italy not too far from the Swiss border (figure 6). Created by Celts in the fourth century BCE, the image of Cernunnos from Val Camonica is not extremely detailed, but it contains most of the tell-tale signs of Cernunnos in art.[85] The most noticeable part of the carving are the antlers on the god's head.

---

85. Serith, "Cernunnos: Looking a Different Way."

Just what the antlers of Cernunnos signify is an open question. For most of us, they suggest a link to the natural world. Over the decades, several scholars have suggested that Cernunnos was a hunting deity, with the antlers supporting that assumption. Certainly in Val Camonica, hunting would have been an important and life-preserving activity. Stags might have simply been seen as powerful animals in their own right, and therefore worthy of adoration. Since stags are a source of meat, clothing, shelter, and tools, there's certainly a lot to honor there.

Less prominent to the untrained eye, but hard to miss for the Cernunnos devotee, are the torcs around the arms of Cernunnos. To the ancient Celts, torcs were more than ornaments or jewelry; they were symbols of wealth, power, and status.[86] The Snettisham Great Torc (found in Norfolk, England) is made of silver and gold and weighs just over a kilogram and incorporates sixty-four separate wires in its design! The torcs being wielded here by Cernunnos must have been thought to be similarly large, judging by their size on his arms. Both torcs and antlers are a part of nearly every Cernunnos image and are one of the primary ways he can be identified in ancient art.

It's also worth noting the posture of Cernunnos's arms in the Val Camonica carving. They appear to be in what's known as the *orans position*, which tends to indicate prayer or supplication. It's a common posture in Christian art and one still used by Catholic priests today, but it was also used by ancient Pagans. The fact that the small figure next to Cernunnos is also in this position also helps to indicate the divine status of the antlered god, in my opinion.

The squiggly line that begins on the left side of the figure and goes behind his back is most likely a snake or serpent. As we will discuss later in this chapter, the ram-headed serpent is a frequent companion of Cernunnos, so this could be a version of that. Cernunnos's garb varies from image to image. Here he is wearing a long robe. The robe is not typical dress for the god, and it's so long that it seems like it would make hunting unlikely, but it shows up in a few other images as well.

---

86. Leins, *Celts: Art and Identity*, 6.

What's really strange about the Val Camonica image is that Cernunnos is standing. In the fifty-plus images we have of Cernunnos from the ancient world, fewer than five have the god standing on his own two feet.[87] Usually the god is sitting in a "Buddhic" posture (legs crossed, seat on the ground). Because this early image features him standing, this suggests that the sitting posture might have come later, or the standing pose might have been chosen simply because it was easier to draw. The Val Camonica image is not a masterpiece.

Regardless of the image's quality, it is still important, because it suggests that all the things that make Cernunnos were in place by the fourth century BCE. It's likely that the god went through some changes over the centuries, but his core essence seems likely to have stayed the same.

Figure 7: Gundestrup cauldron.
The panel featuring Cernunnos is on the inside of the vessel.

Perhaps the most iconic image of the Horned God in antiquity is Cernunnos on the Gundestrup cauldron (figure 7). Unearthed in a peat bog in Denmark and created in Southeastern Europe (most likely modern-day Bulgaria or Romania), the Gundestrup cauldron is unlike any other artifact left by the ancient Celts.[88] In fact, referring to the Gundestrup cauldron simply as a "Celtic" object may not even be accurate. It contains images of elephants

---

87. Serith, "Cernunnos: Looking a Different Way."
88. Leins, *Celts: Art and Identity*, 24.

and hyenas, animals that did not live in Europe when it was created, so whoever created it was clearly well-traveled and worldly.

In 2016 my wife and I saw the Gundestrup cauldron at the National Museum of Scotland. (The cauldron usually resides at the National Museum of Denmark in Copenhagen but was in the UK as part of a touring exhibit called *The Celts*. Before heading to Scotland, it was at the British Museum in London, and today again resides in Copenhagen.) The curators wisely placed the cauldron in the center of the exhibit, and as Ari and I walked through, we could feel the cauldron's energy beckoning us to come closer. It took nearly all my willpower not to run straight toward it the moment I entered the exhibit.

Images of the Gundestrup cauldron do not do it justice. It's far larger than most people imagine, a little over two feet across, and was designed to be taken apart. Instead of it looking like a solid bowl, the panels that make up the cauldron almost look like they are "clipped on" and ready to be disassembled again. (Upon its discovery, the cauldron was found intentionally taken apart.) It was most likely used for ceremonial or religious purposes, with only the very bottom of the bowl below its panels capable of holding liquid.

The cauldron is made almost entirely of silver, though there were once glass beads on the panels to serve as eyes for the figures on them. All of the images on the cauldron's panels are also raised. This is easy enough to see in pictures of the Cauldron, but at the same time, those images do not convey its true 3-D nature.

Of the twelve surviving panels that make up the Gundestrup cauldron, the scene featuring Cernunnos is the most well-known, but the other images are equally striking. They are also in some ways more mysterious, and while they feature deities and scenes that most certainly look "Celtic," no one is actually sure that the deities being represented *are* Celtic. Just what stories the cauldron is trying to tell have yet to be fully deciphered.

Despite what many people think, the panel of the Gundestrup cauldron featuring Cernunnos is not all that prominent (figure 8). Instead of being featured on the outside of the cauldron, where it would most easily be seen, it's an interior panel. Its placement means that to really see it, one must lean over and look into the cauldron. The image of Cernunnos is different from that of the other deities featured on the cauldron, too. The rest of the divine figures are depicted as having large heads and small bodies, while Cernunnos has the proportions of a normal-size man.

Figure 8: Cernunnos panel on the Gundestrup cauldron.
On the cauldron's most famous panel, we see Cernunnos
surrounded by animals and a man riding a dolphin.

Much of what we believe we know about Cernunnos comes directly from the Gundestrup cauldron, so it's worth going over what appears on his specific panel. In the image on the cauldron, Cernunnos is surrounded by a menagerie of animals. Just what species all the animals are in the image is a point of debate. The stag near Cernunnos, though, is crystal clear and shares his headwear (their antlers are the same). To the left of Cernunnos (your right in the image) are what appear to be dogs. Past the dogs there are some large cats, and flanking both sides of the panel are some sort of horned animal, most likely a bull.[89] (The most curious animal depicted is a dolphin who carries a human rider.)

The large number of animals surrounding Cernunnos in the image has led many to proclaim him the "Lord of the Animals," but it's really only

---

89. I feel like I should point out here that my editor disagrees with the idea that these figures are bulls, though they are generally described that way by people who write about the Cauldron. They do have very skinny necks for bulls.

on the Gundestrup cauldron that we see him in such a situation. In other images, he appears either mostly alone (not counting his serpents) or with other deities. Cernunnos surrounded by animals is the exception and not the rule. The proximity of the dogs to Cernunnos, as well as the nearby stag, supports the idea of Cernunnos as god of the hunt, but again, this is more of an outlier than a consistent characteristic in his iconography (though it shouldn't be dismissed).

The meaning of the dolphin and rider image is rife for speculation, but the two figures are often overlooked or left out of many reproductions of the panel. Traditionally, water was a way to reach the Celtic Otherworld, a land of both deities and (most likely) the dead. The dolphin-rider could be an allusion to that idea, or something else entirely. The bovine figures, especially if they are cattle or bulls, could be a symbol of wealth, as livestock were important to the ancient Celts. If I'm correct in my assumptions about the dolphin/rider and the cattle, those ideas complement many of the other ideas represented by Cernunnos on the panel.

The biggest difference between Cernunnos on the Gundestrup cauldron and Cernunnos at Val Camonica is his sitting posture. There are several different theories that might possibly explain why Cernunnos is often depicted sitting with his legs crossed. The easiest one is that the Celts simply sat on the ground a lot. Instead of lounging in chairs or couches, the Celts of Gaul were more likely to sit with their legs crossed on the ground.[90] Cernunnos sitting in a similar fashion might mean that he's simply accessible to those who worship him. Sitting cross-legged on the ground is also a posture a Celtic hunter likely used when at rest.[91]

The most common explanation for the sitting posture of Cernunnos is that his pose is related to Asian or Indian practices. The speculation here is that Cernunnos is meditating; and considering the worldly nature of the Gundestrup cauldron, the idea can't be dismissed out of hand. Most frequently, Cernunnos is compared to an image found on a seal discovered in

---

90. Bober, "Cernunnos: Origin and Transformation of a Celtic Divinity," 21.

91. Stewart, *Celtic Gods, Celtic Goddesses*, 112.

the Indus River Valley (in modern-day Pakistan) dating from about 2000 BCE.[92] Most commonly known as the *Pashupati Seal*, the seal is thought by some to depict an early image of the god we know today as Shiva (or Siva).

There are certainly similarities between Cernunnos and the figure on the seal, but there are differences too. While the figure from the Indus River Valley seems to be wearing horns, a closer look reveals that the horns look as if they are part of a helmet, and not a naturally occurring feature. They also look far more like "horns" than like the antlers of Cernunnos. The figure on the Pashupati Seal might also be female, while the Cernunnos on the Gundestrup cauldron is obviously male.[93]

Could the two figures be related? Most certainly. The Celts and the inhabitants of the early Indus River Valley civilization share common ancestors. Both groups are "Indo-European" (which is a language grouping more than a racial one), which means their individual languages came from the same origin point. The deities among Indo-European groups also seem to have evolved from the same rootstock. So it's possible that Cernunnos and proto-Shiva have a common ancestor. However, the large gap of time between the creation of the Pashupati Seal and the first images of Cernunnos (1,600 years!) is quite large. The gap in time between the creation of the seal and the Gundestrup cauldron is even greater, with most scholars believing the cauldron was created between 150 and 50 BCE.[94]

Along with torcs and the sitting position, the ram-headed serpent is one of the defining characteristics of a Cernunnos image. Unlike our culture's rather problematic relationship with snakes, to the ancient Celts, serpents were positive and generally represented abundance and fertility.[95] The Celts also believed that snakes guarded buried treasure, associating Cernunnos with wealth, much like the torcs he wears and holds. Rams were sacrificial animals in the world of the Celts, making it likely that the ram's head on the serpent's body represents sacrifice or death.[96] As the homes of snakes are

---

92. Serith, "Cernunnos: Looking a Different Way."

93. Serith, "Cernunnos: Looking a Different Way."

94. Leins, *Celts: Art and Identity*, 25.

95. Congail, "Cernunnos and the Ram-Headed Serpent."

96. Bober, "Cernunnos: Origin and Transformation of a Celtic Divinity," 26.

generally underground, the serpent might also be another link to Cernunnos and the Underworld.

Some scholars see the ram-headed serpent as a symbol of chaos or disorder, but that seems unlikely to me since Cernunnos seems to be in charge of the creatures when they are with him.[97] That serpent more likely represents the balance between life and death, since the ram and the serpent together seem to inhabit those two paradigms.

Like the Cernunnos carving at Val Camonica, the god's arms are once more in the orans position, indicating prayer. Even while holding a torc and a serpent, Cernunnos appears serene, perhaps even meditative. For those looking to bolster the god's connection to India or Eastern meditative practices, Cernunnos's expression on the Gundestrup cauldron gives the theory a bit more credence.

The most ambiguous of the signs on the Cernunnos panels might be the vegetative-looking ornamentation that appears between the various figures on the cauldron. I've always felt that the ornamentation looks like flowers, but no one really knows for sure what its meant to represent. What might be most interesting, though, is how the ornamentation is woven between the antlers of Cernunnos and that of the stag to his right. It's by far the largest patch of ornamentation on the cauldron and might suggest some sort of metaphysical link between Cernunnos and the stag.

THE REIMS STELA

Outside of the Gundestrup cauldron, one of the most captivating images of Cernunnos appears on a stela found in the French town of Reims (figure 9). Its similarity to the Cernunnos of the Pillar of the Boatmen suggests that it's of a similar age to that of the monument, making it fifty to a hundred years younger than the Gundestrup cauldron. The Reims stela contains most of the symbolism we associate with Cernunnos, including antlers, sitting posture, a bull, and a stag, but there are other notable differences here as well.

---

97. Serith, "Cernunnos: Looking a Different Way."

The most obvious difference is that here, Cernunnos is flanked by two gods, Apollo on his right and Mercury to his left. If Cernunnos is connected to death, then his proximity to Mercury is appropriate. Mercury, after all, guided the souls of the dead into the Underworld. Mercury was also a god of commerce and money, and the idea of wealth is a frequent motif in Cernunnos art. Apollo's appearance is a bit more problematic, but in his guise as a sun god, both Apollo and Cernunnos share an affinity with the natural world.

Figure 9: The Reims stela.
Here Cernunnos is flanked by two Roman gods,
Apollo to the left and Mercury (Hermes) to the right.

Instead of Cernunnos carrying a serpent or a torc (though he does wear a torc around his neck), there appears to be a large sack of coins on the god's lap. In fact, the bag has so many coins that they are pouring out of his sack and onto the ground. The Reims stela is further indication that Cernunnos had something to do with money and wealth. The coins could also tie Cernunnos to the Underworld, as the metals used to make coinage are mined from the earth. Coins and metal were also associated with the Roman Pluto and Greek Hades, both deities of the Underworld. The fact that the coins fall between a stag and a bull should not be overlooked either. This could be another allusion to fertility, both in the wild and with domesticated animals. The stag might also once again tie Cernunnos to an activity like hunting.

An alternative explanation for the sack in Cernunnos's lap is that it is a cornucopia, and that something other than gold is falling out of it, most likely grain. I don't think this is likely, as those really do look like coins to me, but ancient art is open to a variety of interpretations. If it is a cornucopia, then Cernunnos could be feeding the stag and bull beneath him, suggesting dominion over domesticated animals.

Though sometimes depicted as whole in drawings of the Reims stela, Cernunnos's antlers are broken in the original and appear as small bumps on the top of his head. The tines of his antlers are present in the stela but appear above him, on the top of the temple that the three gods are standing in front of. It's possible they were attached to his head once, or perhaps their broken nature is being used to indicate a time of year. Perhaps Cernunnos has shed his horns in the late winter and they are now being used as decoration to suggest either death or regeneration.

Also, at the top of the temple, between the possibly shed antlers, is a rat. The rat is not a typical companion of Cernunnos but might be here to suggest yet another association with death or the Underworld.[98]

THE GODDESS CERNUNNOS

Just like Pan, Cernunnos also has a female avatar. Though not an especially frequent figure in the archaeological record, she shares several attributes with Cernunnos, and her artifacts have been found in the same geographical area. One of the most interesting female Cernunnos images is a bronze statue from the Franche-Comté region of Eastern France, currently housed at the British Museum in London.

Sometimes interpreted as male, the figure has a clearly defined bosom and what appears to be a face with female features, though it should be noted that androgyny was not uncommon in the ancient world.[99] This version of

98. Bober, "Cernunnos: Origin and Transformation of a Celtic Divinity," 43.

99. Deo Mercurio. "Kapnonoy: to Carnonos."

Cernunnos is depicted in a sitting position and partially resembles a stag. There are horns on top of this figure's head, and I write "horns" here because they don't quite resemble the antlers of a stag. The horns are far too thick to be antlers and lack the points that give antlers their distinct look.

Like similar statues that have been discovered over the years, this female Cernunnos seems to be carrying an offering bowl and a cornucopia on a pole. Her lap also looks like a welcome place for offerings, and on similar statues, offering bowls are often situated on the figure's legs. The cornucopia could represent the abundance shared by the goddess Cernunnos, with the offering bowls serving as a reminder to present her with offerings as a means of thanks. Like most Cernunnos-related images, the cornucopia also suggests wealth.

So was there a female version of Cernunnos? It's certainly possible. It could also be his wife or daughter. Or it might be unrelated to Cernunnos, since among the Celts, sitting with one's legs crossed wasn't all that uncommon. However, among deer and related species, only males grow antlers (with the exception of reindeer), so because it's something not generally seen in the wild, I believe the antlers are most likely a reference to Cernunnos in some way.

WHAT EXACTLY DO WE KNOW ABOUT CERNUNNOS FROM THE ANCIENT WORLD?

Because of how Cernunnos was pictured over the centuries in ancient art, I think we can draw a few strong conclusions about the god.

Cernunnos was a God of Wealth

Between the torcs and the bags of overflowing coinage, I think it's safe to say that Cernunnos had something to do with material prosperity. The fact that he's shown with useful animals (useful for food and clothing) such as the bull and the stag also suggests this, as does the ram-headed serpent.

Cernunnos Was a God of Wild Spaces

The constant presence of the antlers can't be explained away and most likely has something to do with the natural world. There are also some indications that he might have been a god of hunting, most notably the dogs and perhaps the hunting posture.

Cernunnos Was a God of Death and the Underworld

Often overlooked on the Gundestrup cauldron, the image of the dolphin and the rider is suggestive of the Underworld, like much of his other iconography. Modern interpretations of the Horned God, and especially Cernunnos, often overemphasize the natural world connotations, but perhaps more than anything else, Cernunnos had something to do with death. Death is also a complementary companion of hunting and the natural world, since death is a part of those spheres.

Does all of this coincide with how Cernunnos is honored and worshipped by Pagans and Witches today? Not always, but I feel like it's rather close. I also urge people to share their experiences with Cernunnos. As we will see later with the god Pan, deities do adapt and change over time. I don't think anything has stayed exactly as it was two thousand years ago. The gods are not beings preserved in amber; they are active in this world, and that activity suggests agency, and the ability to change and progress.

It's likely that Cernunnos (or at least versions of him) is more popular today than in the time of the Celts from Gaul. As his worship continues to spread, we will find out more about the god through his interactions with us. Anytime I've interacted with a sincere devotee of Cernunnos, I've found that our interpretations of the god have a lot in common. The past gives us a great starting point, but it's just that: a starting point. The power of Cernunnos is growing in our modern world, and as it does so, we will gain a new understanding of him.

Chapter Eight

A DEVOTIONAL ALTAR FOR CERNUNNOS

GROWING CLOSER TO CERNUNNOS can be challenging. As he's a god with no mythology and lacking much of a modern footprint outside of Witchcraft and Pagan circles, materials referencing him are scarce. When people ask me about the best way to grow closer to a deity, I usually tell them to try talking with that deity, which is a great place to start! However, we can take the simple act of speaking with a deity up a notch by building a devotional altar to them.

A devotional altar is just what it sounds like: it's an altar designed as a specific place to pay devotion to a particular deity. But it can also be more than that. My Cernunnos altar not only is a place to show my devotion to "C" (as we call him around the house) but is also a focal point for my personal and magickal interactions with him. I use my Cernunnos altar both to leave him libations and to better my own situation through magick. Since our relationships with the gods are reciprocal, these interactions feel especially appropriate to me.

A devotional altar is different from a working altar used in ritual, as it's meant to be semipermanent. So when setting up your devotional altar, try to find a place that can be dedicated strictly to Cernunnos. This doesn't have to be an elaborate spot in your home. The top of a bookshelf or dresser works especially well, but if that's not an option, then a corner of a living room table or a fireplace mantel will work too. An empty shelf on a bookcase is fine as well, and you could even just put a shelf on your wall and use it for your devotional altar. The larger your space, the more you'll be able to do with your devotional altar, but there are always creative work-arounds if space is at a premium.

ITEMS FOR A CERNUNNOS ALTAR

Once you've found a place for your Cernunnos altar, you'll want to gather items to put on it. Whatever you place on your altar should resonate with *your* personal understanding of Cernunnos. If you just can't view him as a god of death and the afterlife, then don't include anything honoring those aspects of him. While it's an altar for Cernunnos, it's also your space, and you should be comfortable while using it. With that said, these are the items I recommend for a Cernunnos altar:

- *A representation of Cernunnos.* The easiest thing to use here is a statue of Cernunnos. Statues were used as focal points for devotion in the ancient world and are still used by many Witches today. While I am a big fan of statues, they can be prohibitively expensive. In addition, many Witches are uncomfortable using mass-produced items. If either of these conditions applies to you, not using a statue is completely acceptable. An easy alternative is simply using a picture of Cernunnos. This could be something on heavy paper stock such as a postcard, a painting or drawing from a favorite artist (this includes yourself), or something printed off your computer. Candles have long been used to represent deity, so a single green pillar candle that's lit only when you are working with your Cernunnos altar is another good option.

  Natural items work here too. A pair of shed antlers (or even just a single antler) is a perfect representation of a god like Cernunnos. You could also choose a necklace that looks like a torc, which can easily be found online and at Renaissance festivals, or use something from the woods, like a pine cone or a fallen branch. One of my favorite ways to represent Cernunnos on an altar is by gathering a bunch of fallen leaves, fashioning them into something resembling a wide circle (glue works just fine here), and then placing a candle in the center of the leaves. (If you go this route, make sure there's a good amount of distance between your candle and the leaves. Both you and Cernunnos don't want you starting a house fire in his honor.)

- *A libation/offering bowl.* Because a devotional altar is a place to show devotion, you'll want a bowl in which you can leave gifts for Cernunnos. I think the best sort of offerings are liquid ones, and generally alcohol, but you can leave Cernunnos anything you think he'll enjoy. Whatever you offer the god should be something you enjoy or indulge in yourself. If you don't drink beer, then that would be a poor choice to place in an offering bowl. Whatever you use for your libation bowl, be sure it is large enough to hold whatever you choose to pour in it and is leakproof. (This sounds like commonsense stuff, but I have used bowls for libations that had cracks in them that I was unaware of.)

  If you are uncomfortable with physical (or liquid) offerings, incense is another option here. Instead of leaving Cernunnos wine or beer, you could burn incense to honor him. If you choose to go this route, I suggest using earthy scents representative of the outdoors, such as sandalwood. Incenses that suggest wealth, such as frankincense or myrrh, are also good options. Whatever you choose should resonate with both you and the god.

- *Something related to hunting.* This might be the trickiest thing on my list. On my Cernunnos altar, I have a small collection of arrowheads that I've picked up over the years. Another alternative here is an arrow; even better if you made it yourself. You might also choose to go with a tool you already have, such as an athame or other ritual knife. If your altar is especially big, you could probably place a sword, an axe, or a spear on it.

- *A pentacle or other portal.* In Modern Witchcraft, the word *pentacle* most often refers to a disc-shaped working tool made out of metal, clay, or wood, with a star in its center.[100] Most pentacles utilize a five-pointed star, but traditionally pentacles have lots of different symbols in the middle. Though pentacles today are generally used when blessing things like water, salt, and incense during ritual, traditionally pentacles are gateways and portals to other worlds.

I include a pentacle on my Cernunnos altar because he's a god and therefore dwells in the lands that deities dwell in, but also because, as a god of death, he's tied to what lies beyond our world: the Summerlands, or land of the dead. I also think that as a god of death, Cernunnos rules over the land of death in some way, so the pentacle serves another purpose: it's a gateway that my beloved and mighty dead can use to visit with me on my Cernunnos altar.[101]

Is the pentacle too Wiccan for you? If so, there are other options. Basically, you want whatever you use here to be representative of the crossing over from life to death and back again. To that end, you could use a picture of a cemetery, gravestones, or even just a crossroads. You could also design your own sigil here if that works for you.

- *Pictures of your dead.* It's not necessary to place photos of those you've lost on your Cernunnos altar, but as a god of the dead, he doesn't mind sharing his space a bit, I've found. Cernunnos is a great facilitator between the spirits of the dead and those of us here in the world of the living. Because the dead exist in his "other world," learning from them can be a powerful tool for growing closer to Cernunnos.

- *A small dish or jar for coins.* Do you have a small jar or dish lying around the house that will hold a quarter? Then you've got something that will work to represent Cernunnos's power as a god of

---

100. Mankey and Zakroff, *The Witch's Altar*, 48. It always feels really good to be able to cite my own work in the books I write. This particular book has a long chapter on pentacles, including information on how to build one quickly and easily.

101. *Beloved dead* refers to the dead who were family and friends but were not necessarily Witches or Pagans. The term *mighty dead* is used to designate those who are dead and practiced the Craft. It's possible for our beloved and mighty dead to be the same in some instances.

wealth and money. You can use a clear jar here or something picked up from a Witch store. Whatever you use does not have to be fancy. When you set this on your altar, be sure to have a few coins ready to place in or on it.

- *Something from the natural world.* Because Cernunnos is also a god of this world and the wild spaces, you'll want something from nature on your altar. It could be something directly related to him or something that just resonates with you. On my altar I have a Cernunnos statue to represent the god and a pair of antlers that represent his place in the wild. Simpler options are fine too, like seeds, pine cones, or acorns. You could also choose something living, such as a potted plant. If you're capable of keeping your altar clean and maintained, then fresh-cut flowers are another option. However, don't use this option if you are incapable of replacing the flowers regularly. Gods don't want rotting flowers on their altars.

- *Something related to domesticated animals.* Because of the hunting dogs on the Gundestrup cauldron, I've always associated Cernunnos with domesticated animals. If you have an animal companion, putting their picture on your Cernunnos altar is appropriate. You can also put something there that simply reminds you of them, such as one of their toys. If you want to add a little extra magick to whatever you use here, add a piece of your cat's or dog's (or whatever) hair to it. (I know the Gundestrup cauldron only includes dogs, but I'm pretty sure Cernunnos doesn't have a hatred of cats, so don't feel bad if you have a cat and not a dog.)

- *Whatever else works for you.* These are the things on my Cernunnos altar, but feel free to add more items if that works for you.

SETTING UP YOUR DEVOTIONAL ALTAR

There's no one right way to set up an altar. It can be something you do silently in a rather mundane way, or you can turn it into a full-fledged ritual. However you do it, be sure that whatever you're using for your altar is clean, both physically and spiritually. Wipe down your altar space and make sure it's free of dirt and dust. Once that's done, cleanse it with smoke or salted water to remove any negativity from the space.[102]

While you can just place your items on the altar, I think it's far more effective to verbalize your intentions to both yourself and Cernunnos as you set up your new space. Start by deciding where you want to place whatever it is you are using to represent Cernunnos. Most of us will probably want to place him in the middle, but if it makes more sense to you to put him on the left- or right-hand side of your altar, that's fine. As you place him in the spot that works best for you, welcome him to the altar:

> *In the name of Cernunnos, I set up this altar. May it serve as a place to grow my relationship with he who is lord of the wild spaces and keeper of the dead. Great Cernunnos, be welcome in this place for as long as it pleases thee. May we work our will together, O ancient antlered one. So mote it be!*

Next, place your libation bowl on the altar and verbalize its purpose:

> *May this bowl serve as a place for the offerings I freely and gladly give to you, Cernunnos. May my gifts strengthen you and your influence upon this world. So mote it be!*

Pick up whatever it is you have chosen to represent the natural world and let it rest in your hand for a moment. Imagine where exactly it came from and how it connects to the natural world. Feel its energy pulse in your grip and picture it with great Cernunnos. Say:

> *Great Cernunnos, lord and protector of the natural world, I place this (name of item) upon your altar. May it strengthen the relationship we have with each other and our connection to the natural world. So mote it be!*

Place the item you are using to collect coins and place it upon your altar. When it's secure, place a couple of coins in it while saying:

---

102. *The Witch's Altar* has complete instructions for cleansing an altar if you're looking for more detail.

I give these coins to you so that you might create abundance and wealth in my life. As I give to you, I ask that you might also give to me. Bless this altar with your abundance, and may this space help me manifest my true will. So mote it be!

Pick up whatever object you've chosen to represent the idea of the hunt. As you hold it in your hand, visualize the things you hunt for in this life. Most likely it's not for deer or other game animals, but for the things we all desire: a solid job, a partner(s), love, a place to call home, etc. Imagine yourself tracking these things down and overcoming the obstacles that stand between you and your end goals. Place your item upon the altar while saying:

I dedicate this (name of item) to Lord Cernunnos. May it bring me closer to you and your ways and help me to triumph over any adversity that I might experience. So mote it be!

There are several different ways to place your pentacle upon the altar. If your pentacle is large enough, you might want to set whatever you are using to represent Cernunnos on top of it. You might feel more comfortable simply placing it on the altar and then setting Cernunnos on top of it only during certain circumstances, or never at all. Remember, this is your (and Cernunnos's altar), so do what you feel is right. When you set the pentacle down, say:

I place this gateway upon my altar to ever remind me that Cernunnos exists in both this world and the next. Great Cernunnos, help me to understand all of your mysteries, those of the living and the dead. Open wide the portals between this world and those of the Summerlands when I need lessons that can only be provided by the dead and the Lord who watches over the souls that have departed this world. So mote it be!

If you have pictures of your beloved or mighty dead that you want to put on your altar, now is a good time to do so. In my own practice, I place these images to the back of my Cernunnos altar to signify that the altar belongs to C, first and foremost. It sounds petty to say, but even gods can be a bit jealous. As you place the images on your altar, address Cernunnos:

I place these pictures here as reminders of the souls in your care in the world beyond, Cernunnos. Watch over those I've lost and allow them to visit and guide me as you see fit. So mote it be!

The last item for the altar from my list is something representative of a beloved animal companion (and, yes, this could be one who has passed on). This is, of course, completely optional, but for many of us, animal companions are valued members of the family. As you set your item on the altar, say:

Great Cernunnos, watch over my beloved (name of animal companion). May you keep them safe from harm in this world and embrace them in the next. When their animal nature comes to the fore, may I see the natural world and your mysteries reflected within it. Bless my relationship with this creature, and may your protection of it bring us closer together. So mote it be!

At this point, add whatever else you desire to your devotional altar, being sure to verbalize the purpose of each item you place on it. When you have everything set up as you see fit, take a step back and look at your altar. Does anything *feel* out of place? This could be Cernunnos asking you to rearrange things slightly, so be aware of any messages he might be trying to send to you. When you are sure that Cernunnos is comfortable with what you have built, dedicate everything to him one last time and pour him an offering:

I have built this altar to further my relationship with you, great Cernunnos. May it serve as a place of strength for us both and as a space to facilitate our communication. I ask that you share your mysteries with me here and help me to connect with you and your wonders. As I dedicate this altar to you, I pour you this libation [pour an offering], freely and happily given. May my offering strengthen our bond and give you power to bring change to my life and this world. Great Cernunnos, be welcome in this place. So mote it be!

HOW TO USE YOUR CERNUNNOS ALTAR

The easiest way to use your Cernunnos altar is as a focal point for interacting with the god. I think *prayer* is sometimes a dirty word in Witchcraft circles, but prayer is really just speaking with (or to) a deity, and that type of communication is a great way to build any relationship. Having that kind of interaction at a specific spot also makes it more focused. I can chat with Cernunnos anywhere, but doing so in front of my altar links the act more specifically to my Witchcraft practice. Using your altar as a place to talk to Cernunnos is the most important function it will serve.

Pouring libations to the gods in my life is very important to me, and this is probably the second most important part of a devotional altar. I believe the gods want to know that we are thinking about them, and sharing some whisky or wine with them is a good way to show that acknowledgment. Many of us who actively give our gods offerings do so continuously, on a daily or weekly basis. (And when we forget for a day or two, we often break out the "good stuff," such as twenty-one-year-old single malt, as a form of apology.) Others reserve offerings for special occasions, such as the sabbats or after a positive life event they think the deity helped them with. Anytime you ask a god like Cernunnos for assistance with something, it is customary to pour a libation as a thank-you. It's the least we can do!

On my devotional altars, I tend to just leave liquid gifts, generally alcoholic ones, but you should use what you are most comfortable with. Clean spring water is a fine libation, provided it is given with reverence and it means something to you. Unlike an offering of food, which will eventually rot and attract bugs, liquid offerings will typically evaporate on their own. However, unless you are leaving only water to Cernunnos, whatever you pour out to him will eventually leave a sticky residue in the bottom of your bowl. Because of this, you should wash your bowl every couple of weeks. No one wants a gift in a dirty bowl.

While a devotional altar is primarily a place to grow closer to deity, it can also be used for magickal purposes. Not only are the things I have on my Cernunnos altar there in honor of him, but almost all of them have magickal significance as well. Specifically, the items on my Cernunnos altar are representative of the idea of sympathetic magick, or "like attracts like."

Leaving coins to Cernunnos on his altar is a way of attracting wealth into my own life. Every time I leave Cernunnos some spare change, I say:

For the god, may your material blessings fall upon me.

When I find myself (or a friend) in dire financial need, I'll take what I've collected in my bowl and give it to charity, hand it directly to someone in need, or leave it in a place where I feel it will do some good. As I do so, I ask that Cernunnos allow wealth to return to me (or whoever else):

> *As I share with the world, may the world also share with me. Let my needs be met and keep me from want. I make this sacrifice in the name of Cernunnos. So mote it be!*

There's an old adage that says, "It takes money to make money," and giving money to the gods is a way to receive it in return.

When job-searching or simply trying to get my next book picked up by my publisher, I will often write down those desires on a piece of paper and place them in the dish full of arrowheads on my Cernunnos altar. While doing so, I'll say:

> *Let my will fly true as I begin the next project in my life. Illuminate the way and bring to me that which I currently seek. So mote it be!*

I'll repeat that little mantra every day until I obtain my desire or realize I don't want what I originally asked for. Yes, the latter sometimes happens, which is why the mantra begins with "Let my will fly true." Sometimes we are wrong about what we most desire! When what I want has manifested or I've moved on, I then take the piece of paper and either throw it away or burn it to ashes. Then I pour Cernunnos a libation.

I often use my Cernunnos altar as a focal point for working with my beloved dead. I usually begin by placing Cernunnos upon the altar's pentacle and visualizing the star in the pentacle's center opening like an eye. That opening signifies an entryway into the realm of the dead. I then think of the person I wish to feel close to again, visualizing them in my mind's eye and conjuring up memories of their voice. I then invoke Cernunnos:

> *Open wide the gates between this world and the next! Let me feel the presence and the power of those who reside in the realm of the dead. May I feel*

them close to me once more in this, my time of need. I ask these things in the
name of Cernunnos. So mote it be!

I then talk to those I've lost, much like I talk to Cernunnos at his altar. Other times I'm simply still, feeling the energies of those I've lost close to me again while being aware of any communication they might be trying to share with me. When I find myself frightened of death, I sometimes ask this boon of Cernunnos just as reassurance that there's an existence on the other side of the veil.

When I'm feeling disconnected from nature, I visit my Cernunnos altar and touch the item I've placed there to represent the natural world (in my case, a pair of antlers).[103] Holding those antlers in my hands allows me to feel the power and awe of nature, all without having to leave my office. It's an especially powerful piece of magick when I'm trapped inside my house or even just my suburban neighborhood for days on end. It's easy to become separated from the wild pulse of the world; having an anchor to that energy (and having it blessed by Cernunnos) is one of the most important pieces of magick in my life.

I do not think that Cernunnos is a god of health or healing in a traditional sense, but since I believe he looks over domesticated animals, I do ask him to watch over my cats on occasion. The Cernunnos statue on my altar has the god in his traditional sitting posture, and when I worry about one of my cats for whatever reason, I place the object I use to represent my cats on Cernunnos's lap. This is a direct message to the god that I'm looking for assistance and that I trust him with my precious fur-babies. When working magick for my cats, I'm rather direct with Cernunnos:

> *Great Horned Lord, I ask that you look after (name of animal compan-*
> *ion). Keep her healthy, keep her safe, and keep her free from harm. Watch her*
> *as you watched the animal companions of old, offering assistance and care*
> *now when it's needed most. So mote it be!*

---

103. Much of this book was written at the beginning of the Covid-19 pandemic in 2020. I have very much missed nature during this time of sheltering indoors.

Needless to say, I always pour Cernunnos a libation after such a request.

Sometimes, though, all of the prayers and the magick cannot overcome death. Our animal companions will die and move on to the next world, and when they do, I always ask Cernunnos to watch over them:

> *Cernunnos, into your care I place the spirit of my dearly departed (name of animal companion). Welcome her into your other realm and give her the comfort she needs in this time of transition. Through your cauldron, may she be able to continue to feel my love and affection, and may I feel all that she might offer me. Great god of the living and the dead, give us both solace and peace in this time of transition. So mote it be!*

When my longtime cat Princess died, I kept a picture of her cradled in Cernunnos's lap for almost a year.[104] On a near-daily basis for many months, I shed my tears at Cernunnos's altar while thanking him for taking care of my dear one in this next stage of her existence. It's the best use I've ever made of my Cernunnos altar, and he really was right there with me the entire time.

———

While the altar written about in this chapter was designed specifically for Cernunnos, with a few changes you can use it as a template to build a devotional altar to the larger Horned God, or specific deities such as Pan or Herne. The only adjustments you'll really have to make involve swapping out the things on the altar that are specifically for Cernunnos and replacing them with different items to represent the deity you wish to work with, if applicable. If I was building a devotional altar for Pan, for example, I would add something phallic or sexual, a pan flute, and a token representative of his nymphs, while removing the coins, pentacle, and anything else suggestive of death.

---

104. Princess was Siamese, so her name was fitting. She really did believe she was royalty, and so did I.

Chapter Nine
THE GREEN MAN

THERE IS A TENDENCY AMONG Pagans and Witches to assume that every deity we might honor during ritual is old—not just centuries old, but millennia old, and dating back to pagan antiquity. But the world is a complicated place, and there are several gods that fit into the Horned God mythos who are probably just as much a product of the modern age as they are of antiquity, but I don't believe this makes them any less potent as gods or goddesses.

There are purists out there who will argue that a deity first discovered or named in the twentieth or twenty-first century is made-up or fictitious, and in my more pretentious days I was probably one of them. However, every deity starts somewhere, and I like to believe that there are always reasons specific deities make themselves known to us. Much of what we know and believe about gods like Pan and Cernunnos is also tied in to our modern sensibilities and interpretations, so why should other deities in the horned pantheon be any different? The Horned God reveals himself in a variety of ways.

The imagery attached to deities such as the Green Man, Elen of the Ways, and Herne is often very old, even if their myths might be of a more recent origin. Images that resemble the Green Man are nearly two thousand years old, as are statues of antlered goddesses (as we saw with Cernunnos in chapter 7). The god Herne wasn't written about until nearly the year 1600 CE, but even that is over four hundred years ago now. If something speaks to us, it speaks to us, and it doesn't matter if that something was first honored three thousand years ago or three weeks ago.

GREEN MAN ADVENTURES

My wife, Ari, and I had been in the UK for only thirty-six hours when we began gazing at the images of the Green Man in St. Giles' Cathedral in Edinburgh, Scotland.[105] Upon entering the church, we found ourselves in a state of hushed awe (we just love old religious places), and it took us a while before we even contemplated that the Green Man might be around. But eventually it dawned on me that there was probably an image of him in a 650-year-old church, so I took out my phone, did a quick google search, and found out that there are dozens of images of the Green Man at St. Giles'.

The following day, we arose early and took a bus to Rosslyn Chapel (famous for being the alleged burial spot of the Christian Holy Grail in books like *The Da Vinci Code*). I had read extensively on Rosslyn over the years and knew ahead of time that the chapel contained images of the Green Man. Our entrance to the chapel included a small pamphlet pointing out the most famous images at Roslyn, including a rather impish Green Man that's often included in pictures of the chapel. But even with my pamphlet guiding me, I had trouble finding the Green Man in the chapel. Taking pity on me, my wife eventually helped me spot him.

Though I had been reading about the Green Man for years, the written material on the subject does not always do him justice. I had expected majestic, easy-to-spot images of the Green Man smiling pleasantly from atop church walls. The reality was something altogether different. At both St. Giles' and Roslyn, the images of the Green Man are small and often in unexpected places. He is far more ornamentation that main event, and the most well-known Green Man image from Roslyn Chapel is no bigger than a bar napkin; high on the ceiling, he was truly hard to spot! Green Men appear on the sides of church pews, on structural corbels (a type of bracket), and as decorative motifs where wooden support beams come together (known as a ceiling boss).

---

105. St. Giles' Cathedral was established in the twelfth century, though much of the church's current structure was built about two hundred years later. Originally a Catholic church, it's part of the Church of Scotland today.

THE GREEN MAN IN HISTORY

For me, the Green Man has always been symbolic of nature. With his leafy face, he's the power of the natural world that radiates from forests, hills, and streams. On mountain hikes, I can often see his visage in craggy rocks and peaks. I have called to him while indoors performing Spring Equinox rituals, and I have seen his smile as the Oak and Holly Kings do battle on the Summer and Winter Solstices. While the armchair scholar in me recoils at some of the bad history I've read about him over the last thirty years, the Witch in me still embraces it, because much of it represents the truth of how he appears to me and also those I love and practice with.

However, the historical Green Man written about in Pagan books is more fantasy than reality. One of the first Pagan books I ever read that devoted extensive space to the Green Man connected him to ancient Greece and the cults of Pan and Dionysus, and eventually Cernunnos.[106] In her entry on the Green Man in the book *Lord of Light and Shadow*, writer D. J. Conway lists other names for the Green Man, including Arddhu, Atho, and the Horned God. She concludes the entry with "see Cernunnos," implying that Cernunnos and the Green Man are in fact the same deity.[107]

The truth of the matter is that we don't know very much about the images that today we call the Green Man. Let me stress the word *images* here, because representations of the Green Man are exceedingly variable. The majority of them look nothing like the Green Men we encounter in art related to Modern Witchcraft; the expressions are far more agonized in appearance, and some are scary-looking. One of the words once used to describe Green Man images in British churches was *grotesque*, due to the rather sinister appearance of many Green Men.[108]

---

106. Conway, *Lord of Light and Shadow*, 58. Arddhu and Atho are allegedly names of Welsh Underworld gods. Arddhu is sometimes honored in the Anderson Feri Tradition, and Atho was the name of the god in an English Witchcraft tradition that existed in England during the late 1950s.

107. Conway, *Lord of Light and Shadow*, 151.

108. Anderson, *Green Man*, 20.

Up until 1939, the name generally used to refer to images of the Green Man was *foliate head*, a reference to the plant material that can often be seen spewing from the mouth of many Green Men. The name *Green Man* in reference to foliate heads comes from a paper submitted in 1939 by Julia Somerset (1901–1971), more commonly known as Lady Raglan (she was the wife of the 4th Baron Raglan), to the Folklore Society in London. Raglan's paper was based on previous work by Margaret Murray (there's that name again!) that had suggested that foliate heads were Pagan fertility figures placed in Christian churches by still devout Witches looking to honor the old religion in the cathedrals of the new.[109] The term *Green Man* was then adopted by the art historian Sir Nikolaus Pevsner and included in his 46-volume Buildings of England series, which helped to popularize the term.[110]

Not surprisingly, there are a whole host of issues with such an assumption, the first being that the heyday of the Green Man occurred while Christianity was ascendant in Europe. The Green Man really only became a fixture in Christian churches during the late Middle Ages and into the early modern period (from 1200 to 1500 CE or so), though references in Christian materials dates back to the tenth century.[111] If the Green Man was meant to be a quiet Pagan prayer hidden above the church pews, it was one that went underground for hundreds of years. It's not completely out of the question that Green Man images are in some way related to ancient paganism(s), but considering the era, it's a difficult case to make.

So if the Green Man was not originally a relic of the Pagan past, what does he symbolize? Christian sources are just as quiet on that count as any alleged Pagan ones. The most logical explanation for the Green Man (and remember, many of these images do not look friendly) is that the figure represents a soul entangled in sinful behaviors, or perhaps a soul stuck in purgatory. Other less than hopeful interpretations suggest that the figure might

---

109. Hutton, *Pagan Britain*, 347.

110. Livingstone, "The Remarkable Persistence of the Green Man."

111. Hutton, *Pagan* Britain, 349.

represent a decaying corpse, illustrating the consequences of sin and the snares of the Christian Devil.[112]

But not all Green Man images are negative-looking. There are some that are quite inspiring and truly suggest our modern interpretations of him. In a Christian context, those images might represent immortality, salvation, resurrection of the body after death, or something to do with love.[113] They could also be representative of something agrarian, such as the yearly return of life in the spring or the beauty of the green earth. Christianity has very little that expresses the wonder of the natural world, so the beautiful Green Men could be a remedy for that.

The term *Green Man* is actually an old one, even if its attachment to the foliate-head image is of a more recent vintage. In England, there are dozens of old pubs founded centuries ago that use "Green Man" in their title. However, the term Green Man was usually in reference to Robin Hood and similar figures who were believed to have lived in the woods during the Middle Ages.[114] Considering how individuals like Margaret Murray have connected the Horned God to figures like Robin Hood, the reference is especially appealing to Modern Witches.

Green Men were also frequent visitors in the courts of both the Tudors and the Stuarts, who ruled England during most of the period from 1485 to 1714. In royal courts, Green Men were generally leaf-covered men who carried clubs, most likely in reference to drunkenness. Branches and pieces of brush were used as signs indicating the sale of alcohol in England during this period, which explains the dress of these Green Men.[115]

Despite what I've shared with you so far, it remains possible that many Green Man images were inspired by pagan antiquity. There are several ancient images that bear a striking similarity to several Green Men. One of the most remarkable dates from the year 300 CE (sometimes dated as early as 200 CE) and is part of the Mildenhall hoard (or treasure), currently on

---

112. Hutton, *Pagan Britain*, 349 and 350.

113. Hutton, *Pagan Britain*, 350.

114. Anderson, *Green Man*, 20.

115. Hutton, *Pagan Britain*, 349.

display at the British Museum in London. The "Great Dish" or "Great Plate of Bacchus" features the Greek Titan Oceanus (a deity of rivers and the sea) in its center, his visage appearing as if made of fallen leaves. The depiction of Oceanus with a leaf-like face was not limited to the Great Dish, and a fifth-century representation in present-day Turkey has similar features.[116]

There are a whole host of images alleged to be precursors to the Green Man, and this is not surprising due to his varied appearance in churches throughout Europe. One of the more convincing arguments is a third-century depiction of Dionysus from modern Germany. Featuring a wilting head, this image foreshadows many of the "grotesques" that would appear over a thousand years later. Though Christian references to foliate heads can't be found before the tenth century, there appears to be a Green Man on the tomb of Saint Abre in France dating back to the year 400 CE.[117]

Perhaps the most logical explanation for the image of the Green Man is that it was inspired by similar images found in India. Green Man images began to show up in Europe just as trade with India and China was starting to pick up across the continent. This was followed shortly thereafter by the Crusades, which made the world even smaller. Images from India and China could easily have been found among the Arab population of the Middle East and then transported back to Europe from there.

Images from Hindu temples sometimes feature heads expelling something similar to the plant matter that would soon be found in churches across Europe from Scotland to Russia. Images of demons from Nepal also bear a similarity to many of the more frightening Green Man images. While we often think the world is a huge, hard-to-traverse place, even twelve hundred years ago there were several links between Europe and Asia, and it's not out of the question to wonder if art from India had an influence on the cathedrals of Europe.

---

116. Anderson, *Green Man*, 47.

117. Anderson, *Green Man*, 46.

*Figure 10: The haunting image of the Green Man.
This image of the Green Man was inspired by a Green Man
from Norwich Cathedral in Norwich, England. Unlike most
other Green Men, his image adorns the back of a
folding chair instead of a church wall.*

The name *Green Man* is a bit of a misnomer too, because (and this should not be a surprise by now) there are also a few Green Men who are clearly Green Women. Whatever the Green Men in churches were meant to represent (and it's likely they represented a variety of things), they weren't necessarily limited to male faces.

Green Men generally go unmarked in European churches, with no words identifying who they are meant to be or their meaning (figure 10). However, one church in France includes the name *Silvanus* on a Green Man image on a fountain at the Abbey of Saint-Denis in France around the year 1200.[118] Silvanus was the Roman god of the forest.

THE GREEN MAN TODAY

By the 1970s, the Green Man as a symbol of fertility and the sacredness of nature had become a dominant talking point in most literature mentioning him. Even scholarly publications often commented on the Green Man as a relic of the Pagan past, so it's no surprise that such ideas were repeated in the Witch and Pagan materials of the day. By the 1990s, the Green Man had even begun settling into shopping malls, and his face was being used by environmental groups as representative of their goals.

Polytheist Witches often talk about the gods as having "agency," meaning they possess power in this world and are directly influencing events that concern them. Generally, the idea of agency is limited to deities who have ancient and traceable pedigrees, but this feels limiting to me. Whatever foliate heads meant in 1300 is immaterial to what the Green Man represents now. He is the soul of nature, and a connection to wild spaces, and this is something believed by millions of people.

Green Man images appear in hundreds of churches in Great Britain, and many of those churches are proud of their Green Men. They aren't proud of them for representing sin, or even hope, but because they are symbols of wildness and the natural world. Many churches with Green Men even comment on their alleged origins among pagan antiquity, and they are proud of

---

118. Anderson, *Green Man*, 111–112.

that! Perhaps images of the Green Man were placed on high church walls five hundred years ago in order to inspire us today!

And make no mistake that the voice of the Green Man (and Green Woman) is louder today than ever before. When I visit a church with their image, I can hear them whispering to me, no matter how anguished they appear to be. Perhaps some of that anguish was in anticipation over just how much of a mess we've made of our world today. (If I were a symbol of nature, I probably wouldn't be happy in the twenty-first century either!)

Today people from all sorts of life believe that the Green Man is a representative of Paganism's past and present, and because of that, it's true! His origins may not be exactly that, but when I see a Green Man today, I know I'm either in a Witch-friendly place or among those who care for the earth. Today the Green Man is often drawn with horns on his head by contemporary artists, bringing the Green Man even closer to Modern Witchcraft and Pagan practices.

JACK IN THE GREEN

Often thought to be related to the Green Man, the figure known as Jack in the Green has been a part of English May Day celebrations for nearly two hundred years.[119] The English anthropologist Sir James Frazer (1854–1941) called Jack "a vernal spirit of vegetation" and believed he represented an ancient tree spirit.[120] Writing a few decades later, Lady Raglan would link the figure to the Green Man, and the two have been intertwined in the Pagan imagination ever since. The band Jethro Tull would include a song named after the figure on their 1977 album *Songs from the Wood*. (Pick this one up. It's a Pagan classic.)

Jack in the Green certainly looks like some sort of vestige of ancient Paganism. Traditionally a Jack in the Green costume consists of a woven wicker (or wood) frame designed to cover the top half of a person's body, intertwined with greenery and flowers. Jacks in the Green traditionally march and dance in May Day parades, where for much of the nineteenth century

---

119. Hutton, *The Stations of the Sun*, 242.

120. Frazer, *The Golden Bough*, 247.

they were portrayed by chimney sweeps. With their merry and very green appearance, it's easy to see a figure symbolic of spring fertility and renewal, but the truth of the matter is far stranger.

The origin of Jack in the Green lies with English milkmaids of the seventeenth century who once danced door to door on May Day with greenery and flowers in their hair and on their milk pails in search of cash. Eventually their May Day outfits grew more sophisticated (or odd), and they began to wear wooden pyramids on top of their head, again adorned with flowers and greenery. The warmer weather accompanying May also traditionally increased milk yields in England, a fact the maids probably wanted to draw attention to. Eventually the costumes of the milkmaids were adopted by English rag-pickers and chimney sweeps.[121]

In the hands of the chimney sweeps, the costumes grew larger and more elaborate, transforming into the Jack of the Green that many of us are familiar with today.[122] Since the summer months were traditionally bad for chimney sweeps, the Jack in the Green costumes attracted a lot of attention and were a rather successful form of advertising. Taking this a step further, many chimney sweeps dressed young boys as Jack in the Green, attracting more sympathy and money from May Day revelers.[123]

While the Jack in the Green is not a vestige of paganisms past, it has become a symbol of spring, and in that sense is certainly "Pagan." Seeing a chimney sweep dressed up as Jack in the Green on a May Day morning in the 1850s was most certainly a sign of the spring's power and a promise of the summer to come. As the decades rolled along, Jack in the Green gradually fell out of favor in many parts of England, but came roaring back at the start of the twentieth century in a revival of folk customs that has continued to the present day.

---

121. Hutton, *The Stations of the Sun*, 242.
122. Hutton, *The Stations of the Sun*, 242.
123. Hutton, *The Stations of the Sun*, 242.

CONNECTING WITH THE GREEN MAN

With a wide array of conflicting images and no mythology, the Green Man can sometimes feel like a difficult figure to connect to. But as the soul of nature and the heartbeat of the natural world, he's actually a pretty easy figure to grow close to. The Green Man can not only be seen in some of Europe's oldest churches but can be found anyplace where we connect to nature.

The following exercise can be used as a guided meditation in a group setting, but if it's something you choose to work with alone, you'll want to commit an outline of it to memory. Reading something is never the same as actively participating in it! And if you find, when doing this alone, that you veer wildly from what's on the printed page, that's probably a good thing. Let the Green Man and the wild dictate your experience, not a book!

Ideally you'll want to perform this activity outdoors, but if that's not an option, indoors can be equally effective. If you do find yourself looking for the Green Man indoors, you'll need:

- A forest-scented oil, such as pine, cedarwood, or sandalwood—Alternatively, you can also use a similarly scented incense. I like to use an oil diffuser when possible, but as an alternative, you can use a diluted version of these oils and just place a dab under your nose.
- Nature sounds—This can be a CD or from a streaming music service. If your neighborhood is quiet, you could also just open up the window, though you risk letting in invasive car and/or pedestrian noise.

If you are doing this exercise indoors, find a comfortable spot where you can sit on the floor, or choose a chair where you can sit upright, with your feet firmly on the floor. If you can position yourself in such a way that it's possible to feel sunlight/moonlight or the breeze on your face and body from a window or door, take advantage of that. Before you sit down, get your nature sounds going, along with whatever you are using to create a woodland/forest scent. Once that's all taken care of, sit down and begin the exercise.

If you are doing this outdoors, find a comfortable spot on the ground to sit. The ideal here is a forest or a woodland clearing of some kind, but even a public park with a couple of trees will work pretty well. If you can, sit with your back against a tree, with your spine straight and your legs straight in front of you touching the ground. It's okay to lay a blanket on the ground for comfort, but even better if it's just you (your clothes) and the natural world.

As you sit down and get comfortable, close your eyes and focus on the world around you. What do you hear? What do you feel? What do you sense? Do you notice the warmth of the sun or a cool breeze upon your skin? Are there birds chirping or crickets humming? Breathe deeply and pay attention to what your nose detects. Do you smell a forest floor, cut grass, or fresh flowers? All that you are sensing is in the domain of the Green Man, the spirit of nature.

With your back straight, focus inward on your own body; wiggle your toes, notice your diaphragm moving up and down as you breathe, and gently move your fingers. Concentrate on your spinal column for a moment, and feel the energy that moves up and down through it. Visualize that energy moving through your body, and picture it moving downward from your shoulder blades to the small of your back. When that energy reaches the end of your spinal column, push it out through your body, to extend into the ground beneath you. As that energy moves out of your body and into the earth, keep your consciousness with it.

As your energy slips into the earth, feel what is around you there. Depending on the time of year, the soil you feel might be holding on to life, waiting for it to be reborn in the spring, or perhaps that soil is alive with green growing things. Whatever is there, take notice of it and feel its energy. Alive or dead, it is of this world, and a part of the cycle we are all connected to.

(If you are indoors while doing this exercise, you'll have to push your energy out through the floor you are sitting on, through your home's foundation, etc. Eventually, though, you will find the natural world, even if it's buried under a couple of feet of concrete.)

Move your consciousness and energy through the ground around you, being especially aware of any roots you might encounter—and you will encounter roots eventually, no matter where you begin your journey. As you become aware of the roots in the ground, travel up those roots, letting your energy mix with that of the plants you are experiencing. When you reach the top of one of those plants, are you a blade of glass wiggling in the room? Or perhaps a flower in bloom with a bee on it searching for nectar? Feel the plants around you, allow yourself to feel for a moment what being a dandelion or a clover in a field might be like.

(Depending on where you are, it's possible that the energy you feel might not be pleasant. If a plant is sick, dying, or poisoned, then being inside its shoots and leaves will be uncomfortable. If this is the case, reflect for a moment on what we humans have done to the world. You may want to release a little bit of your own energy into what you are feeling as a way to give that plant strength and as an apology for the shortsightedness of humanity.)

When your energy reaches the top of one plant, descend back into the earth in search of your next root. Eventually you will find roots that just feel older, wiser, and more powerful than anything you've previously encountered. Certain species of trees interlock their roots, making it hard to determine where one tree begins and another ends; make your way through the tangle of roots until your consciousness and energy reside in the trunk of a powerful tree.[124]

As you enter the tree, stop for a moment to feel all of the energy around you. If you concentrate hard enough, you should be able to hear and feel something that sounds similar to a human heartbeat. *Thumm, thumm, thumm, thumm* ... that's the power of the tree and the heart of nature. Feel the pulsing power of the nutrients and the water that the roots of your tree bring in from deep inside the earth. Allow your consciousness to slowly move up the trunk of the tree, diverging from the tree's trunk occasionally to let your energy run through the trees branches.

There in the branches, let your energy go into the leaves and fruits of the tree. As a leaf, feel the sun on your surface taking in the solar energy that sustains life. As a seed, pine cone, or fruit, feel the potential for creation that

---

124. Interlocking roots are especially true of redwood trees on the Pacific Coast. In most redwood groves, all of the trees there are connected, and the healthy ones will help keep the weaker ones alive. If you ever get a chance to do this meditation near the Pacific Ocean, I highly recommend it!

exists within you. Feel the wind rustle along your surface, or feel a bird or insect perch upon you as you sway there.

Move up the tree, through branches that reach ever higher, then back to the tree's trunk…up, up, up until you reach the top of the tree. When you arrive there, push the edge of your consciousness just out of and over the highest branch, while holding onto your connection to the tree's energy. Looking down from the top of the tree, you should be able to see the wonder of the natural world below. Still connected to your tree, you should truly feel like a part of the earth and all of creation.

Thumm, thumm, thumm … That energy you feel, the awe that you feel, that is the power of the Green Man (or Green Woman). They are the heart of nature, pulsating, powerful, and full of life. Even when we feel disconnected from them, they are there with us in some way, if we are but willing to look. The image of the Green Man is how people have expressed their continued devotion to the wild spaces and the green growing things of the earth, but to experience and feel the Green Man, we must look to Earth herself.

As you look down upon the world from the top of your tree, listen to and sense the energies around you. In trees, the powers of earth (soil), air (the breeze that pollinates), fire (the sun's rays), and water all come together. Here in this space, it's possible to hear or feel a message from the Green Man. Open yourself up to whatever wisdom might be shared with you, or simply revel in the power of being one with the trees and the wild, for it is in these spaces that the Green Man lives.

When you are comfortable with all you have explored, move back down through your tree, perhaps leaving some of your energy as a gift. Sink down into the roots of the tree, your consciousness and remaining energy moving once more through the ground. When you arrive at where you started your journey, let your energy reenter your spinal column, and feel it reintegrating with your body. As the energy begins to move through your arms and legs, recall what it felt like to be at one with the earth, at one with the Green Man.

It's highly possible that the first time you do this exercise, you will feel absolutely nothing. If that's the case, there's no need to worry; simply try again! It might take three or four tries until you get it right, especially if you've never experienced anything outside of your body. Besides, this meditation is not the only way to feel the mysteries of the Green Man. The same experiences are waiting for you outside in the wild of nature. There we can feel his call too!

Chapter Ten
HERNE THE HUNTER AND ELEN OF THE WAYS

THE FIGURE KNOWN AS Herne the Hunter has been a part of Modern Witchcraft from the very start. Gerald Gardner called him a "British example par excellence of a surviving tradition of the Old God of the Witches" in 1959's *The Meaning of Witchcraft*. Since then, Herne has most often been equated with the Gaulish Cernunnos, with many authors arguing that the two figures are the same god with different names. I disagree with that premise, but I understand why many people continually conflate the two deities.

Books about male Pagan deities have always been in short supply, and one of the earliest and most influential of those very limited number of books was *The Witches' God* by Janet and Stewart Farrar. In that book, Cernunnos and Herne share a chapter and are basically written about as the same deity. I understand the confusion; because of Cernunnos's association with all things "Celtic" and Britain's large Celtic population in antiquity, the idea makes some sense. But while a few ancient images of Cernunnos have been found in Britain, he doesn't seem to have been a particularly popular (or even well-known) god there. The two names also sort of sound alike when one drops the "ous" from Cernunnos, but other than that superficial similarity and their antlers, the two deities have very little in common.

Unlike Cernunnos, whose name and visage appear on altars and statues, the first mention of Herne occurs in William Shakespeare's play *The Merry Wives of Windsor*, most likely written between 1597 and 1599 and first mentioned in print in 1602.[125] By that date, England had long been Christianized, suggesting an even more tenuous link to Cernunnos. In that play, Herne is more ghost than deity and is written about in a way that's drastically different from how most people view him as a deity:

> There is an old tale goes, that Herne the Hunter,
> Sometimes a keeper in Windsor Forest,
> Doth all the winter-time, at still midnight,
> Walk round about an oak, with great ragg'd horns;
> And there he blasts the tree, and takes the cattle,
> And makes milche-kine yield blood, and shakes a chain
> In a most hideous and dreadful manner.
> You have heard of such a spirit, and well you know
> The superstitious idle-headed eld
> Receiv'd and did deliver to our age,
> This tale of Herne the Hunter for a truth.[126]

It's possible that Shakespeare made up the figure of Herne specifically for his play, but I find that unlikely. *The Merry Wives of Windsor* is full of references to places and names from the area, which suggests Shakespeare knew Windsor well, or at least had an informant who did. In addition, there are several folk tales that mention Herne (though it's possible they were created in reaction to Shakespeare), along with the remains of a tree that was associated with him in England's Windsor Forest.

For most of the last four hundred years, sightings of Herne in the Windsor Forest have been similar to his appearance in *The Merry Wives of Windsor*: he's been more ghost than god (figure 11). Folklore about Herne from the Berkshire area (next to Windsor Forest) has generally focused on the hunter as a figure to be feared, not worshipped. To call Herne the local "bogeyman" of the area would not be an exaggeration. But the gods of the old religion often become the devils of the new, so it's worth looking at the history of

---

125. The editors of *The Yale Shakespeare* believe the play was probably written in 1599, but the 1597 date shows up in multiple works, including Fitch's *In Search of Herne the Hunter*, 253.

126. Shakespeare, *The Merry Wives of Windsor,* in *The Yale Shakespeare: The Complete Works*, 274.

Herne to discern both his character and where his origins might lie outside of Shakespeare's quill.

Figure 11: Herne the Hunter.
A spectral Herne the Hunter hunts by night in the great Windsor Forest.

There are several versions of the Herne story. The one I'm most familiar with appears in William Harrison Ainsworth's (1805–1882) novel *Windsor
Castle*, published in 1842. In that version of the tale, Herne is a gamekeeper
at Windsor Forest, employed by the monarch Richard III (1452–1485). Herne
was a favorite of Richard, and as a result the other gamekeepers became
jealous. On one particularly tragic day, Herne and Richard went off on their
own in pursuit of a prized buck, but instead of being easily subdued, the
buck gored the horse of the king. As the king fell from his horse, the buck
attempted to strike a killing blow, but Herne lept between the buck and the
king with his knife out. Herne delivered a lethal blow upon the deer, but not
before he himself was mortally wounded.

Now gored, Herne lay dying, and the King was distraught. When the rest
of the hunting party caught up to Richard and the dying Herne, the king
promised a large reward to whoever could restore Herne to life. As Herne prepared to take his last breath, a wizard appeared promising to bring Herne back
from the precipice of death. The king readily agreed, but the other keepers
conspired against Herne, asking the wizard to take away the woodland skills
that Herne used in service to the king upon his return. The wizard agreed for
a price, and Herne was revived after one month in stasis. Curiously, the wizard
grafted the antlers of the buck killed by Herne onto the keeper's head.

Stripped of his woodland skills, the revived Herne went mad and eventually hung himself from a mighty oak in the forest that later became known
as "Herne's Oak." After this second death, Herne returned to both curse the
keepers who had taken his woodcraft away and the forest, causing hunting in
Windsor Forest to cease for lack of game. With nothing to hunt, Richard III
grew concerned and met with Herne. At that meeting, Herne revealed the
duplicity of the other keepers and demanded justice. Richard agreed and had
Herne's tormentors hung on the very oak Herne had used to take his own
life. His quest for vengeance satisfied, Herne took up permanent residence in
Windsor Forest, where he leads the hunt as a ghostly presence, often accompanied by other spectral hunters and hunting dogs.

There are a few variations on the tale of how the mortal Herne became
Herne the Hunter, the most shocking of which has Herne returning after

death to the realm of the living to seek vengeance upon the English king who defiled his daughter. Other versions of the story have Herne hanging himself to atone for either hunting illegally or committing some other sort of foul deed in Windsor Forest that betrays his king.[127] Whatever the variation, most of these stories involve Herne hanging himself, a noteworthy end that we will come back to later.

One of the details that makes the story of Herne so interesting to me is that there is further evidence of the reality of Herne beyond Shakespeare and folklore.

Several different versions of Shakespeare's plays have been published over the centuries, and the versions that most of us are familiar with come from the *First Folio*, the collection of his plays published in 1623. An earlier version of *The Merry Wives of Windsor* from 1602 features a slightly different take on Herne, here called *Horne*. While he still remains a ghostlike figure, in addition to having antlers atop his head, Horne also takes the appearance of a stag:

> Oft haue you heard since Horne the hunter dyed,
>
> That women to affright their litle children,
>
> Ses that he walkes in shape of a great stagge.
>
> Now for that Falstaffe hath bene so deceiued,
>
> As that he dares not venture to the house,
>
> Weele send him word to meet vs in the field,
>
> Disguised like Horne, with huge horns on his head.[128]

The spelling of Herne as *Horne* is most likely not an accident. In the first half of the sixteenth century during the reign of King Henry VIII, a parchment currently in the British Museum tells of a man named Rycharde Horne, who, along with several compatriots, was caught poaching in Windsor Forest.[129] The punishment for poaching was most often death, and if that death involved hanging, it's possible that Horne is at least one part of Herne's

---

127. Fitch, *In Search of Herne the Hunter*, 9.

128. Shakespeare, quarto 1 of *The Merry Wives of Windsor*, in *The Yale Shakespeare: The Complete Works*, 43.

129. Fitch, *In Search of Herne the Hunter*, 11–12.

myth. Rycharde could be the original ghostly source of Herne, or perhaps his name was added to an already existing myth.

Herne's Oak was the name given to a particular oak tree in Windsor Forest where Herne was alleged to have hung himself. Sadly the tree itself was cut down in 1796 (most likely by mistake), but its location was marked on a map dating back to 1742, where it's called *Sir John Falstaff's Oak*, named after a character in Shakespeare's play. A few pieces of wood survive from Herne's Oak, along with drawings of what it looked like in the eighteenth century.[130] Upon the tree's demise, the local newspaper, the *Whitehall Evening Post*, published a poem commemorating the oak "that nightly Herne walk'd round."[131]

If Herne is more than a figure of folklore and literature, where might his true origins lie? Instead of looking at figures such as Pan and Cernunnos, I prefer to look further afield at deities whose stories contain at least a little bit of Herne's myth. While it's popular to think of Britain as being one of the homes of the Celts, other pagan groups settled there too. The area around Windsor Forest was settled extensively by one of those groups, the Vikings, who imported their own myths and legends. One of those myths involves the god Woden (or Odin) hanging himself from Yggdrasil, the World Tree, in order to gain the wisdom of the runes.

If Herne is directly related to an ancient pagan deity, it's far more likely to be Odin than Cernunnos, an idea I first came across in the work of Eric Fitch (author of *In Search of Herne the Hunter*). The two deities share being hung from a tree, and both figures have been linked to spectral hunting parties. The Vikings settled in England during the ninth and tenth centuries, which means the figure known as Herne would have spent less time "underground" before being written about than if he were related to Cernunnos. Perhaps myths of Odin mixed with ghost stories of executed poachers, creating the figure we know today as Herne. We'll never know for sure, but this seems likely to me.

---

130. Fitch, *In Search of Herne the Hunter*, 23–24.
131. Fitch, *In Search of Herne the Hunter*, 146.

WORKING WITH HERNE

The tales of Herne's origins reveal a figure focused on vengeance and atonement. He's vengeful toward those who have wronged him (either his fellow keepers or the king) or he seeks atonement for his past misdeeds. Among Modern Witches who worship Herne, he tends to be worshipped as a rather generic version of the Horned God or as Cernunnos. But I think it's worth noting these two additional characteristics that make Herne unique in the annals of horned and antlered deities.

Certainly a figure associated with forests is very much an "earth deity," but to look at or honor only that part of Herne feels shortsighted. If the deities we worship are real entities, then it behooves us to explore their mythologies in order to better understand them. Herne is more than just another name people sometimes use in place of Cernunnos; he's a completely different god, born on a different shore during a different period of time. And if he is connected to Odin, he's also a god of wisdom and prophecy, in addition to his other attributes.

Because of Herne's unique qualities as a horned deity, I often call upon him when seeking justice or trying to right a wrong in my life. While I'm not someone to actively go and toss curses and hexes at others, I do believe in defending myself and shining a light on the truth when falsehoods have gotten in the way of it. Several years ago, an old acquaintance of mine began spreading rumors about me and calling me a liar. When circumstances like that arise, it's time for Witchcraft, and on this particular occasion I looked to Herne for help.

HERNE'S WITCH BOTTLE SPELL

Traditionally Witch bottles are buried under windows and doors to reflect any negative energy directed toward a particular household. This spell is a variation on the classic Witch bottle, and sends all negativity, lies, and bad deeds back to the person instigating those things. It's not necessary to know who the source of your problems is to work this spell, and it might even be more effective if you don't. If you name the wrong person to receive the negative energies being directed at you, then that person will suffer need-lessly, so certainty is a must!

Here are the items needed for this spell:

- A small jar with a wide mouth, such as a spaghetti jar
- A small length of chain or cord to wrap around the object represent-ing the cause of your problems (I recommend using something that resembles a chain, such as a small chain-link necklace.)
- Something representing the cause of your problems (If you know the exact individual who is at fault, a printed picture of them works very well, as does writing their name on a sheet of paper. If you don't know their name, that's fine too. In that case, just use some-thing that represents the cause of the problem, such as a picture of lips if you are trying to fend off gossip, the word "LIES!" if someone is lying about you, etc.)
- Seven shiny dimes
- A reflective item, such as a very small mirrored item or a coin or rock wrapped tightly in a piece of aluminum foil (Aluminum foil is an easy way to create a reflective surface for your magick.)
- Stones of protection, such as black tourmaline, black obsidian, hema-tite, fluorite, smoky quartz, jet, or amethyst (If there's a stone you associate with protection that is not listed here, you can use that too.)
- Vinegar
- Something from your body (This can be a strand of hair, a fingernail, or urine. If you want to take your magick up a notch, you can also use vaginal secretions, semen, or blood, including menstrual blood.)
- Anything else you want to add (Everything is on the table with a Witch bottle.)
- A libation to offer to Herne after the spell is complete (I suggest ale or cider.)

If you prefer to do magick in sacred space, begin by casting a circle and calling the quarters. Once everything is set up to your liking, invoke Herne:

I call to Herne to assist me today with my magick! May justice be swift and may those who have tried to wrong me feel the full brunt of their misdeeds. I ask for the protection and assistance of the great hunter Herne! Lend your power to mine so that I may be free from my tormentors and those who work against me shall be silenced. So mote it be!

Start by taking whatever it is that you are using to represent the negativity being sent against you and wrapping it in your small chain. If you can tie the chain into a knot around the object, all the better. If you are using a picture or a small piece of paper, inserting that into one of the links of the chain and then tying the chain with a knot will work nicely here. As you wrap and knot the chain, speak these words:

> *With Herne's chains, I bind you,*
> *To stop the damage you do.*
> *All harm toward me will cease,*
> *And all will be at peace.*

Repeat the above four lines as you wrap your chain around the object representing your troubles. When you reach the end of the chain, speak these final two lines:

> *In the name of Herne, I cast this spell.*
> *My will be done. So mote it be!*

While wrapping your chain around the object representing your troubles, imagine all of the negativity being directed toward you ceasing. Visualize mouths being shut, whispers not being shared, and only good coming your way. When you are through with this mini binding, put the chain and your bound item into your Witch bottle.

Pick up the dimes you have gathered for this ritual. Notice their reflective surface and imagine any negative energy being directed toward you being reflected back to its source. Think about yourself being surrounded by good luck and being free from all negativity and evil thoughts. Slowly place each of the dimes into your Witch bottle while reciting the following:

One dime for good luck in all I do.
A second for my wishes to come true.
The third for being seen as I am.
Four to stop all who would curse and damn.
A fifth to reflect that which vexes.
Their will turned into this Witch's hexes [drop in the sixth dime].
Seven for the power of the horn'd one, Herne.
Protect from me all that which I spurn!
Horned one, protector and power,
Bless this work with your earthen glower!

Now pick up your small mirror or reflective item, and again visualize any unwanted energy being directed at you being sent back to the source. As you place that item in your Witch bottle, say:

I use against you what you would use to hurt me.
Through Herne, all shall bounce back to you. So mote it be!

Pick up the stone you are using to represent protection. Feel its energy and let that energy throb in the palm of your hand for a moment. Visualize yourself being free from strife and worry and anything that would harm you. See yourself safe and secure in your home and with your loved ones. Know that you are loved and that there are people out there who have a vested interest in your welfare. When you are ready, add the stone to your Witch bottle and say:

I shall be free from strife, safe and secure.
With the power of Herne, this I ensure!

I usually fill my Witch bottles with vinegar and sometimes a small amount of urine. If you want to use strictly vinegar, that's great! If you are using vinegar in conjunction with something else, be sure not to fill your bottle all the way up in this next step. If you want to add anything else to your Witch bottle (other than that which represents you), do so before adding the vinegar.

The idea behind using vinegar to fill up your Witch bottle is to make sure the negative energy that will bounce back to your tormentor is rotten and nasty. People tend to stop being assholes when that sort of behavior results in bad luck for them! As you fill your bottle with vinegar, say the following:

> *Vile, sour, disgusting, unwanted, and rude,*
> *I send back to you what you used to intrude!*
> *May you be the victim of your own evil and malice.*
> *The scales of justice I now put back in balance!*

Finally, add your piece of hair, fingernail, or urine to the Witch bottle and say:

> *Through the power of Herne, this bottle serves only me.*
> *From torments and pain, I shall soon be free.*
> *All sent toward me now goes back to its source.*
> *That is the way of my magick, the path and the course.*
> *With the power of Herne, god of justice and right,*
> *I now have my tormentors in my sight!*
> *All will be good, from negativity I shall be free,*
> *This spell is now cast, I say so mote it be!*

Witch bottles are usually buried under windows and doorways. Since this is not a typical Witch bottle, best to keep it on your altar for as long as you need it. When those who wish you harm have ceased working against you, take the bottle off your altar and bury its contents outside, or pour the contents somewhere outside where they are unlikely to be disturbed for a while, such as near a bush. The bottle can be recycled or reused after it has been washed.

When the spell is over, be sure to thank Herne with some sort of offering. Ideally you should pour out your offering near an oak tree in his honor. If that's not an option, simply place your offering in a chalice or bowl, direct the god to it, and place the offering on your altar for at least a few hours, or better yet a day. When removing the offering, thank Herne again and dispose of the cup's contents.

ELEN OF THE WAYS

Currently, one of the most popular faces of the Horned God belongs to a female version of the deity, a reindeer-antlered goddess known as Elen of the Ways (figure 12). Although Elen was virtually unheard of before the 1980s, it's now possible to buy statues, T-shirts, and books featuring her online and in many Witch shops. Much like Cernunnos, there are no myths that feature Elen by name (or with her antlers), but unlike Cernunnos, there's also no archaeological evidence for Elen of the Ways. The story of Elen of the Ways is unlike that of any other deity featured in this book.

Elen is what I think of as a *revealed* deity. She was brought into the light by reading between the lines of mythology and through personal *gnosis*, meaning direct contact with a deity by a human being. The revealer of Elen is British goddess historian Caroline Wise, whose essays (and later books) on the subject of Elen of the Ways form the backbone of the deity's mythology and character. According to Wise, Elen of the Ways is the British goddess of the natural world, fertility, gardens, underground sources of water, ley lines,[132] roads, migratory routes, and, not surprisingly, reindeer.[133] Since Elen is the goddess of such a vast array of ideas and energies, it's not surprising that she's become popular since she was introduced to the modern world in 1986 (the year Wise first published information on the subject of Elen).

The biggest piece of evidence for the existence of Elen in the ancient world comes from the Welsh collection of stories and tales known as the *Mabinogion* in the United States and the *Mabinogi* in the United Kingdom. The stories that make up the Mabinogion were compiled in the twelfth and thirteenth centuries and are based on much older oral legends. The first written version of the Mabinogion (apart from a few fragments) appears toward the end of that time frame. The stories that make up this collection deal primarily with heroes and kings, but it's believed by many that those heroes and kings were once most likely Welsh-Celtic deities. The Mabinogion also contains characters familiar to us from other mythologies, such as King Arthur,

---

132. Ley lines are allegedly paths through which intense amounts of earth energy run. Places of special religious or spiritual significance, such as Stonehenge, are thought to be built on top of ley lines.

133. Wise, "Elen of the Ways, Part 1."

along with historical figures such as Magnus Maximus (c. 335–388 CE), who ruled the western half of the Roman Empire in the late fourth century.

Figure 12: Elen of the Ways.
Because there are no ancient depictions of Elen,
every image of the goddess is a modern one.

It's in the Mabinogion story of Maximus (who is referred to in the text as Macsen Wledig) that Elen appears. According to the tale, known as *The Dream of Macsen Wledig*, Maximus dreams of a beautiful red-haired woman who lives in a faraway land. Being an emperor, he sends out men all across the world to find this woman. After much searching, they find her in present-day Wales. This is, of course, Elen (or sometimes Helen), and once she's located, Maximus travels with haste to be at her side. The two fall in love, and Elen's father is given dominion over the island of Britain and three new castles are built in honor of Elen. Elen also convinces her new husband to build an extensive series of roads in her native land to make the defense of Britain easier. Before Elen and Maximus can live happily ever after, the emperor has his throne stolen from him while he's away, but thanks to his new allies, he quickly regains it, and gives the Britons the province of Brittany in Gaul (present-day France).

In Wales, Elen, the wife of Maximus, has become Saint Elen and is thought to have built the first Christian churches in Wales. (While hailed as a saint in Wales, Elen has never formally been canonized by the Roman Catholic Church.) Elen is the patron saint of roads and their builders, a tidbit that aligns nicely with her role in the Mabinogion. The ancient Roman road *Sarn Helen* is named after Saint Elen, though the road predates the time of Maximus, lending more credence to the idea that the Elen of the Mabinogion was a Celtic-Welsh goddess.

The Mabinogion and the story of Elen as a saint are our best clues to the goddess's ancient existence. In her writings on Elen of the Ways, Wise offers more justifications for the existence of Elen in the ancient world. Some of those are problematic (such as linking Santa's reindeer to Elen; Santa didn't use reindeer until the nineteenth century), but a good argument can be made for a goddess of British roads related to reindeer. As we've already seen in this book, there were female versions of Cernunnos: could these have possibly been Elen of the Ways?

Wise has always been very adamant that Elen has reindeer antlers atop her head, and for good reason. Reindeer are the only species of animal where females, in addition to males, grow antlers. Interestingly, males shed their antlers shortly after mating season in November/December, while female reindeer keep their antlers until their calves are born in late spring. Because of this, Santa's reindeer are far more likely to be female than male.

The first "roads" among ancient humans were probably the migratory trails of animals like reindeer. These tracks help link Elen as a reindeer goddess to her role as a goddess (and saint) of roads. While the physical and literary evidence for Elen of the Ways is scant, there's a pretty good circumstantial case for her being an ancient goddess of some sort, even if I find much of the historical evidence for Elen of the Ways rather dubious (and I urge you to read about Elen and draw your own conclusions; links are in the bibliography).

Though some of the mythology and reasoning used to establish the existence of Elen in the modern world feels a bit suspect to me, I don't doubt the existence of the goddess. I've read critics of Wise and Elen of the Ways call Elen a made-up deity, but I think that's far too dismissive. I have friends who have had experiences with Elen of the Ways, and judging by her current popularity, I have to believe there is some sort of collective energy pushing her to a place of prominence in our society. It's also worth noting that every deity starts from somewhere, and whether that's in the ancient or the more modern world is immaterial. As a believer in a truly universal Horned God, I find that Elen provides another entry into the Horned One's mysteries.

Chapter Eleven
THE REBIRTH OF PAN

IN GREEK, THE WORD *pan* means all or everything, which is also one of the word's many meanings in English.[134] Because of pan's meaning in Greek, the word is also often applied to the god of the same name. This has led a lot of Pagan and Witchcraft writers over the years to argue that the meaning of pan in Greek today is related to the god. That *pan* and *Pan* would mean the same thing is a logical assumption, even if it's wrong. (As we've seen previously, the name of the god Pan means shepherd; see chapter 5.)

Several years ago, I was talking about Pan with an acquaintance of mine who practices primarily as a Hellenic Reconstructionist (meaning she tries to do rituals in honor of the Greek gods in a way that approximates how those rituals would have been done 2,500 years ago). Somehow we got caught up in a discussion on the origins of Pan's name, and when I told her about its links to shepherds, she exhaled deeply and then tried to suppress a chuckle. "You know," she said, "I chose not to attend a workshop on Pan you did a few years ago because you called it "Pan: The God of All," because I just assumed you had no idea what you were talking about."

I laughed in response, because what else could I do? Besides, she was right: by using that name, I *was* suggesting to the well-informed that I probably didn't know what I was talking about. But in some ways, Pan—and, by extension, the Horned God—*has* become the god of everything or all. The

---

134. Online Etymology Dictionary, s.v. "pan," https://www.etymonline.com/word/pan.

Horned God today is viewed primarily as a god of the natural world, and as a nature deity with few equals. He's been written about that way for several centuries now, and the idea was even hinted at in some classical sources.

As we've seen in this book, Pan was most certainly not the god of everything, but there was something very appealing to people about that association. In the early first century CE, the Stoic philosopher Lucius Annaeus Cornutus (first century CE) wrote of Pan:

> And it is 'Pan' as well, since it is identical with *everything* [*pan*]. He is hairy and goat-like in his lower parts because of the roughness of the earth; his upper parts have the form of a human because the ruling part of the cosmos, which is rational, is in the aether. ... His skittish and playful nature points to the ceaseless motion of the universe. He is clad in fawn skin or leopard skin because of the variety of the stars, and of the other things which are observed in it.[135]

Cornutus is not calling Pan "everything" here, but the linkage of heaven and earth does imply an awful lot of territory.

PAN IN THE ORPHIC HYMNS AND INTO THE RENAISSANCE

An ode to Pan found in the Orphic Hymns suggests a universal Pan similar to the Pan identified by Cornutus. The Orphic Hymns are a series of poems that most likely represent much of the text used in a single all-night ritual held by an Orphic cult located in present-day Turkey.[136] We know very little about the Orphics because initiates were sworn to secrecy regarding the mysteries of the cult, just like with the mysteries of Demeter at Eleusis and in some Witchcraft traditions today. In addition, there were probably several different Orphic cults, each with its own unique liturgy and practices. We do know that, like the cult at Eleusis, Orphics were concerned primarily with the survival of the soul after death, and were inspired by the Greek musician Orpheus, hence the name.

---

135. Boys-Stones, *L. Annaeus Cornutus*, 16.

136. Dunn, *The Orphic Hymns*, 1–3.

The primary god in the Orphic tradition was the Greek Dionysus, but Dionysus wasn't the only deity honored by the Orphics. In the Hymns, several dozen deities are all given their own poem, along with natural phenomena such as the sky and the sea. In addition, most of the eighty-plus poems that make up the Orphic Hymns include an "aromatic suggestion," or scent to be burned during the reading of each particular hymn. Many of those scents are familiar to us, such as frankincense and myrrh, but others can only be guessed at. Luckily for us, the incense suggested for Pan is "mixed," so the Pan devotee is free to use whatever they like.

Here is the Orphic Hymn for Pan, as translated by Patrick Dunn in his 2018 book *The Orphic Hymns.*

The Orphic Hymn for Pan

I call mighty Pan, the god of shepherds
and the whole universe together; sky
and sea, the all-regal earth, and deathless
fire: for these are the limbs of Pan himself.
Come, blessed, spinning, cavorting, enthroned
with the Seasons, goat-limbed, Bacchic, frenzy
of gods' inspiration under the stars.
You strike cosmic harmony with playful
song. You, the aid of imagination
and bringer of terrible images
to mortal fears, delighting in shepherds
and herdsmen among the fountains. Sharp-eyed
hunter, the lover of Echo, you dance
with the nymphs. All-growing god, the father
of all, many-named daimon,[137] the ruler
of the cosmos, increaser, light-bringer,
fruitful Paian, cave-haunting god, heavy
with wrath, truly the horned Zeus, for through you

---

137. A Greek *daimon* was generally a lesser god, such as a nature spirit or a deified mortal.

the boundless plain of the earth lies firm, but
deeply flowing waters of the tireless
seas yield, and Ocean, surrounding the earth
with waters, and the air that we share for
nourishment, the spark of all life, the eye
of most nimble fire high above: For these
holy things stand apart by your command;
you change the natures of all by your wise
will, nourishing the human race throughout
the boundless world. So come, blessed one, frenzied
with divine inspiration to this most
holy libation: give life a good end
and send out Pan's passion to the earth's ends.[138]

The Pan written about here is generally how we encountered him earlier in this book. He's the god of shepherds as well as his usual dancing, frenzied self, but there's something more to him hinted at in the text. This is not just the rustic god of Arcadia; the Orphic Pan is "truly the horned Zeus" and, as such, the "ruler of the cosmos" and the god of "the whole universe together." There's something sinister to this Pan as the "bringer of terrible images to mortal fears," but also something positive and triumphant. He's the "increaser," the god who controls the natural world and the "spark of all life." The language of the Orphics in regard to Pan was radically different from that of the Pan worshipped in classical Greece.

Despite the familiarity many of us have today with the Orphic Hymns, they were not widely known in the ancient world. The sect that wrote these was probably very small, and the version we have of them today comes to us by way of Constantinople (current-day Istanbul in Turkey), and from there to Italy and then the rest of Europe beginning in 1423.[139] The first English translations of the Hymns wouldn't appear until 1792, in a translation by Thomas

---

138. Dunn, *The Orphic Hymns*, 63.

139. Dunn, *The Orphic Hymns*, 1.

"the Pagan" Taylor (1738–1835) in 1792.[140] It's most likely not a coincidence that the reemergence of the Orphic Hymns in Italy and finally Great Britain coincided with a renewed interest in the great god Pan.

Perhaps the most beautiful expression of Pan as "everything" came from the Christian Bishop (and Saint) Isidore of Seville (560–636). Seville's greatest contribution to history was his *Etymologiae*, an etymological encyclopedia containing writings from classical antiquity that would have otherwise not survived to the present day. Isidore's writings on Pan were probably based on the writings of the fifth-century Roman writer Maurus Servius Honoratus, who was not a convert to Christianity.[141] Isidore's work is worth sharing here because of both its beauty and its lasting influence. Later writers who wrote about Pan as "all" were very likely influenced by Servius, or others influenced by him.

> The Greeks call the god of country people, whom they fashioned in the likeness of nature, Pan. ... He is called Pan, that is, 'everything,' for they fashion him out of every sort of element. He has horns in the likeness of the rays of the sun and moon. He has a pelt marked by spots, on account of the stars of the sky. ... He holds a pipe of seven reeds, on account of the harmony of heaven, in which there are seven tones and seven intervals of sound. He is hairy, because the earth is clothed and agitated by the winds. ... He has goat's hooves, so as to show the solidity of the earth. They claim he is the god of all things and of all nature, whence they say Pan, 'everything' as it were.[142]

Seven hundred years after Servius, the European Renaissance began in present-day Italy, and with it came the return of the Greek and Roman gods of antiquity. For the first time in a thousand years, the goddesses and gods of antiquity could be found once more in European art and literature.[143] By

---

140. Taylor was a Neo-Platonist and was called "the Pagan" by his contemporaries. Seriously, I can't make this stuff up.

141. Merivale, *Pan the Goat-God*, 10.

142. Isidore of Seville, *The Etymologies of Isidore of Seville*, 188.

143. Godwin, *The Pagan Dream of the Renaissance*, 3.

the middle of the fifteenth century, cities such as Rome were overrun with images of classical deities, including, of course, Pan. This does not mean that people were actively worshipping the gods of antiquity, at least not intentionally. The reflowering of pagan imagery probably stemmed from a desire to express ideas such as romantic love, joy, drunkenness, and passion, things that Christian icons and figures are poor at bringing to life.

When writing about Pan during the Renaissance, many writers picked up where Servius left off. Encyclopedists of the Renaissance wrote about Pan in a variety of ways, but their favorite seemed to be as the god of everything or all. The English encyclopedist Francis Bacon (1561–1626) was full of praise for the god Pan and found symbolism in every hoof and horn of the god.

To Bacon, Pan had pyramidal horns reaching to the heavens, "since the sublimities of nature, or abstract ideas, reach in a manner to things divine; for there is a short and ready passage from metaphysics to natural theology."[144] He calls Pan's physical body "the body of nature" and equates his beard to the power of the sun. Like Servius, the panpipe is representative of the heavens and denotes "consent and harmony." Pan's shepherd's crook represents the ways of nature, "which are partly straight and partly crooked."

Bacon's Pan is also cosmic, related to nearly all the goings-on in the world. Pan's sisters are the "Destinies, or the natures and fates of things," because the "chain of natural causes links together the rise duration, and corruption; the exaltation, degeneration, and workings; the processes, the effects, and changes, of all that can any way happen to things." Bacon finishes his ruminations by once more equating Pan directly with nature and labeling them both "perfection."[145]

PAN'S REBIRTH IN THE ENGLISH COUNTRYSIDE

The most important reflowering of Pan took place not in Greece or Rome but in England, where he would become the most written about male deity in all of English literature.[146] That achievement is especially notable when

---

144. Bacon, *Bacon's Essays & Wisdom of the Ancients*, 333–343.

145. Bacon, *Bacon's Essays & Wisdom of the Ancients*, 333–343.

146. Hutton, *The Triumph of the Moon*, 45.

one considers that Pan was rarely written about in England before the nineteenth century. For most of us, the poetry of the Romantic (1798–1837) and Victorian (1838–1901) eras was something we were forced to read in high school English class and then quickly forgot about. But the poetry produced during those hundred or so years would have a tremendous impact not just on Pan but on the Horned God as a whole.

To quote British historian Ronald Hutton, the poets and writers of those eras provided a "language" that we still use today when talking about the Horned One.[147] The flowery words many of us use about and to the Horned God were directly inspired by this period of literature; and many of the works written about Pan two hundred years ago continue to fit nicely into modern Witch ritual. We also know that early Witches such as Gerald Gardner and Doreen Valiente read the poems and literature that helped set Pan's cloven hooves firmly in the modern world.

There's a very real-world reason Pan reemerged in nineteenth-century England: the Industrial Revolution. In 1810 about 20 percent of the population in England lived in large cities, while the other 80 percent lived in more rural areas. One hundred years later, the rural-urban divide had effectively flipped, with 80 percent of England's population now living in cities and only 20 percent continuing to live in the country and other rural settings.[148] That's a drastic sea change in culture, especially to have happened in such a short period of time. The result of this was that people began to feel disconnected from the countryside they (or their forebears) had once inhabited and began looking for an entry back into that world.

It should be pointed out that the majority of poets were city dwellers, but like the Greeks of Athens and the poets of Rome who romanticized Arcadia, English poets began to romanticize England's lost rural landscape. Many attempted to find a connection to the natural world through Christianity,

---

147. Hutton, *The Triumph of the Moon*, 3. In the first chapter of this book, Hutton describes how the writings of the Romantic poets provided a framework for describing modern Paganism and its deities, including the Horned God. The title of that chapter is "Finding a Language."

148. Hutton, *The Triumph of the Moon*, 141.

but not surprisingly, Jesus as a wild god of the forest just doesn't work very well. Because Christianity lacks an explicit connection to the natural world, they turned to classical Greece and found Pan as the god of all in the Orphic Hymns (which had recently been translated into English) and in the works of Bacon and other Renaissance-era encyclopedists. It also helped that many of England's most prominent poets chose to write about Pan, inspiring those who came after them.

There were two different "Pan motifs" during this era, and both of them are still with us today when we talk about the Horned God. The first is the "Orphic" or "Cosmic" Pan; this is the Pan of everything or all, who is the very embodiment of nature. Often this is a god who can be heard or felt but seldom seen. When people today write about the Horned God in the abstract or as an all-powerful, always-present deity, they are referencing this version of Pan.

The second version was (and is) the "Rustic" or "Intimate" Pan. To the poets of the nineteenth century, this was the Pan who ruled over the eternal English countryside, preserving nature and keeping the industrial world away from what was left of England's romanticized pristine wilderness. This was a Pan who could be seen if one knew just where to look. This was also the Pan whom people prayed to (then and now) and who was a presence and force in people's lives.

English poets also presented the world with a much more sanitized version of the god. Nymphs were mentioned in passing, but generally as a way to lament lost love. The Pan of the English countryside was not the god of rape or panic sexuality, but a god of love and natural beauty. This is an important change, and another example of how the Pan of this period reflects how many Witches talk about and understand the Horned God today.

There's another dimension to the return of Pan that can be written about only in a book for Witches: I have to assume that Pan's reemergence in the modern world was something that he desired, or perhaps the world needed. Why were people suddenly writing about Pan? Could it be that the god was whispering in their ears once more? Did Mother Earth choose to awaken Pan from his nap in an effort to save the earth or at least remind humans just how beautiful the natural world is? When writing about history, it's easy to place the emphasis on human agency, but my gods aren't passive. In most cases, they have sought me out, not the other way around. Romantics and Victorians may have been looking for something like Pan, but I also think he was looking for them.

Since Pan is a deity who has inspired tens of thousands of poems, essays, and novels, it would be easy for me to quote from those materials extensively for the next forty or so pages. However, that seems like overkill, so instead I'll simply share some of my favorite examples of Pan in English literature, focusing on more prominent poets whose works have had a lasting impact. It's also my hope that what's shared here will inspire you as a follower of the Horned One, and that you'll love all of it as much as I do.

PAN IN ENGLISH POETRY AND LITERATURE

The first major poet to adopt Pan as a continuing motif was William Wordsworth (1770–1850), who most often wrote about Pan in the Orphic style, as a god heard and felt but never truly seen. Wordsworth's most famous poem is the multi-volume *The Prelude*, an autobiographical work detailing his development as a poet and human being. The eighth book of the *Prelude* is titled *Retrospect: Love of Nature Leading to Love of Man,* and it's here that the reader discovers Pan the "Invisible God, thrilling the rocks/With tutelary music," protecting a flock of goats from "all harm."[149] *The Prelude* was written over a period of fifty years, but the lines above about Pan most likely date from sometime between 1799 and 1805.

Contemporary with Pan as the "Invisible God" is the depiction of the god in Wordsworth's 1806 poem "Composed by the Side of Grasmere Lake," where Pan as nature offers solace from a world full of violence and misery:

> Clouds, lingering yet, extend in solid bars
> Through the grey west; and lo! these waters, steeled
> By breezeless air to smoothest polish, yield

---

149. Wordsworth, *The Complete Works of William Wordsworth,* from *Book 8: Retrospect: Love of Nature Leading to Love of Man* in *The Prelude.*

A vivid repetition of the stars;

Jove, Venus, and the ruddy crest of Mars

Amid his fellows beauteously revealed

At happy distance from earth's groaning field,

Where ruthless mortals wage incessant wars.

Is it a mirror?—or the nether Sphere

Opening to view the abyss in which she feeds

Her own calm fires?—But list! a voice is near;

Great Pan himself low-whispering through the reeds,

"Be thankful, thou; for, if unholy deeds

Ravage the world, tranquility is here!"[150] (emphasis mine)

A little less than ten years later, Wordsworth would write in the poem "O'er the Wide Earth" how the longing for nature dwells within the hearts of all people and how we all quest for something like Pan:

O'er the wide earth, on mountain and on plain,

Dwells in the affections and the soul of man

A Godhead, like the universal PAN;

But more exalted, with a brighter train.[151]

While there's nothing to suggest that Wordsworth ever worshipped the god Pan, the same can't be said for English poet and essayist Leigh Hunt (1784–1859). Today Hunt is mostly a footnote in the careers of the much more gifted poets he influenced, John Keats (1795–1821) and Percy Bysshe Shelley[152] (1792–1822), an influence that included the god Pan. Though most scholars tend to scoff at the idea that Hunt worshipped the god Pan, his surviving correspondence sometimes suggests otherwise. In a letter to friend and fellow writer Thomas Jefferson Hogg (1792–1862), Hunt connects dec-

---

150. Wordsworth, *The Complete Works of William Wordsworth.*

151. Wordsworth, *The Complete Works of William Wordsworth.*

152. Percy Bysshe Shelley is immensely famous in literary circles, but he's probably better known today as the husband of the novelist Mary Shelley, who wrote *Frankenstein.*

orating with evergreen branches to ancient paganism and suggests to his friend the following:

> If you all go on so, there will be a hope some day that old Vansit-tart[153] and others will be struck with a Panic Terror and that a voice will be heard along the water saying—"The Great God Pan is alive again!"—upon which the villagers will leave off starving, and singing profane hymns, and fall to dancing again.[154]

It's hard to tell exactly if Hunt and those in his orbit truly worshipped Pan in a religious sense, but they most certainly felt drawn to the god and classical paganism. The poetry and prose that arose from their quill pens expressed an undeniable appreciation of the god. In 1821 Shelley wrote to a friend that "I am glad to hear that you do not neglect the rites of the true religion. ... I ascended alone, the high mountain behind my house, & suspended a garland & raised a small turf altar to the mountain-walking Pan."[155]

Shelley's "Hymn of Pan" (1820) portrays not a universal god, but a god whose primary gift to the world is his music. Pan's pipings in the poem are so sweet that even the god Apollo is envious of them. What touches me in the poem are how Pan's songs tell the story of the world:

> I sang of the dancing stars,
> I sang of the daedal Earth,
> And of Heaven, and the giant wars,
> And Love, and Death, and Birth.[156]

Sadly, at the end of the poem, Pan's pipings turn sorrowful when his heart is broken, but that too is the story of life.

---

153. Nicholas Vansittart, 1st Baron Bexley and one of Britain's longest-serving Chancellors of the Exchequer, was the person to whom Hunt referred in this letter. The Chancellor of the Exchequer is the keeper of the purse, essentially the UK's minister of finance.

154. Merivale, *Pan the Goat-God*, 63.

155. Shelley, *The Letters of Percy Bysshe Shelley: Vol. 2, Shelley in Italy*, 361.

156. Shelley, *The Complete Poetical Works of Percy Bysshe Shelley, Vol. 1*, location 12631, from the poem "Hymn of Pan."

Written the same year as "Hymn of Pan" but not released until after the poet's death in 1824, Shelley's "The Witch of Atlas" also features Pan, but a god more akin to Wordsworth's version of the Arcadian:

> And universal Pan, 'tis said, was there,
> And though none saw him,—through the adamant
> Of the deep mountains, through the trackless air,
> And through those living spirits, like a want,
> He passed out of his everlasting lair
> Where the quick heart of the great world doth pant,
> And felt that wondrous lady all alone,—
> And she felt him, upon her emerald throne.[157]

John Keats's "Hymn to Pan" (1818) is part of a much longer work, the *Endymion*, which begins with a group of shepherds gathering around an altar to pray to Pan. This "Hymn to Pan" nearly reads like an invocation to the god of Arcadia, touching upon most of the qualities attributed to Pan in the ancient world (minus the more unsavory ones, of course):

> Thou, to whom every fawn and satyr flies
> For willing service; whether to surprise
> The squatted hare while in half sleeping fit;
> Or upward ragged precipices flit
> To save poor lambkins from the eagle's maw;
> Or by mysterious enticement draw
> Bewildered shepherds to their path again;
> Or to tread breathless round the frothy main
> And gather up all fancifullest shells
> For thee to tumble into Naiads' cells,
> And, being hidden, laugh at their out-peeping;
> Or to delight thee with fantastic leaping,
> The while they pelt each other on the crown

---

157. Shelley, *The Complete Poetical Works of Percy Bysshe Shelley, Vol. 1*, location 7849, from the poem "The Witch of Atlas."

With silvery oak apples, and fir cones brown—
By all the echoes that about thee ring,
Hear us, O satyr king![158]

The work focused specifically on Pan spans four stanzas, each as long as the one reprinted above and each just as beautiful.

Before the *Endymion*, Pan featured in Keats's "I Stood Tip-Toe upon a Little Hill," published in an 1817 collection dedicated to Leigh Hunt. Here the poet's love of Pan is not quite as evident, but Keats paints a beautiful picture of what lies just outside of our mundane field of vision. When peeking through a tangle of branches or bushes, I often feel like Keats's narrator:

So did he feel, who pull'd the boughs aside,
That we might look into a forest wide,
To catch a glimpse of Fawns, and Dryades
Coming with softest rustle through the trees;
And garlands woven of flowers wild, and sweet,
Upheld on ivory wrists, or sporting feet:
Telling us how fair, trembling Syrinx fled
Arcadian Pan, with such a fearful dread.
Poor Nymph,—poor Pan,—how he did weep to find,
Nought but a lovely sighing of the wind
Along the reedy stream; a half heard strain,
Full of sweet desolation—balmy pain.[159]

Here it's not just Syrinx who is broken at the end of Pan's chase, but the goat-god as well. And those first six lines! They read like the perfect start to a Beltane or Midsummer rite.

The literary cult of Pan begun by Wordsworth, Keats, Shelley, and Hunt only grew in intensity as the nineteenth century progressed. By the end of the century, it nearly turned into something of a requirement that the aspiring poet

---

158. Keats, *The Poetical Works and Other Writings of John Keats*, 134–135.

159. Keats, *The Poetical Works and Other Writings of John Keats*, 13.

dedicate a few verses to the goat god of Arcady.[160] In addition to inhabiting the eternal English countryside, Pan's power began to be felt in cities as well. Poet Matthew Arnold (1822–1888) finds just enough of the natural world in London's busy Kensington Gardens park in 1852 to invoke the god:

> In the huge world, which roars hard by,
> Be others happy if they can!
> But in my helpless cradle I
> Was breathed on by the rural Pan.[161]

In his poem "Oak and Olive," James Elroy Flecker's (1884–1915) encounters with the god in the urban landscape of the early twentieth century include a full menagerie of nymphs and maenads:

> When I go down the Gloucester lanes
> My friends are deaf and blind:
> Fast as they turn their foolish eyes
> The Mænads leap behind,
> And when I hear the fire-winged feet,
> They only hear the wind.

> Have I not chased the fluting Pan
> Through Cranham's sober trees?
> Have I not sat on Painswick Hill
> With a nymph upon my knees,
> And she as rosy as the dawn,
> And naked as the breeze?[162]

Flecker's ability to see the divine all around while his mundane friends are "deaf and blind" to the wonders of nature and the gods should be a familiar

---

160. Hutton, *The Triumph of the Moon*, 46.

161. Arnold, *Complete Poetical Works of Matthew Arnold*, from the imaginatively titled poem "Lines Written in Kensington Gardens."

162. Flecker, *The Collected Poems of James Elroy Flecker*, location 2362, "Oak and Olive."

refrain to most Witches. How many of us have found a place full of wonder only for our nonmagickal friends to dismiss it out of hand?

The power of Pan to enchant the urban landscape, as related by poets such as Arnold and Flecker, was not the isolated work of a few minor writers, but was an especially common motif in the late nineteenth and early twentieth centuries. The novelist W. Somerset Maugham wrote of this period, "Poets saw him lurking in the twilight on London commons, and literary ladies in Surrey and New England, nymphs of an industrial age, mysteriously surrendered their virginity to his rough embrace."[163] But Pan embraced more than just the nymphs of the industrial age; he also embraced the gay men of the era.[164] The result was a third facet to Pan by the end of the Victorian era: a god who embraced the (then) forbidden.

Before concluding this chapter, there are three specific portrayals of Pan in the late nineteenth and early twentieth centuries that I think deserve some special attention. This first is from the poet Algernon Charles Swinburne (1837–1909), who wrote so beautifully of Pan and his fellow Olympians that his 1866 collection of poetry, *Poems and Ballads*, was a genuine sensation on college campuses.[165] Students at Cambridge and Oxford defiantly chanted excerpts in the late 1860s while much of the establishment looked on in horror. Swinburne's praise of Pagan deity paints a picture of gods in love with joy and beauty, while Jesus and his father are portrayed as the architects of worldwide sadness.

For our purposes, Swinburne's most important poem might be "A Nympholept," published in 1894 as part of the collection *Astrophel and Other Poems*. What makes "A Nympholept" so noteworthy is the near-absolute power of the god Pan. In Swinburne we see how the Horned God will be called to in the decades to come:

> I dare not sleep for delight of the perfect hour,
> Lest God be wroth that his gift should be scorned of man.

---

163. Maugham, *Cakes and Ale; or, The Skeleton in the Cupboard*, 121–122.

164. Hutton, *The Triumph of the Moon*, 50.

165. Hutton, *The Triumph of the Moon*, 26.

The face of the warm bright world is the face of a flower,
The word of the wind and the leaves that the light winds fan
As the word that quickened at first into flame, and ran,
Creative and subtle and fierce with invasive power,
Through darkness and cloud, from the breath of the one God, Pan.

[... *There's a lot of space between these two verses.*]

Thee, thee the supreme dim godhead, approved afar,
Perceived of the soul and conceived of the sense of man,
We scarce dare love, and we dare not fear: the star
We call the sun, that lit us when life began
To brood on the world that is thine by his grace for a span,
Conceals and reveals in the semblance of things that are
Thine immanent presence, the pulse of thy heart's life, Pan.[166]

PAN AND ALEISTER CROWLEY

Though not a Pagan or a Witch (despite the conspiracy-theory nonsense of some in the Witchcraft community), British occultist Aleister Crowley (1875–1947) would have a huge impact on what many Witches do. A skilled ceremonial magician and an accomplished poet, Crowley's writings on magick went on to influence generations, and many of his words were recycled by the earliest public Witches and inserted into their rituals. In some ways, Crowley and Pan were very much alike. They both pursued pleasures, taking advantage of whatever was available, and loved the outdoors. Crowley was an avid mountaineer, especially in his early years.

In Witch circles, Crowley's most well-known poem is his "Hymn to Pan" (1907), which can be read either with a sly smirk and a wink or as a full-throated endorsement of the lustiness of Pan. Unlike other poets of the era, Crowley fully embraced all of Pan's rough edges, and his embrace is not subtle. Crowley also added rhetorical flourishes from his work *The Book of the Law* (1904), which would later feature prominently in the rites of the Ordo

---

166. Swinburne, *Selected Poems*.

Temple Orientis (O.T.O.) and other occult groups inspired by Crowley. By the time Crowley wrote his famous paean to Pan, he was quite familiar with the god in a spiritual context. Crowley's *Liber VII* from 1904 (dictated to the occultist by Aiwass, his Holy Guardian Angel) contains a vision of the god:[167]

Into my loneliness comes—
The sound of a flute in dim groves that haunt the uttermost hills.
Even from the brave river they reach to the edge of the wilderness.
And I behold Pan.[168]

Crowley's "Hymn to Pan" can be read as a prelude to the calls to the lusty Horned God that would arise from many Witches just a few decades later:

Hymn to Pan (Crowley)

Thrill with lissome lust of the light,
O man! My man!
Come careering out of the night
Of Pan! Io Pan!
Io Pan! Io Pan! Come over the sea
From Sicily and from Arcady!
Roaming as Bacchus, with fauns and pards
And nymphs and satyrs for thy guards,
On a milk-white ass, come over the sea
To me, to me!
Come with Apollo in bridal dress
(Shepherdess and pythoness)
Come with Artemis, silken shod,
And wash thy white thigh, beautiful god,
In the moon, of the woods, on the marble mount,
The dimpled dawn of the amber fount!
Dip the purple of passionate prayer
In the crimson shrine, the scarlet snare,

---

167. Kaczynski, *Perdurabo: The Life of Aleister Crowley*, 138.
168. Crowley, *Liber Liberi vel Lapidis Lazuli*.

The soul that startles in eyes of blue
To watch thy wantonness weeping through
The tangled grove, the gnarled bole
Of the living tree that is spirit and soul
And body and brain—come over the sea,
(Io Pan! Io Pan!)
Devil or god, to me, to me,
My man! my man!
Come with trumpets sounding shrill
Over the hill!
Come with drums low muttering
From the spring!
Come with flute and come with pipe!
Am I not ripe?
I, who wait and writhe and wrestle
With air that hath no boughs to nestle
My body, weary of empty clasp,
Strong as a lion and sharp as an asp—
Come, O come!
I am numb
With the lonely lust of devildom.
Thrust the sword through the galling fetter,
All-devourer, all-begetter;
Give me the sign of the Open Eye,
And the token erect of thorny thigh,
And the word of madness and mystery,
O Pan! Io Pan!
Io Pan! Io Pan Pan! Pan Pan! Pan,
I am a man:
Do as thou wilt, as a great god can,
O Pan! Io Pan!
Io Pan! Io Pan Pan! I am awake
In the grip of the snake.
The eagle slashes with beak and claw;

The gods withdraw:
The great beasts come, Io Pan! I am borne
To death on the horn
Of the Unicorn.
I am Pan! Io Pan! Io Pan Pan! Pan!
I am thy mate, I am thy man,
Goat of thy flock, I am gold, I am god,
Flesh to thy bone, flower to thy rod.
With hoofs of steel I race on the rocks
Through solstice stubborn to equinox.
And I rave; and I rape and I rip and I rend
Everlasting, world without end,
Mannikin, maiden, maenad, man,
In the might of Pan.
Io Pan! Io Pan Pan! Pan! Io Pan![169]

Crowley was not the first magickal person to cry "Io Pan," but he would turn it into something of a catchphrase to many in the magickal and Witch communities.

Despite its familiarity to many in the occult community, Crowley's "Hymn to Pan" lost the wider battle for how the Horned God would later be viewed by most Witches. Instead of Pan as the "lissome lust of the night," the most lasting image of Pan from the early twentieth century would be one far more serene and in line with the Pan of Keats and Shelley. That it would show up in a children's book makes the triumph of this version of Pan all that much more interesting.

THE PIPER AT THE GATES OF DAWN

To me, the fullest flowering of Pan as a literary phenomenon appears in Kenneth Grahame's (1859–1932) *The Wind in the Willows* from 1908. I'm sure most of you are familiar with *Willows* today because of the many movie and TV adaptations that have flourished in its wake. (It even inspired a ride at Disneyland.) But what most of those adaptations fail to address is the story's

---

169. Crowley, *The Equinox: Volume 3, Number 1 (The Blue Equinox)*, 5–7.

seventh chapter, "The Piper at the Gates of Dawn," which features Pan as the soul of nature.

Without even writing the god's name in his novel, Grahame perfectly captures the new kinder, gentler Pan, and does it in a way so powerful that reading it sometimes makes me weep. Grahame's Pan was how I first embraced the Horned God and is the vision I most often return to when experiencing the god in nature. I'm not alone in this reverence; the Pan conceived of in *The Wind in the Willows* would become the dominant version of the god in Pagan and Witch circles. (A part of me wonders how many Witches were born after hearing about Pan for the first time in Grahame's work.)

The reverence Grahame has for Pan is inescapable. He is "the Friend" and "the Helper" and an "august Presence" radiating love, kindness, and the overwhelming force of the natural world. Grahame is clearly writing about a god in his novel, which is why many Christian websites recommend that parents skip this particular chapter when reading the book to their children. The entire passage is worth perusing, but most especially these few paragraphs:

'This is the place of my song-dream, the place the music played to me,' whispered the Rat, as if in a trance. 'Here, in this holy place, here if anywhere, surely we shall find Him!'

Then suddenly the Mole felt a great Awe fall upon him, an awe that turned his muscles to water, bowed his head, and rooted his feet to the ground. It was no panic terror—indeed he felt wonderfully at peace and happy—but it was an awe that smote and held him and, without seeing, he knew it could only mean that some august Presence was very, very near. With difficulty he turned to look for his friend and saw him at his side cowed, stricken, and trembling violently. And still there was utter silence in the populous bird-haunted branches around them; and still the light grew and grew.

Perhaps he would never have dared to raise his eyes, but that, though the piping was now hushed, the call and the summons seemed still dominant and imperious. He might not refuse, were Death himself waiting to strike him instantly, once he had looked with mortal eye on things rightly kept hidden. Trembling he obeyed, and raised his humble head; and then, in that utter clearness of the imminent dawn, while Nature, flushed with fullness of incredible colour, seemed to hold her breath for the event, he looked in the very eyes of the Friend and Helper; saw the backward sweep of the curved horns, gleaming in the growing daylight; saw the stern, hooked nose between the kindly eyes that were looking down on them humourously, while the bearded mouth broke into a half-smile at the corners; saw the rippling muscles on the arm that lay across the broad chest, the long supple hand still holding the pan-pipes only just fallen away from the parted lips; saw the splendid curves of the shaggy limbs disposed in majestic ease on the sward; saw … All this he saw, for one moment breathless and intense, vivid on the morning sky; and still, as he looked, he lived; and still, as he lived, he wondered.

'Rat!' he found breath to whisper, shaking. 'Are you afraid?'

'Afraid?' murmured the Rat, his eyes shining with unutterable love. 'Afraid! Of *Him*? O, never, never! And yet—and yet—O, Mole, I am afraid!'

Then the two animals, crouching to the earth, bowed their heads and did worship.[170]

THE REBIRTH OF PAN AND THE HORNED GOD OF NATURE

The Horned God as a nature deity is perhaps his most obvious manifestation and yet is often the most difficult one to articulate. That difficulty most likely arises from the various ways we each see the Horned God's role in the natural world. For some Witches *he is the natural world*, and to others he is a shepherd of it, guiding the yearly turn of the Wheel, sometimes at the expense of himself. Others might interpret the Horned God's role in a more intimate way: perhaps he is the power that connects us directly to nature?

I would argue that the writers of the nineteenth and early twentieth centuries also saw Pan in these ways. As the decades progressed and these new

---

170. Grahame, *The Wind in the Willows*, 181–182.

interpretations of Pan got caught up in the much bigger Horned God, they became ways to interpret our own personal experiences with him. It's fitting that the Horned God's role as a nature deity has been so perfectly captured in poetry and prose over the years.

Not all of us unknowingly met the Horned God in English literature class, but the way we most often talk about him in Witch (and especially) Pagan circles reflects the influence writers from the last two hundred years have had on his myth. Mostly gone was the idea of a raging panic terror, and in its place we found a power that sings to us in the woods and comforts us when we find ourselves disconnected from nature. As a young Witch, it was this version of the Horned God that led me to his mysteries, and while my understanding of him has greatly increased over the decades since, it's still a part of his character that calls to me. It's hard for me to imagine a ritual in the outdoors where I don't feel his heartbeat near my own.

For many Witches today, the Horned God of *The Wind in the Willows* probably feels like an anachronism. Instead of seeing him as the benign "Friend" and "Helper," it's become popular in many Witch spaces to focus on the Horned God's role in death and to explore his connections to the Devil of Margaret Murray's Witches. Certainly the Horned God is more complicated than "happy Pan running through the forest," but I would argue that "happy Pan" remains a part of his character.

The Horned God of nature is what connects us to the bigger world. For many of us who live in an urban environment, the Horned God is the presence that takes us away from the mundane concerns that go along with that sort of lifestyle. Not everyone wants to go and live in the woods, but there is beauty in the wild spaces, and we can feel and experience that beauty through the Horned God's power. There's something wild and primal that exists within many Witches, and the Horned God helps us understand and experience that urge. Wanting to throw off one's clothes and howl at the moon is not a character flaw; it's a way to connect with the energies of the earth. For many of us, the Horned God is our guide through those mysteries.

Chapter Twelve
THE DEVILISH HORNED GOD

MODERN WITCHES HAVE A strange relationship with Christianity and the Devil. Many Witches who say they believe in a wide variety of deities often doubt the existence of the monotheistic God(s) of Christianity, Islam, and Judaism. They tend to scoff even louder at the demigods found in those faiths, such as the figure most of us today call the Devil. When a Witch is speaking to those outside of the Witch and Pagan worlds, I often hear, "Witches don't believe in the Devil," but that's not entirely true.

There are a lot of Witches who believe in the Devil (see chapter 17), just as they believe in any other entity who has been around for thousands of years. It's also worth pointing out that when a Christian accuses a Witch of worshipping the Devil, they aren't necessarily wrong in the context of their own faith. To many Christians, any deity outside of Jesus and his dad are either the Devil or one of his demons.

Try as we might, most Modern Witches can't completely escape the Devil. If we are being honest with ourselves, we also have to admit that he's in the very DNA of the Horned God. This does not mean that when someone is worshipping the Horned God, they are consciously worshipping an entity that wants to destroy the world. It just means that the texts and ideas that helped shape Modern Witchcraft and give rise to the Horned God contained a few devilish ideas.

LUCIFER, THE LIGHT BEARER

There are even many Witches today who actively worship the figure of Lucifer, who is often linked to the Devil. Lucifer is not a name found in original versions of the Old or New Testaments of the Christian Bible, but instead is the Greek translation of the term *Day Star*, which in Greek was most often translated as "light bearer" and often linked to the Morning Star, which is the planet Venus.[171] In the Old Testament book of Isaiah, a prophet writes that a corrupt Babylonian king will fall from his high perch ("How are you fallen from heaven, O Day Star, son of Dawn!").[172] This idea was misinterpreted as being about the Devil, with people erroneously thinking that *light bearer* was another name for this figure.

The idea of the falling Day Star led to the myth of "Satan falling from heaven" in many Christian traditions (figure 13). Jealous of humanity, this version of Satan leads a rebellion against the Christian God, loses his fight, and is thrown out of heaven along with his followers. Satan then takes command of hell and spreads evil around the world. None of this is really in the Bible and contradicts the actual use of Satan in the Old Testament, which simply means "obstacle."[173]

As a "light bearer," the figure of Lucifer began to be associated with wisdom, which tends to be the version of Lucifer generally honored by some Witches. On occasion this Lucifer is seen as being in conflict with the Christian God, but only because the God of the Christians would prefer to see us live in ignorance. The first book ever published on the subject of Modern Witchcraft included Lucifer as a god of the skies who was kicked out of heaven for disagreeing with the Christian God.

Charles Leland's (1824–1903) 1899 work *Aradia, or the Gospel of the Witches* purports to contain the rites and rituals of a group of Italian Witches who worship the goddess Aradia and her parents, Lucifer and Diana. The beginning of the book opens with a passage documenting the birth of Aradia:

---

171. Wray and Mobley, *The Birth of Satan*, 109.

172. Wray and Mobley, *The Birth of Satan*, 109 and 110.

173. Pagels, *The Origin of Satan*.

Diana greatly loved her brother Lucifer, the god of the Sun and the Moon, the god of Light (Splendor), who was so proud of his beauty, and who for his pride was driven from Paradise.[174]

Lucifer shows up as a light bearer and the source of wisdom in the writings of several other nineteenth- and early-twentieth-century occultists who would go on to influence Modern Witchcraft. Aleister Crowley called Lucifer "not the enemy of Man, but he who made Gods of our race, knowing Good and Evil; ... 'Know Thyself!'" Helena Blavatsky, the founder of the Theosophical Society, wrote that Lucifer was "the angelic Entity presiding over the light of truth," and called him our redeemer, intelligence, and savior.[175]

Figure 13: Lucifer.
Lucifer is most often depicted in Christian art not as
a light bearer but as a falling angel cast out of heaven.

---

174. Leland, *Aradia*, 1.

175. Oates, *Tubelo's Green Fire*, 18. Both quotes are taken from this book.

Several well-known Witches have expressed their admiration for Lucifer over the years. The Clan of Tubal Cain in England, founded by Robert Cochrane (born Roy Bowers 1931–1966) and later run by Shani Oates, honors Lucifer as the "Young Horn King" in their rites. In her written work, Oates states that the group's Magister (ritual leader) acts as "the 'son' of the Morning Star" and align themselves to the "potencies of Lucifer."[176] She later states that Lucifer is seen by some in the Craft as the "supreme deity" of Witches. Such devotion to Lucifer among Witches is not typical, but to some Witch traditions he's most certainly an important figure. Ignoring that to make a small group of Christians feel better about what we do as Witches feels dishonest.

In art, Lucifer tends to be pictured as a beautiful young man, lining up with the idea that he's a fallen angel. Due to the belief in some circles that Lucifer is the equivalent of Satan, he is sometimes shown with horns. But what really links Lucifer to the Horned God is that both figures are deities of the earth. If Lucifer is a fallen star, then he's a part of this planet, not off sitting on a cloud or waving a pitchfork around several miles underground. That the Horned God is a part of the earth is essential to understanding him, which is why some Witches see Lucifer as a part of the Horned One.

As we've seen, Margaret Murray's influence on the Horned God in Witch circles has been enormous, and while Murray believed that the Witches of the early modern period were worshipping a survival from pagan antiquity, she also believed that figure had been corrupted and confused with the Christian Devil. That confusion was not limited to those fighting against Witchcraft; it was also part of the Witch religion she believed she was documenting. Murray believed that at some point the Pagan Horned God absorbed the Christian Devil, with Witches actively worshipping the Horned One as the Devil. In her book, Murray equates nicknames for the Devil (such as "Old Hornie") with nicknames for the Horned God, further muddying the waters.

Most of Murray's ideas about how the "Witch-cult" operated are looked at with skepticism by modern scholars and by many Witches. But one of the

---

176. Oates, *Tubelo's Green Fire*, 44.

things that has made Murray so influential over the last hundred years is the fact that she quoted actual witch trials, and the things she quoted sometimes end up in our own rituals. Several years ago, I was at a ritual where I was told to put my left hand on top of my head and my right hand on the sole of my right foot, which is an awkward pose that comes straight from one of Margaret Murray's books.[177] Did actual Witches in 1601 do that? It's hard to trust any sort of "confession" that comes from someone being tortured, so probably not, but it's a tidbit that comes straight from someone believed to have worshipped the Devil.

In *The God of the Witches*, Murray lists six activities of Witches: admission ceremonies, dances, feasting, sacrifices (of both human children and the leader of the Witch-cult), orgies, and magick. None of us today are engaging in any human sacrifices, but the Horned God as a willing sacrifice figures in many Witchcraft traditions (something we'll get to in chapter 14). The other five activities Murray lists are all things engaged in (or at least not frowned upon, in the case of orgies) by Modern Witches, and many of them are called demonic by those lacking a sense of humor or sympathy toward the Craft of the Witch. I'm also of the opinion that the Horned God has a role to play in all of them.

A GOD OF SEX AND PLEASURE

After nature, the one thing I see most associated with the Horned God is sex. Even horned gods not generally depicted in a sexual way in pagan antiquity, such as Cernunnos, are sometimes pictured with erect penises to bring them more in line with the greater image of the Horned God. Without question, I think sex is important to the Horned One (Pan wouldn't want it any other way!), but I believe it comes with certain caveats.

As a god of nature, the Horned One lives in harmony with the earth. On occasion he takes from it, such as when hunting or harvesting food, but then he also gives back to it. As a sacrificial god, he gives his essence back to the earth so that crops might ripen in the field. He also takes care of and respects

---

177. Mankey, *Transformative Witchcraft*, 66.

the natural world. To be a true follower of the Horned God, one has to accept responsibility for one's actions and attempt to live a life that respects others. And this same type of behavior also applies to sex.

To be blessed by the Horned One, sex, at a bare minimum, should take place only between consenting adults. Ideally, any set of sexual partners should look upon one another with respect, all while taking responsibility for their actions. This means everyone agreeing verbally to sex, and then taking the necessary steps to ensure that sex is safe. The Horned God is down with blessing condoms! Sex should not be the end result of lies or false pretenses. Sex is an act that should uplift the people having it, not degrade them or be used as a way to gain dominance over another individual.

Occasionally I'll hear other Witches talk about sex in the context of the Horned God as something having to do exclusively with fertility, but this is wrong. Yes, the end result of certain types of sex is children, but thinking that sex is simply for procreation is limiting. Many human beings like to have sex simply because of the pleasure that it brings. If one is actively seeking a child, then sure, fertility is a part of sex, but the vast majority of sexual encounters between adult humans have nothing to do with trying to create a baby. And since the Horned God embraces all forms of sexuality and sexual identity, sex in the context of the Horned One can't be limited to strictly vaginal intercourse.

Unlike members of some other religious traditions, Witches view sex as a sacred gift. It's not a cosmic test of morality; it's simply an enjoyable part of human existence that we are free to engage in with a consenting partner(s). I see sex as a blessing from the Horned God, and when we engage in it responsibly, we grow closer to him.

Feasting

As a deity tied in the bounty of the earth, the Horned God can certainly be seen as a god of feasting. While I don't think wasting food is a responsible or neighborly activity to engage in, we all overeat on occasion, and I think it's safe to say that such indulgence is part of the human condition. Nearly all the major holidays celebrated in the world today include some sort of feasting; a desire to share food and drink is nearly imprinted upon our DNA. Not surprisingly, Christians during the period of the witch trials tended to look at anything that brought joy into people's lives as sinful, and equated feasting among Witches with the sin of gluttony.

While most Modern Witches don't sit down to a gigantic meal during the course of an average ritual, feasting, at least in a metaphorical sense, is still a part of most Witch ritual. The rite of cakes and ale (or cakes and wine) is a celebration of the earth's abundance and fertility and is traditionally blessed by the gods of the coven celebrating it. For many of us, that means blessings from the Horned One, or from directly named deities such as Dionysus or Cernunnos.

A simple feast during ritual serves a variety of purposes. It's a mini celebration of thanksgiving and, through libations, provides us with an opportunity to honor our gods. Food and drink also helps to ground the body after raising energy and working magick, but perhaps most importantly, cakes and ale is a bonding exercise. Sharing food and drink is one of the most intimate things we can do with other people.

The original sabbat celebrations of many Modern Witches didn't include much in the way of work and were generally about celebrating the change of seasons. That celebration often involved feasting. Even today, there are Witch covens that enjoy a bit of feasting after ritual, which is why most open circles in the Pagan world feature a potluck dinner at the conclusion of their rites.

Food and drink also bring us joy, and I've always believed that the Horned God wants us to experience joy. I'll admit that some of the happiest moments in my life have involved a bottle of wine or Scotch, always shared with friends and loved ones. But I've also been incredibly happy while sharing a magnificent meal with my family. Holiday meals spent around my grandma's dining room are some of my most cherished memories.

Magick

Like Modern Witches, the Witches of Margaret Murray's Witch-cult practiced magick. That magick generally involved their Horned God as a source of, contributor to, or instigator of that magick. While it's hard to imagine

Pan sitting still long enough to cast a candle spell, magick is about more than spells. Aleister Crowley defined magick as "the Science and Art of causing Change to occur in conformity with Will," and if there is one thing the Horned God can do, it's act as an agent of change.

Though not often thought of as magick, the power of gods such as Pan and Dionysus is something I can't help but think of in a magickal context. With a well-placed scare, Pan could get well-trained armies to turn on themselves, and today his presence in the circles of many Witches helps to lower inhibitions. (Have you ever seen a hundred people after a Pan ritual? It's going to be a good night for a lot of them!) Dionysus brought divine madness to his followers, helping them to experience ecstasy in his name. If that's not magickal, I don't know what is.

The Horned God's connection to magick goes deeper than just practice. In some Witchcraft traditions he's seen as the force that gave magick to the world, and more specifically, to we humans. Certainly, Lucifer as a god of wisdom might fulfill this role; the gift of knowledge includes the gift of magick after all. Other figures related to the Devil and Lucifer, such as Azazel from the apocryphal Book of Enoch, were said to share magick with the world. Azazel was said to have given magick specifically to women, in effect creating the first Witches. (We'll deal more with Azazel in chapter 17.)

In a broader cosmic sense, it's the magick of the Horned God that helps the seed to sprout and the leaf to fall. As the heart of nature, he's the magickal essence that turns the seasons and brings about the annual rise and fall of the world's wild spaces. Magick is about more than spells on the altar, it's about the energy that moves the world and the universe. As a figure connected to that essence, it's the Horned God who helps keep the world spinning round.

Dancing

Traditionally Pan was a god of the dance, and today the Horned God is seen as one too. Dancing during ritual serves a variety of purposes, but perhaps most importantly is an excellent way to raise energy.[178] When we contract and relax our muscles, we are creating energy, and what's left over from moving our bodies can be infused with intent and then used for magickal purposes. Dancing to raise energy is especially common at the public rituals of many Witches because it's easy and something most people can do.

But dance is about more than raising energy; it can be trance-inducing. In a trancelike state, we are often more receptive to seeing the gods and experiencing magickal energies. In the rites of many Traditional Witches, dance is used expressly for this purpose and often leads to sightings of the Horned God during ritual.

Dancing is also simply something that's full of joy. Dancing allows us to truly live in our bodies, and with every footfall we are connecting to the earth. When used as a communal activity, dancing helps us to connect with one another, and we all know the Horned God likes it when we connect with each other! Dancing indulges all of our senses: it's a whirlwind of sights, physical sensations, sounds, and even smells! Dancing is also something we do simply because it brings joy, and joy is a feeling the Horned God wants us to experience.

Initiation

The first modern public Witches were generally part of initiatory groups. At the time it was believed that for one to receive the rituals of Witchcraft one must join a coven, and the only way to join a coven was to undergo a rite of initiation. The Witches documented in Margaret Murray's work also allegedly underwent the process of initiation, but instead of one simply being allowed to join a coven afterward, the initiation ritual involved giving one's soul to Satan for eternity. Often this involved kissing Satan (or his representative) on the bare buttocks or signing one's name in a book. (If anyone ever suggests to you that you should sign away your soul or kiss them in an inappropriate area, run far away as quickly as possible. No real Witch would ever suggest a thing.)

---

178. I spend a lot more time talking about the power of dancing as a way to raise energy in *Transformative Witchcraft*.

Today's initiation rituals don't include any ass-kissing or soul-selling, and they are no longer the only entryway into Witchcraft, but I believe they still have purpose. According to Merriam-Webster, to initiate someone facilitates a beginning, instructs in the learning of something, and also means "to induct into membership by or as if by special rites."[179] All three of those definitions play a part in Modern Witchcraft initiation traditions. Most often initiations aren't just an entryway into a tradition, but are also used to share knowledge and provide instruction in a ritual setting.[180]

In Witchcraft, initiation rituals can be complex (especially if one is joining an established tradition) or exceedingly simple. In some ways the first spell we ever cast as a Witch is an initiation into the mysteries of magick. Likewise, our first-ever meeting with the Horned God is an initiation into his mysteries.

Christian churches often have trouble with groups and institutions they can't control, and frequently accuse those groups of being un-Christian and perhaps even Satanic. The medieval order of the Knights Templar was wiped out by the French monarchy working in tandem with the Catholic Church, for example. Most likely the Church and Crown coveted the wealth and influence of the Templars and used allegations of Devil worship to destroy the order. Most specifically, the Templars were accused of worshipping Baphomet, who was later reimagined as a goatlike entity in the nineteenth century. (We will spend a bit more time with Baphomet later in this chapter.)

Even in the twenty-first century, allegations of Devil worship plague fraternal orders, especially the Freemasons, the most influential initiatory order of the modern era. Established in the seventeenth century and descending from Scottish stonemason guilds, the Masons have influenced countless fraternal orders and religious and spiritual groups, such as the Latter-Day Saints (the Mormons) and today's Witches. Initiation rites within Wiccan-Witchcraft have

---

179. Merriam-Webster Online Dictionary, s.v. "initiate," https://www.merriam-webster.com/dictionary/initiate.

180. I feel pretty comfortable stating this, because all three of those were a part of my initiation into Gardnerian Witchcraft. Not surprisingly, I spend a lot of time discussing initiations in my book *Transformative Witchcraft*.

been strongly influenced by the Masons and contain many Masonic terms and initiation techniques.

For our purposes, what's most important within Masonry is the idea that some sort of Devil or Horned God lies at heart of the order, and according to some influential Masons, it very well might. Albert Pike (1809–1891) was one of the most influential American Masons in history, and is hugely responsible for much of the occult imagery and ideas found within some Masonic rites. Pike joined the Masons in 1850 and served in the order until he died over forty years later. For much of that time, he served as the head of the Southern Jurisdiction of the Scottish Rite (a role he would play from 1859 until his death).[181]

(While Pike is an influential figure in many occult circles, he is not someone to idolize, and if I met him today, I'd probably punch him in the face. He was extremely racist, and there are many who believe he had a hand in creating the Ku Klux Klan, which in its original incarnation used rituals also inspired and adapted by Masonry. Pike's inclusion in this book is by no means an endorsement.)

There are several different orders within Masonry that contain additional initiation and elevation rituals apart from the regular three degrees. The two most well-known of those inner orders are the Scottish and York Rites. When Albert Pike joined the Masons, there were very few active participants in the Scottish Rite, and most likely less than a thousand in the United States.[182] In order to revive the Scottish Rite, Pike began reworking the thirty-three degrees of the Scottish Rite, and in the process infused the rites with an abundance of esoteric knowledge and symbolism.

In addition to rewriting the rituals of Scottish Rite Freemasonry, Pike also produced a companion volume designed to illuminate some of the mysteries in his rituals. That book, *Morals and Dogma of the Ancient and Accepted Order of the Scottish Rite of Freemasonry* (most commonly known as just *Morals and Dogma*), was first published in 1871 and given to everyone who received the Scottish

---

181. Stavish, *Freemasonry*, 130.

182. Stavish, *Freemasonry*, 130.

Rite's thirty-second degree from the Scottish Rite's Supreme Council of the Southern Jurisdiction until 1974.[183] *Morals and Dogma* is an absolutely massive tome, much of it plagiarized from the work of the tremendously influential French occultist Éliphas Lévi (born Alphonse Louis Constant, 1810–1875). Like many occultists of his day, Lévi was comfortable placing Lucifer in the role of "knowledge revealer," and Pike followed suit. The problem for Pike (and Masonry) was that Pike's use of Lucifer in *Morals and Dogma* was considered proof by critics of Masonry that the group was Satanic. (*Morals and Dogma* is over seven hundred pages and not an easy read. I doubt that most copies of it have been thoroughly read by their owners.)

Quotations from Pike's work have been used to paint all Masons as Satanists and Luciferians, and it certainly does seem that way when one reads some of Pike's quotes from the book:

> LUCIFER, the Light-bearer! Strange and mysterious name to give to the Spirit of Darkness! Lucifer, the Son of the Morning! Is it he who bears the Light, and with its splendors intolerable blinds feeble, sensual, or selfish Souls? Doubt it not.[184]

Pike's writings about Lucifer were not anything revolutionary, and simply depict Lucifer as the idea of light and wisdom. However, the very name alone seems to absolutely terrify some people, and Pike's inclusion of it in *Morals and Dogma* didn't do Masonry many favors. Another passage from Pike includes the god Pan:

> The true name of Satan, the Kabbalists say, is that of Yahveh reversed; for Satan is not a black god, but the negation of God. The Devil is the personification of Atheism or Idolatry.
>
> For the initiates, this not a *Person*, but a *Force*, created for good, but which *may* serve for evil. *It is the instrument of Liberty or Free Will.* They represent this Force, which presides over the physical generation, under the mythologic and horned form of the God PAN; thence

183. Stavish, *Freemasonry*, 131–132.
184. Parfrey and Heimbichner, *Ritual America*, 73.

came the he-goat of the Sabbat, brother of the Ancient Serpent, and the Light-bearer or *Phosphor*, of which the poets have made the false Lucifer of the legend."[185]

Even where he's probably unwanted, the Horned God has a history of showing up in initiation rites.

The fraternal order that might bear the most similarity to many Modern Witchcraft traditions could be the Society of Horsemen, or the Horseman's Word. Most likely established in Scotland during the eighteenth century, the Horseman's Word is sometimes thought of as a survival from pagan antiquity, but it most likely was inspired by the Miller's Word, and before that the original Freemasons.[186] Unlike the Masons, who did their best to present a welcoming public face, both the Horseman's Word and the Miller's Word embraced more diabolical elements, cultivating an air of mystery and sometimes even fear about the group and their members.

Initiates into the Horseman's Word were made to walk a "crooked path" (a term used by many Witches to describe their practice) on their way to initiation ceremonies. Once those ceremonies had begun, potential initiates had to shake hands with individuals portraying figures such as Lucifer and *Auld Nick*, which is another name for the Devil.[187] Society members dressed up as Lucifer often sported an impressive pair of antlers on top of their head, and sometimes reached out to the hands of potential initiates with a hoof (on a stick, of course) instead of a hand.[188]

The initiatory rituals of groups like the Horsemen and the Millers were inspired not just by the rites of the Masons but also by folklore and by legends about the witch trials that had occurred just a century or two earlier. It's often suggested that the rituals of the Horsemen were taken from Witchcraft, an unlikely proposition, as the alleged rites of medieval Witches were generally fiction. However, stories about Witchcraft did influence the rites of

---

185. Pike, *Morals and Dogma*, 102.
186. Hutton, *The Triumph of the Moon*, 63.
187. Mankey, *Transformative Witchcraft*, 143.
188. Mankey, *Transformative Witchcraft*, 144.

the Horsemen, and later the rituals of the Horsemen would inspire today's Witches.

IMAGES OF THE DEVIL DURING THE WITCH TRIALS

The leaders of Murray's theorized Witch-cult were more than just High Priests; they were believed to be the Devil himself. When Murray's Witches gathered with their Grand Magister (the leader of the Witch covens), they saw him as a god "manifest and incarnate," and they praised him while on their knees, and even prayed to him.[189] The materials she quotes from the witch trials suggest a supernatural entity; one poor victim of the witch trials related meeting the Devil and being told that he "was her God."[190]

Murray suggests that the Grand Magisters who were supposed to literally be the Devil were instead con men of the highest order. She writes that the "so-called Devil was a human being, generally a man and occasionally a woman."[191] She later quotes a contemporary who calls the leaders of the Witch-cult "unscrupulous and designing knaves who personated Satan."[192] In other words, Murray's Witch-cult was perpetuated by shysters who pretended to be the Devil for profit and sex.

If the Witches of Murray's alleged Witch-cult truly believed they were honoring the Devil in their circles, it stands to reason that the Grand Magister would look like either Satan or some sort of horned god. But that's just not the case. Murray's Grand Magisters always lack horns and any real connection to the Horned God or the Devil in appearance. The closest her Magisters come to looking like the Devil is when on a couple of occasions some were said to have "cloven feete."[193] Depictions of the Devil in popular art at the time of the witch trials also fail to show much in the way of a horned deity.

---

189. Murray, *The God of the Witches*, 28.

190. Murray, *The God of the Witches*, 30.

191. Murray, *The Witch-Cult in Western Europe*, 31.

192. Murray, *The Witch-Cult in Western Europe*, 32.

193. Murray, *The Witch-Cult in Western Europe*, 32.

It's assumed by many Christians and Witches that depictions of the Devil from the time of the witch trials were influenced by the Pagan gods of antiquity, especially Pan. But the idea of Pan (or any other horned god) as a prototype for art featuring the Devil is erroneous.[194] If we truly examine depictions of the Devil in art, we get something very different from the god of Arcadia.

It's true that most depictions of the Devil from the 1400s onward contain horns, and some even show a figure with cloven feet, but the Devil is linked to all sorts of animals in the art of the period of the Witch Trials. Sometimes his face is like that of a bird or a cat, and in addition to goat legs he also sometimes has chicken feet. But the thing he resembles most often is something reptilian (figure 14).

Figure 14: A delightful Devil.
This Devil looks downright captivating. Look at that smile!

In most art of the period, the Devil simply looks like a gargoyle inspired by lizards, often complete with wings and claws. When he is shown with hair, that hair generally covers his entire body, which is drastically different from Pan, whose chest was generally bare. Like Pan, the Devil does sometimes wear a beard, but most biblical figures are shown with beards, so that means

---

194. Link, *The Devil*, 45.

very little. There are a few isolated incidents where the Devil looks like Pan, but they are just that, isolated, and are the exception rather than the norm.[195]

Many classic illustrations featuring the Devil leading a band of Witches depict the figure as completely black. In woodcuts during the period of the Witch Trials, he is the only figure to be fully shaded in. This was probably done to reflect the contrast between the Devil (or a demon) with the angels of the Christian heaven. Since angels were traditionally garbed in white, the denizens of hell had to wear the color that contrasted most with it.[196]

Murray's Grand Magisters were most often described in ways that contrasted with their depiction in art during the Witch Trials. Instead of appearing reptilian or animal-like, they were far more likely to be thought of as handsome. They were also dapper dressers, and instead of having horns on their heads, they wore stylish hats.[197] Their clothes were most often black, and in keeping with the racist attitudes of the times, they were often said to be a "black man."[198]

There are accounts of the Devil appearing in animal form during the witch trials, and in France he sometimes appeared as a goat or sheep, but in England he generally took forms unrelated to the Horned God.[199] In Britain he was most likely to assume the form of a cat, dog, horse, or bull, all either common pets or farm animals.[200] Murray explained the Devil changing his shape by suggesting that her Grand Magisters commonly wore the masks of animals, especially at large rituals.[201] I don't know how anyone could confuse the average cat with a man standing upright dressed in black clothes and wearing a cat mask, but to Murray this idea was plausible.

---

195. Pierre Boaistuau, in his *Histoires prodigieuses*, depicts a very hairy near-Pan in 1597, but it's far more goat-man than any classical depiction of the god. This is the most Pan-like Devil image that overlaps with the Witch Trials.

196. Link, *The Devil*, 55.

197. Murray, *The Witch-Cult in Western Europe*, 32.

198. Murray, *The Witch-Cult in Western Europe*, 29.

199. Murray, *The Witch-Cult in Western Europe*, 61.

200. Murray, *The Witch-Cult in Western Europe*, 61.

201. Murray, *The Witch-Cult in Western Europe*, 61.

OTHER DEVILISH FIGURES: ROBIN GOODFELLOW AND BAPHOMET

One of the most common pictures of the "Devil" seen today in books and online comes from seventeenth-century England and is actually not the Devil at all, but a figure known as Robin Goodfellow or Puck. Like Pan, Robin Goodfellow has horns, the (unhairy) torso of a man, the hind legs and cloven hooves of a goat, and often an erect phallus (or a pretty impressive codpiece). But despite the physical similarities, Robin Goodfellow is not Pan nor the Devil (figure 15). Goodfellow is often called a *hobgoblin*, from a term (*goblin*) used to describe an ugly, prank-playing fairy, but not necessarily an evil one.[202]

Figure 15: Robin Goodfellow.
Images of Robin Goodfellow are often
mistaken for those of the Christian Devil.

---

202. Online Etymology Dictionary, s.v. "goblin," https://www.etymonline.com/word/goblin;
s.v. "hogoblin," https://www.etymonline.com/word/hobgoblin.

In literature, Robin Goodfellow is a good-natured house spirit who rewards those who do hard work and punishes the lazy. He's a prankster, and his tales are always far more whimsical than diabolical. A 1639 edition of a book dedicated to the figure is subtitled *His Mad Prankes and Merry Jests*, and the title page promises that the work is "Full of honest Mirth, and is a fit Medicine for Melancholy."[203]

The most famous account of Robin Goodfellow is as Puck in William Shakespeare's (1564–1616) *A Midsummer Night's Dream*, written in 1595/96. As Puck, Robin Goodfellow is a member of the fairy court ruled by King Oberon and Queen Titania. He's a magickal and mischievous presence, but certainly not evil.

Pan as a stand-in for the Devil did not become particularly common until the nineteenth century, and that's likely because of the French occultist Éliphas Lévi. In the second volume of his work *Dogma and Ritual of High Magic*, Lévi includes an illustration of a figure he calls Baphomet. Lévi's Baphomet has the head of a goat, a pentagram on his forehead, cloven hooves for feet, and a delightful bosom. Lévi's illustration of Baphomet is so captivating and unique that it's been used as a figure of the Devil ever since its initial publication.

To Lévi, the figure had nothing to do with Satanism or the Devil, and instead represented the entire universe: sex, sin, redemption, revelation, parenthood, intelligence, and the four elements of earth, air, fire, and water.[204] Two crescent moons flanking Lévi's Baphomet, one dark and one illuminated, are also present, representing good and evil. Lévi's original illustration of Baphomet is not particularly evil-looking, unless one is scared of goats, but it has been reimagined over the last 150 years to appear more sinister.

The figure of Baphomet does not stem directly from any horned god of pagan antiquity. Instead, the name Baphomet is most likely a corruption of Mahomet (Mohammed), the founder of Islam. During the Middle Ages, a

---

203. *Robin Good-Fellow: His Mad Prankes and Merry Jests.* 2nd edition printed in London by Thomas Cotes in 1639. https://www.bl.uk/collection-items/robin-goodfellow-his-mad-pranks-and-merry-jests-1639.

204. Guiley, *The Encyclopedia of Witches and Witchcraft*, 17.

Baphomet was an idol, generally thought to be represented by a skull or a head.[205] The legendary Knights Templar were accused of worshipping a Baphomet and put to death for it. Lévi's version of Baphomet introduced the figure to a completely new audience, and today there are many Witches and occultists who honor Baphomet in their circles as Lévi described him: as a figure representative of the entire universe (figure 16).

Figure 16: Baphomet.
This might be the most misinterpreted image of the last two hundred years.
Baphomet doesn't represent evil; he simply represents everything.

Modern depictions of the Devil looking much like the present-day Horned God are really a product of the nineteenth century, and most likely evolved from the popularity of Pan in the poetry of that era. The figure of the Devil in red with a pitchfork is also rather contemporary, with the Devil's red skin representing the fires of the Christian hell. The Horned God of the Witches

---

205. Guiley, *The Encyclopedia of Witches and Witchcraft*, 16.

looking like the Christian Satan is something that has come about due to the power and popularity of our Horned One today and over the last hundred years.

KRAMPUS, THE HORNED GOD OF YULE AND THE CHRISTMAS DEVIL

Currently one of the most popular faces of the Horned God is that of the Krampus, the "Christmas Devil." The Krampus is a figure from European folklore and can be found throughout Central Europe (including Germany, the Czech Republic, Austria, and Slovakia), in Northern Italy, and as far south as Croatia. In recent years, he's become a more familiar presence in Canada and the United States. The appearance of the Krampus varies from country to country, but almost always includes goat horns and cloven hooves. He is often depicted with brown and black fur, though that can vary (figure 17).

Figure 17: Krampus.
He's making a list and checking it twice,
and then putting you in a basket to take you to hell.

Traditionally the Krampus is a very threatening figure and is known to spank bad kids with a switch and chain the worst offenders and place them in a basket on his back and whisk them to hell. If all of this sounds a little silly, I have it on good authority that children in many parts of Europe are legitimately terrified of the Krampus. A coven member of mine who grew up in Croatia once expressed to me just how much she feared the Krampus every December.

Though the Krampus is often perceived as a Yuletide bad guy, he's really just the opposite. He's basically the "bad cop" to Santa's "good cop," simply trying to coax the best behavior out of young people the best way he knows how, which in this case is with fear. Traditionally the Krampus makes his rounds on *Krampusnacht* (Krampus Night), celebrated on December 5, directly before the Feast of Saint Nicholas on December 6 (which is a gift-giving day in many places). In smaller towns and villages, he's known to visit with children as early as November 15, and he's also been known to make appearances on Christmas Eve.

I think it's worth pointing out that the Krampus doesn't punish the good, but only the wicked. No one has any reason to fear the Krampus as long as they are treating others with kindness and respect. While the Krampus is a part of many nominally "Christian" celebrations, I've never read or seen anything depicting him as the avenging arm of Jesus or a demon in the employ of Satan (even if he is called a devil sometimes). The great thing about most Christmastime traditions is that most of them aren't really linked to anything particularly religious. They are simply another manifestation of the magickal time that is the holiday season.

The name *Krampus* most likely derives from the German word *krampen*, which translates as "claw." As to the actual origins of the Krampus, no one is completely sure. Recently the idea that he's the son of the Norse goddess Hel has been making its way around the Witch world, but there's no real documented evidence of this. (Even reputable websites who sometimes make this claim provide no evidence for it.) The Krampus could also have his origin in ancient pagan "mumming" traditions, which often involved people dressing up as animals. Given the wide geographic range of the Krampus, it's quite possible that he has a myriad of origin points.

What we do know is that the Krampus didn't become a common holiday figure until the sixteenth century, several centuries after the establishment of Christianity in Central Europe. One of the reasons for the Krampus's increase in popularity during that period can be linked to his role as an "assistant" to other gift-givers.[206] Saint Nicholas has always been the most popular gift-giver at Christmas, but during the Protestant Reformation, Martin Luther (1483–1546), in an attempt to remove all traces of Catholicism from the Protestant version of the faith, replaced Saint Nick with the baby Jesus, a figure that became known as the *Christkind*.[207] The baby Jesus as a gift-giver presented several challenges, the most obvious one being "how does a baby carry a sack of toys?" Figures like the Krampus helped fill that void, and when Nicholas returned as gift-giver in many areas, the Krampus stayed right beside him.

In some areas of Europe, Nicholas was replaced by figures like the German Belsnickel. The Belsnickel gets his name from the German *Pelznickel*, which translates roughly as "Nicholas in Furs." Like the Krampus, the Belsnickel is a rather severe figure known for punishing children and carrying a chain.[208] This is a much more threatening and wild version of Nicholas, and is another possible origin point for the Krampus.

Both the Belsnickel and the Krampus could also have their origin in the European "Wild Man" tradition. Wild Men are similar to the North American Bigfoot but are generally depicted as more civilized and less like a giant ape. Wild Men were thought to live on the remote edges of society and were an extremely popular motif in art in the fifteenth and sixteenth centuries. They also served a role very similar to that of the Krampus: they were often the bogeyman that parents would threaten their children with. Wild Men varied in appearance from place to place, and many of them might have

---

206. Bowler, *Santa Claus*, 24.

207. Over time, the Christkind morphed from the baby Jesus into an angelic-looking young woman. It's just hard to find babies capable of portraying holiday characters. I write more about the Christkind in my 2020 book *Llewellyn's Little Book of Yule*.

208. Bowler, *The World Encyclopedia of Christmas*, "Belsnickel" entry.

pagan origins too. People dressing up as Wild Men were also a part of many mummers parades.

Due to his rather threatening appearance, the Krampus eventually became known as the Christmas Devil (or Demon). This idea has been reinforced by much of the art surrounding the Krampus over the last 140 years. Vintage post-cards often feature the Krampus with red skin (or fur) and looking very much like the Christian Devil. He's even depicted with a pitchfork on some occasions. This is a relatively recent development and doesn't reflect how he was traditionally depicted.

Though originally a figure concerned mostly with children, the Krampus began to be featured as the "id" of Christmas in the early twentieth century. Postcards at the turn of the century often show him in the company of housewives, with many of the women looking at him with adoration and perhaps lust. In addition to his horns and cloven hooves, the Krampus is known for his long tongue, which could be part of his appeal.

There's a blurry line between figures from folklore such as the Krampus and gods who are known to us through mythology and archaeological remains, but in my own practice I honor the Krampus as a very real figure. He's the naughty side of the holiday season, the mayhem that makes New Year's Eve or the office Christmas party just a little more fun and sensual than it might otherwise be. The Krampus also helps us connect to what Yuletide used to be: a season for parties, frolicking, fun, and most often heavy drinking and gluttonous eating.

When my coven's Yule rituals are just a little too serious for my own taste, I invoke the Krampus to lighten them up. The Krampus is an extremely confident figure; I think one would have to be in order to wave chains in the faces of strangers while in their homes. Because of that, when I find myself in awkward or unwelcoming social situations during the holidays, I invoke the Krampus. The Christmas Devil always gives me the energy and confidence to get through whatever social obligation I find myself obliged to undertake.

Chapter Thirteen
THE LIGHT OF LUCIFER RITUAL

THE ONLY THING WE have to fear when working with Lucifer is the truth. Lucifer is the great illuminator: he brings to light our wants, needs, desires, foibles, and inadequacies. If you want to get to the heart of a matter, Lucifer is a fine god to call upon. If finding out your heart's true desire brings with it a sense of dread, then you might find yourself a bit dismayed with what he has to tell you.

For this ritual you'll need four things: a deck of tarot cards, a candle, a glass of wine (or other beverage to leave as an offering), and a question you seek an answer to. I also think it works better in dark or dim light (which might require an extra candle or two). This rite can be done as a full ritual with a circle casting and quarter calling, or it can simply be done in a quiet place where no one will bother or interrupt you. Although a lot of Witches are comfortable reading tarot at parties and other social gatherings, this tarot reading does not lend itself to that.

The question you ask can be about anything, but tarot rarely offers overly specific answers. You most likely aren't going to get the name of your next lover out of this exercise, nor will it end with the knowledge of a precise date when something will happen. If you are new to tarot, there are many books out there that can help you with the meanings of the cards; however, the interpretation that matters most is your own. As you do this exercise, trust your own intuition and that of Lucifer. That's what he's there for: to help guide you and offer wisdom.

I've written this ritual for one person, but it can easily be done for or with someone. Be warned, though, that you should probably inform anyone with whom you might perform this rite that you'll be calling on Lucifer. Even some of the most open-minded Witches I know have negative reactions where they hear that name!

THE RITUAL

Set up your working area as you see fit. Create a magickal container, if you wish, and if you've chosen to do this ritual in a darkened space, make sure there are enough lit candles around so that you can see clearly. Usually two large pillar candles safely lit on your reading table or altar will do the trick, but make sure you are set up properly before beginning the actual tarot reading.

Begin by calling Lucifer to help guide you through your reading. I like to try and light my candle for Lucifer as I'm calling him, but do what works best for you (and will reduce any chance that you'll light something on fire). When your candle is lit, envision its glow as the clear light of Lucifer coming to your aid. Say:

> *Lucifer, I call to you this night to aid me in my work. Day Star, illuminate the path that I should take going forward. Clear away the shadows so that all may be clear before me. May your wisdom guide me and help me to understand the obstacles that may be in my way. Allow me to look in the past, present, and future so that I may best determine a path of action. Great Lucifer, Shining One, be with me in this space. So mote it be!*

Once Lucifer has been called and his candle lit, shuffle your deck of tarot cards. As you shuffle the deck in your hands, contemplate the question that you wish to ask. Form that question clearly in your mind, and let it travel down your body, through your shoulders and arms, into your hands, and into the cards. Infuse the cards with your energy (and if you do this exercise for someone else, let them shuffle the cards and do the same thing), and while you are holding the cards in your hands, say Lucifer's name again out loud, asking him for guidance.

As I contemplate my question and shuffle the cards, I often chant the following mantra:

> *O Day Star, aid me this night,*
> *Lucifer, show me what is right.*
> *Let my work be blessed by your sight,*
> *As I bring my truth out into the light!*

When you feel that the cards are sufficiently shuffled, spread them out in a big messy pile in front of you (facedown) and pull out four cards. As you pull out the cards, ask Lucifer to help guide your hand:

> *Bright One, steady my hand as I draw these cards. Let my intuition guide me down the proper path so that all may be illuminated before me. I pull the first card for the past so that I might see how I've come to this place. The second card will show me what stands in my way: what satan (obstacle) must I overcome? The third card for my will and what it is inside of me that will get me through this journey. And finally the fourth card, that I might see what lies before me.*

While you are asking Lucifer to guide your hand, draw and place your four cards in front of you, facedown. Resist the urge to look at your cards all at once; instead, they will be turned over one by one. Each of the four cards represents a part of the journey before you. The first card is the past, how you came to have the question you are now posing to Lucifer and the tarot. The second card will show you what difficulties lie ahead. These can be external or internal problems. Sometimes we are our own biggest hurdle. The third card will show you what you have to defeat those obstacles. What will assist you might come from others or from yourself. Every query is different. And finally, the last card represents a probable outcome.

Place your dominant hand just above your first card, and keep it there for a few moments. Do you feel the energy coming up from the card? Once you've felt the card's energy reach your hand, state your question out loud once more, clearly and succinctly. When you are done speaking, ask Lucifer for his guidance once more:

With this card, I look into the past.
Lucifer, guide this Witch in their Craft!

Flip the card over and study it. What is it saying to you? Is there a message there about what has brought you to this point in your life? Study it closely to see if it hints at other people who might be involved. Is that a family in the background? A house that might belong to someone you know? Let your mind drift, and trust in Lucifer's guidance to interpret the card.

Place your hand above the second card and feel its energy. Before turning it over, say:

What is this that blocks my path?
O Lucifer, what must I now dispatch?

Examine the card for signs of the obstacles that lie in your way. Take notice of any people on the card. Again, could they be someone you know, or perhaps something inside of yourself? If you are unsure of the answer in your card, hold it up to Lucifer's light and ask him for assistance.

Place your hand over the third card and ask the Day Star once again for assistance:

The Witch overcomes all that is in their way.
Lucifer, what do I have to make the assay?

This card should show you what powers you have to draw upon as you proceed toward your outcome. As Witches, those powers are often internal, both our strong will and our magickal abilities. But there are others out there who might assist us. A Witch who has allies is never truly alone. There are always spirits, gods, fairy folk, and friends all willing to assist from time to time.

And finally place your hand above the fourth card and feel its energy. By now the energy radiating from the cards should be a steady throb or pulse. As the energies of the cards radiate upward, they should feel stronger and more pronounced. When they are at their peak, say the following words and then flip your final card over:

> *Now is the time I ask thee for your sacred sight.*
> *Lucifer, illuminate the future with your shining light!*

This last card should illustrate what might yet come. The card might tell you that the time is not right for whatever it is you seek, or that your quest will end in heartbreak. The cards are not all-seeing or all-knowing, but they do provide insight into what might come to us. Travel down the road shown by your card, but also look for other pathways. Your card might suggest many different outcomes.

When you are satisfied with your reading, thank Lucifer for his assistance:

> *Day Star, shining bright, I thank you for your guidance this night! May the lessons learned here illuminate the road ahead and help me to make the best decisions and arrive at the best outcome. Shining One, great Lucifer, I thank thee!*

Blow out the candle you've lit for Lucifer, along with any others. Take your wine glass and pour its contents outside as a libation to thank Lucifer for his assistance.

Chapter Fourteen
THE HORNED GOD OF DEATH

ON ONE UNSEASONABLY WARM Samhain night in Michigan, I came face-to-face with the Horned God as the Lord of Death and Resurrection. A friend had asked me to play a humorous role in her Samhain ritual that year, but I declined and asked for something else. After a few moments of thinking, she asked if I would be interested in opening the gate between this world and the next and acting as the god of death's representative here on earth. That all felt like a giant step forward in the look for "something serious during ritual" department, and I replied in the affirmative.

Our ritual that evening took place in a small clearing deep in the woods, where the moon shined brightly overhead. We began the ritual in our usual way, calling the quarters, casting the circle, and calling on the gods. While our ritual container was being set up, I reached out for Pan, the primary deity I worked with at the time, only to find him uncharacteristically absent. His silence frightened me, as I really needed him with me for this particular operation.

When it came time for my role in the ritual, I opened by tentatively reading my lines, a mix of apprehension and uncertainty in my voice. "On this Samhain night, I open up the gates of death, the entryway into the realm of spirit …" As the words spilled out of me, I felt a steadying hand on my right shoulder. That touch filled me with strength, and as my voice steadied, I felt a quiet and powerful confidence engulf me.

The hand on my shoulder guided my every action, and suddenly I could feel the spirits of my group's beloved dead all around us. I hesitated for a moment before looking over my shoulder to see the deity who was standing next to me. I was surprised to see it was Cernunnos. His face was slightly obscured to my eyes, but there was no hiding the stag's antlers on the top of his head or the torc around his neck. As the ritual continued, I proceeded to interact with every participant in the circle, with Cernunnos telling me what to say as he led the dead back to the living.

When the ritual was over, I felt contented, but I wasn't exactly sure why. After the god revealed himself to me, I remember very little about the rest of the night; all that I was left with was a feeling that everything had gone well. That night I met with Cernunnos again in my dreams. He urged me join him on his nighttime hunt and race through the forest with him.

The following year at a different Samhain ritual, I was asked again to open a portal between the worlds. When my time to lead ritual began, I felt Cernunnos's hand once more upon my shoulder, with him guiding me through what needed to be done, and we've shared this moment together nearly every Samhain since. Cernunnos as the god of death is as familiar to me as the sun on a summer's day, and yet many Witches I talk to are confused by this.

Witchcraft has placed an overwhelming emphasis on the Horned God as the god of wild spaces and the natural world, so much so that his role in death often gets overlooked. From a very young age, we are taught to fear death and that anything having to do with death is most likely negative. But a Witch knows death is not only inevitable but is a part of the natural order. There is no new life without death, and both life and death are necessary for the world to function effectively.

DEATH AND THE HORNED ONE

Cernunnos has links to death as a god of hunting. Several well-known Horned God–adjacent deities also have connections to the afterlife. Hermes (father of Pan) guided mortal souls to the realm of the dead, as did Faunus, the Roman equivalent of Pan. Dionysus (often depicted as a bull) actually ruled over the land of death in the cosmology of the Orphics, a Greek mystery tradition. But despite these links between horned gods and the realm of death, the Horned One's role beyond the grave is often neglected.

That oversight is especially surprising since the Horned God has been associated with death since the publication of the first book on Modern Witchcraft back in 1954. Gerald Gardner's *Witchcraft Today* is not particularly useful to most Witches today, but it was the first book to ever include information on what would become known as *Wicca* (Gardner uses the term *Wica* in his book, and even then only four times), and mostly contains a lot of inaccurate and fanciful Witch history. However, there are a few brief ritual interludes in the book, and in those isolated moments, its contents not only feel familiar, but shine.

Gardner's books on Witchcraft (he released a follow-up in 1959 titled *The Meaning of Witchcraft*) both owe a huge debt to Margaret Murray (who actually wrote the introduction to *Witchcraft Today*), especially when it comes to the Horned God. The majority of Gardner's references to the "horned god" (he doesn't capitalize the phrase until 1959) emphasize that Horn Head is not the Devil and that such ideas arose out of confusion, again borrowing a page from Murray.

Aside from Gardner's use of the "horned god" as one of Wiccan-Witchcraft's primary deities, his most notable contribution to the development of the Horned God is his linking of the Horned One to death. Ruminating on the development of religion, Gardner writes of the Horned God:

> Primitive man feared to be born again outside his own tribe, so his ritual prayers to his god were that he might be born again in the same place and at the same time as his loved ones, and that he might remember and love them again. The god who rules this paradise must, I think, have been Death, but somehow he is identified with the hunting god and wears his horns. This god of death and hunting, or his representative, seems at one time to have taken the lead in the cult, and man became the master.[209]

---

209. Gardner, *Witchcraft Today*, chap. 2.

Gardner would further elaborate on the Horned God as a god of both life and death in *The Meaning of Witchcraft*. In this book, Gardner seems far surer of his deity: "Horned God" is now capitalized throughout the text, and the links to death are much firmer. Gardner writes of the Horned One as "the dealer of death" and "the Lord of the Gates of Death."[210] Gardner also establishes the Horned God's role as a provider of plenty and spells out his role (along with that of the Goddess) in Witchcraft:

> Witches say that they came because man wanted magical rites for hunting; the proper rites to procure increase in flocks and herds, to assure good fishing, and to make women fruitful; then, later, rites for good farming, etc., and whatever the clan needed, including help in time of war, to cure the sick, and to hold and regulate the greater and lesser festivals, to conduct the worship of the Goddess and the Horned God. They considered it good that men should dance and be happy, and that this worship and initiation was necessary for obtaining a favourable place in the After-World, and a reincarnation into your own tribe again, among those whom you loved and who loved you, and that you would remember, know, and love them again.[211]

For me, Gardner's emphasis on the Horned God as a deity of both life and death forever changed how we see the Horned One. Gardner established that the Horned God of the Witches was not just a deity of the forest or an initiator of sex. Gardner's Horned God was a truly liminal figure, operating in both this world and the next. His presence was not limited to just this world, but was also a part of the rest.

What's fascinating to me about Gardner's focus on death and the Horned God is how unique it is. There's no precedent for it in the poetry of the Romantics and Victorians, and it's not a guiding principle in Margaret Murray's works on Witchcraft. There are some precedents in the ancient world for a deity of both the living and the dead. The Roman Faunus, for example, escorted the souls of the dead to the underworld, and has much in common

---

210. Gardner, *The Meaning of Witchcraft*, 25.

211. Gardner, *The Meaning of Witchcraft*, 25.

with Pan, and as we've seen, Cernunnos has ties to the dead as well. But it's unlikely that Gardner would have been all that familiar with interpretations of Cernunnos outside of Murray. In other words, Gardner's conception of the Horned God hints at something else: personal experience and/or the agency of the Horned One himself.

As someone whose first experience of the Horned One as a god of death came during ritual, I can't help but wonder if Gardner had similar experiences that influenced his perception of the Horned God. Also not to be discounted is the possibility that Old Hornie himself was whispering in Gardner's ear, imparting wisdom and an understanding that was probably surprising to many. It would have been easy enough for Gardner to depict a Horned God in the style of Margaret Murray or Kenneth Grahame, but that's not what happened. Instead, Gardner wrote of a much richer and multi-layered deity.

Acknowledgment of the Horned God as a deity of life and death would continue after Gardner, but starting in the 1970s the idea began to fall out of favor among many Witches. It didn't disappear entirely, and could still be easily found in many of the traditions close to Gardner's original version of Wiccan-Witchcraft, but in more eclectic materials the Horned God's connection was largely overlooked or marginalized. In the practice of Traditional Witchcraft, the Horned God as a Lord of Death has remained close to the surface. Later in this book, we'll look further at the evolution of the Horned God within both Wicca and Trad Craft.

DREAD LORD OF SHADOWS

Witchcraft is a life-affirming religion, but it's also a practical one. Every Witch knows that eventually they are going to die. My hope for all of us is that death will happen a long time from now, but make no mistake, death is coming for us all. Some people deal with death by ignoring it, but those of us who honor the Horned God embrace its eventuality, for we know that our god is a deity of both the living and the dead.

There are no absolutes in Witchcraft, and no hard-and-fast rules about what happens to us when we die. There are those who think we simply cease to be, and others who believe that our spirit will eventually reside in a land of eternal peace and contentment. The most common belief in Witchcraft circles tends to be in reincarnation. Those of us who hold to this view believe that the soul survives death, rests and recharges in a place often called the Summerlands,[212] and is then reborn in a new body on this earth.

It's not necessary to believe in reincarnation or an afterlife, but the Horned God's role as the Dread Lord of Shadows is directly tied into this belief (figure 18). If you aren't a believer, I hope the following information is still helpful. The Dread Lord of Shadows exists to make death easier, on both the living and the now dead.

Figure 18: A shadowy-looking horned god, most likely resembling Cernunnos. The Horned God in his role as the Dread Lord of Shadows.

When addressing the Horned God as the Dread Lord of Shadows at public Samhain rituals, I'm often surprised by how many people are taken

---

212. The term Summerlands to signify a place in the afterlife comes from nineteenth century Spiritualism and later the Theosophical Society, both groups who most likely had a tremendous impact on Modern Witchcraft.

aback by it. For many, their image of the Horned God is simply Pan running around a perfect summer field, or perhaps the Horned God in the middle of lovemaking. But there's more to the Horned One than this mortal coil, and the promises he makes for us in death are just as important as the promises he has made for us here.

Losing a loved one is perhaps one of the biggest pains most of us face in life. Knowing that tomorrow a friend, lover, or family member will not be there is hard to face. The adjustment those we've lost have to go through is most likely equally difficult. To be taken to another realm and place, away from most everything you've known and loved, is terrifying.

While the title *Dread Lord of Shadows* sounds ominous and frightening, the Horned God in this role is a comforter. He welcomes those who have departed our world and makes them feel at home in the next. He is a shoulder to cry on and a place to set one's burdens. As a god who walks between the worlds, he provides comfort not only to the dead but also to the living. When we struggle with questions and pain, he is there to help us with our grief.

There are many who die in great pain, and while their loss hurts us, we know that their passing is for the best. When the dying are embraced by the Dread Lord of Shadows, know that their pain and suffering is being taken away. His touch in such instances is one of love and release and serves to make those who cross over to the realms of death whole once more.

In invocations to the Lord of Shadows at Samhain, the word *rest* is often invoked. The Horned One provides a place for us in death to reflect on what we have done in our lives, and to rest. He has prepared a place where our soul might be renewed and refreshed for what lies ahead on our further journeys.

What lies ahead is important when it comes to understanding the Dread Lord of Shadows, for he is also a god of rebirth and return. He watches over the portal that connects this world and the next, and sends back to this earth the souls that are ready for the next phase of their journey. It is the Dread Lord of Shadows who guards the mysteries of the End and the wonder of beginnings.

At Samhain time, it's the Dread Lord of Shadows who opens the veil between the worlds, allowing his current charges (the dead) to visit with those whom they are apart from. It's his magick and wisdom that allows us to experience reunion with those we've loved, even if that reunion is brief.

Perhaps most important of all is that when we are reborn, the Horned One will reunite us with those we love. There's an idea common among many Witches who believe in reincarnation that we will be reborn in the same place and time as those that we've loved in this lifetime (and other lifetimes). This happens through the grace of the Dread Lord of Shadows, who rules the lands of death and return.

THE DYING AND RISING GOD

The Golden Bough: A Study in Comparative Religion (1890) by the Scottish academic Sir James Frazer (1854–1941) has been one of the most influential books of the Modern Pagan and Witch revivals. Frazer's work has influenced how we celebrate and view the sabbats and is full of magickal practices and rituals.[213] *The Golden Bough* was an ongoing project for Frazer and would occupy much of his life; he would release updated and expanded editions of the work in 1900 and a third edition over the years of 1907–1915.

Frazer's work was written mainly for an academic audience, but his prose is so elegant that the book eventually became a bestseller, with an abridged version going through fifty-one printings between 1922 and 1955.[214] Its popularity in Witch circles was no doubt helped by its extreme readability; compared to Margaret Murray's *The Witch-Cult in Western Europe*, reading *The Golden Bough* is like reading Dr. Seuss. It's also extensively footnoted, and Frazer shares hundreds of religious and spiritual anecdotes from all over the world.

Many of the more agrarian and rural traditions shared by Frazer feel right at home in Modern Witchcraft. Rituals to care for the earth, the home, and the hearth are a part of what many of us do on a daily basis, but Frazer was

---

213. I mention Frazer's influence on the sabbats in my 2019 book *Witch's Wheel of the Year: Rituals for Circles, Solitaries & Covens*, also published by Llewellyn.

214. Hutton, *The Triumph of the Moon*, 116.

most likely surprised that such ideas resonated with people in the twentieth century. Most of Frazer's biographers believe he was an atheist (and many of his early writings allude to this) or at least an agnostic.[215] Instead of finding silliness and superstition in his work, many people, even beyond the Witch and Pagan worlds, have found rituals full of love, joy, and meaning.

One of the primary areas of focus in *The Golden Bough* is on a figure Frazer called the "god of vegetation," who annually died and then rose again in order to ensure the earth's fertility. In Frazer's view, popular deities such as Dionysus, Osiris, Attis, and Adonis were simply stand-ins for grape fields and cereal crops, with the mythology surrounding such gods being just metaphorical tales of the yearly agricultural cycle. Though mostly winked at throughout the text, the endgame of Frazer's work was to discredit Christianity by suggesting that Jesus was nothing more than a reimagined Pagan deity. In Frazer's view, the gods of ancient paganism were silly, so by extension, Jesus was silly too.

The idea of dying and rising gods is common in Witchcraft today, though the idea has been mostly dismissed by scholars of religion. (As one religious scholar put it, "There is no unambiguous instance in the history of religion of a dying and rising deity."[216]) Whether or not dying and rising gods occupy a real place in history is inconsequential here; what's important is just how poetic Frazer made such figures sound. It's also an idea that resonates today with so many of us because most of us can see it every year in microcosm.

I grew up near corn and soybean fields, and as my family drove around central Illinois every year, I learned to appreciate their yearly rise and fall. In late autumn the fields would appear dug up and picked over. In the winter they'd be covered with snow, and then in the spring you'd notice them slowly return to life. In the summer it was possible to literally get lost in rows of corn, and by the start of July the corn crop in my Great-Aunt Gene's fields was always taller than I was. Eventually the corn would fully ripen, and it

---

215. Hutton, *The Triumph of the Moon*, 114.

216. That quote comes from the article "Dying and Rising Gods" by Jonathan Z. Smith, in volume 4 of *Encyclopedia of Religion*. I first came across the quote in *Did Jesus Exist?* by Bart Ehrman on page 227.

would be harvested by the middle of September. Then the whole cycle would start again.

Frazer thought of his dying and rising vegetation god as a worldwide deity simply worshipped by different names. His ideas here are similar to how Margaret Murray would later conceive of the Horned God. Due to just how beautiful and practical Frazer's idea of a dying and rising god was to many early Witches, the idea would become a common one in Witch circles. And when Witches were looking to embody that figure physically, they naturally looked to the Horned God.

Like Frazer's dying and rising god, the Horned God was also a part of the natural landscape, and intimately connected to the turn of the seasons. It had already been established that the Horned God was a god of fertility and abundance, and what could be more fertile and abundant than a ripe field full of grain? The end result was that Frazer's figure ended up wearing horns in many Witch circles, and there are scores of Witches who now see the Horned God as a deity who annually sacrifices himself to preserve the earth's fertility.

In a break with Frazer, most Witches view this sacrifice as happening in the autumn, while Frazer believed it could happen at any point in the agricultural cycle. Frazer also believed that gifts, sacrifices, and offerings to deity were all originally meant to be acts signifying the slaying of a deity.[217] I'm not sure Pan would appreciate me sharing my wine with him if he thought it was meant to symbolize killing him, but most of Frazer's other ideas feel at home in the circle.

An even more poetic spin on Frazer's ideas would appear a few decades later in Robert Graves's (1895–1985) *The White Goddess* (1948). Like *The Golden Bough*, *The White Goddess* has been tremendously influential in the Pagan world over the last seventy years and shows up in all sorts of different contexts. Like Frazer, Graves didn't quite give us a horned or antlered deity in his text, but he did introduce two figures who are often depicted with antlers.

---

217. Frazer, *The Golden Bough: The Roots of Religion and Folklore*, 328.

Taking the idea of the dying and rising god one step further, Graves proposed that ancient myth contained a legend most of us know today as the story of the Oak and Holly Kings. At the Winter Solstice every year, a newly reborn Oak King challenges his old and decrepit brother, the Holly King, for control of the earth and the seasons. Once his brother has been dispatched, the Oak King reigns during the waning half of the year (from the Winter Solstice to the Summer Solstice). The Holly King leaves to lick his wounds, then returns reborn in the summer to conquer his brother. The cycle then continues (and continues and continues).

The idea of the Holly and Oak Kings as universal or even common motifs is dismissed by most scholars, and Graves's work was meant to be a piece of prose poetry, not a historical work. But Graves's work is important when it comes to the Horned God because the brothers are most often depicted these days with antlers. Their tale is also a captivating story that makes for effective ritual.

THE WHEEL OF THE YEAR MYTH

Witches have always built rituals around the change of seasons. Inspired by the work of Frazer and others, the story of the courtship between the Great Goddess and the Horned God has been central to myths reflecting the Wheel of the Year since at least the 1960s. There is no one version of this story, but it generally incorporates the idea of the Goddess as Maiden, Mother, and Crone, with the Horned God developing physically along similar lines.

As I write this book (in 2019), I find this rather common myth to be somewhat troubling. Its limited scope leaves out the experiences of many Witches who are a part of the LGBTQ+ community. (Don't we want to see deities who reflect all of our lives when we gather together in circle? Think for a moment just how disheartening it would be never to see yourself in ritual.) As this book has tried to make clear, the Horned God is not straight, nor is "he" even always a he!

I also find the idea that a woman's life can be summed up in the idea of Maiden, Mother, and Crone to be a little too uterus-centric. I know many women who have chosen not to have children and forgo being labeled a

"Mother." And some of the youngest and most joyful energy I've ever experienced has come from women who are most likely thought of as Crones. I've also found profound wisdom in the words of those much younger than me.

In most versions of this particular myth, the Horned God dies, is reborn, grows in wisdom and experience, courts the Goddess, and then sacrifices himself to ensure the continued fertility of the earth. Before his final sacrifice, he impregnates the Goddess, thus ensuring that he will be reborn. Generally, specific life events are linked to each of the eight sabbats, though those life events are often shuffled around depending on the needs of the ritual.

The story of the Horned God on the Wheel of the Year begins at Yule, when he is reborn, emerging from the womb of the Goddess. While the God has horns atop his head, it's the sun that the Horned One is most connected to on the Winter Solstice. The God's birth is representative of the sun being "reborn" on the solstice, and it's thought that the God will only grow stronger and more powerful as the days grow longer, coming fully into his power at the Summer Solstice.

After his birth, the Horned One is raised by his mother, before she mysteriously disappears, only to be reborn herself. One of the more vexing problems in this myth is that the Goddess would be an older woman by the time she gives birth. There is also no one moment where she is reborn. She simply reappears at Imbolc as a young lady, where she first catches the eye of the Horned God.

The first meeting of the Young Goddess and the Horned One is chaste, nothing more than a bit of infatuation on the part of the Horned God. The Lady returns his flirtations but also keeps her suitor at a distance. Early February is not a time for sexual license, but a time for blushing and fumbled words.

At the Spring Equinox, the two figures most likely share a kiss. They are becoming aware of their sexual selves, and it's likely that both have discovered masturbation by this point in their existence. By the end of March, both figures are returning knowing glances and they begin to become inseparable. Remember here, too, that the Horned God is a gentleman, no matter how strong his sexual urges might be. While his longing is intense, he respects the boundaries and the rules of others.

As spring progresses, the love of the Goddess and God has reawakened the earth, and the trees bud and the flowers bloom. Their relationship has also grown more passionate, and on Beltane night, under the maypole, they consummate their desires. It's the Goddess here who leads the way, guiding and instructing her lover as they indulge in the pleasures of the flesh.

It's after this experience that the Goddess transitions from Maiden to Mother. In some versions of the story, the Goddess becomes pregnant at Beltane. As someone who believes that sex should not always be tethered to reproduction, I find this part of the story especially troubling. (Why can't it wait until the Summer Solstice?) The use of the term *Mother* here can also be problematic. Why can't she be a Warrior? A Queen? Or whatever she wants?

At Midsummer, the coupling of the Goddess and God has progressed enough that their nuptials are celebrated on the Summer Solstice. This might also be the time when the Horned One ensures his survival by impregnating his Lady. One of the first Witchcraft books I read as a young adult advised against ever planning a wedding in June, because the entire month was reserved for the Goddess and God. That's an interesting idea, but not a very accurate piece of folklore.

It's in August when this myth has the most variance. Depending on the person or group telling the story, the Horned God generally sacrifices himself for the good of the harvest at Lammas (Lughnasadh), the Autumn Equinox (Mabon), or Samhain. Just when the Horned One makes his sacrifice likely depends on the story being told at the ritual, and what and when certain cereal crops are being harvested. The majority of grain in Ireland, for example, is harvested by the end of August, while in the American Midwest it's usually closer to the end of September.[218]

Lammas, as a festival celebrating the first harvest of cereal crops, is a popular time for the sacrifice of the God. The sabbat's focus on bread also

---

218. Information on Ireland's harvest season comes from the website of Teagasc: The Agriculture and Food Development Authority. My family owns a farm in Indiana, so the rest comes from more personal experience.

provides a tangible end result of his sacrifice. For many of us, September is the busiest month of the year agriculturally, making the Autumn Equinox (often celebrated as Mabon) one of the most popular sabbat celebrations to mark the passing of the Horned One.

Many Witches choose to honor the demise of the God on Samhain, and with Samhain's heavy emphasis on death, it's a choice that makes a great deal of sense. However, many covens also celebrate the veil being thin at Samhain, and focus almost exclusively on their beloved dead (generally close friends and loved ones who have been lost), which makes the God's sacrifice a sideshow or mostly an afterthought. The sacrifice of the Horned God can most certainly be honored at Samhain, but make sure to do it with the care and reverence that's required.

In my own take on the story, I see the Horned God as making his sacrifice on the Autumn Equinox, and then retreating to the realm of the dead so that he can open the gates for our dearly departed at Samhain. Told this way, the story emphasizes his need and duty to visit the realm of the dead, with his sacrifice in the world of the living also acting as a gift to those no longer with us.

After the Horned God's sacrifice, it's thought that he resides in the realm of the dead, waiting to be born again at Yule. For some Witches, the period between Samhain and Yule is a liminal time that exists outside of the natural order of things due to his absence. However one chooses to tell this story, it's important to remember that it's just a story. Life and death are both a part of this world, and as a result the Horned God always has one foot in each realm. He doesn't die in autumn in any sort of literal way; it's a metaphor, but one that helps us prepare for our own inevitable end.

Even with its shortcomings and limitations, the story of the Goddess and Horned God growing up side by side often makes for good ritual. If this is a myth you choose to embrace, just remember that the Horned God is as likely to take a male lover as a female one. The Goddess is no different, and good Witches know that gender is more than just male-female. There are all sorts of varying gender identities and those who identify with no gender. All of these are valid expressions and are a part of the deities of Witchcraft.

The story of the Goddess and God can be told with two Goddesses or two Gods. It can be told using more than two individuals as well. The only limit to this tale is our own imagination. It's also a story that can be thrown out altogether, and one that can be mined simply for its most personally evocative and meaningful truths. Though often told in Witchcraft circles, the myth of the Sacrificial God and the Lady is not holy writ, and never was.

THE (WILD) HUNT

Hunting has been on the decline for several decades now, and at the time of this writing, only about 5 percent of Americans sixteen and older engage in the practice.[219] But even though interest in hunting is decreasing, over eleven million people still hunt every year. The Witch world is an extremely diverse one, and while I know many Witches who are vegans and vegetarians, there are also Witches who hunt animals for food, and they often honor the Horned God in the midst of their endeavors.

Most hunters strive to live in harmony with the land and the animals they hunt. They tend to be good stewards of the earth, and they only harvest from the woods what they can eat. The Horned God is the god of responsible hunters, not the assholes we read about on social media who spend tens of thousands so they can kill a lion in Africa. Witches who hunt do so to feed their families and preserve the wild spaces where they live. An overabundance of deer can destroy a forest, and with few natural predators left, hunters fill a valuable void.

As a god of both life and death, the Horned God is the balance in the natural world. He brings new life into this world, but also takes life out of it. A well-functioning ecosystem requires both predators and prey, and a healthy respect for those that are prey. Through his connection to Cernunnos, the Horned God has always been a god of the ethical hunt. He's the deity to petition and thank whenever heading into the woods for a hunting adventure. (That includes those who simply "hunt" with cameras too!) But there's

---

219. Rott, "Decline in Hunters Threatens How U.S. Pays for Conservation."

another hunt the Horned God has been connected to over the last few hundred years: the Wild Hunt.

The Wild Hunt is a name given to a wide variety of unexplained apparitions and phenomena that are said to be led by several different deities and historical figures. The term *Wild Hunt* was coined by Jacob Grimm (1785–1863) in his 1835 book *Deutsche Mythologie* (which translates as *German Mythology*—and in case you were wondering, Jacob is one of the Grimms connected to some of your favorite fairy tales). Grimm's book argued that the Wild Hunt (in German, *Wilde Jagd*) was generally a night ride of dead heroes led by a Pagan god and goddess.[220]

Depending on one's location in Europe, the Wild Hunt was known by several different names. It was sometimes connected to the idea of a spectral army, with names such as the Furious Army, Herlewin's Army, and Hellequin's Army.[221] The most terrifying name for the Wild Hunt comes from Cornwall, England, where it's known as the Devil's Dandy Dogs and, not surprisingly, features dogs and hunters hunting the world for human souls.[222] The Wild Hunt is often connected to ancient paganisms, but the first recorded instance of something like the Wild Hunt seems to date only from 1120 CE.[223]

In Modern Witchcraft, there are a couple of very different interpretations of the Wild Hunt. The most common reflects the ideas of Grimm and features a spectral army of the dead generally led by a deity of some kind. In addition to spectral figures on horseback, the Hunt often includes dogs. The Wild Hunt is often linked to the Horned God because one of the most common leaders of the Hunt tends to be Herne. Also showing up with frequency at the head of the Hunt is Odin (or Woden), which, as we've seen, could most certainly be related to Herne.

Just what the purpose of the Wild Hunt is depends on whom one asks. In folklore, the spirits of the Hunt are mostly terrifying and are generally souls

220. Hutton, *The Witch*, 126.

221. Hutton, *the Witch*, 125.

222. Guiley, *The Encyclopedia of Witches and Witchcraft*, 361

223. Hutton, *The Witch*, 128.

condemned to wander the earth, perhaps due to misdeeds. These souls are out to either simply enjoy the act of hunting or gather up human souls. In some traditions, the Wild Hunt appears before a time of great calamity, such as a war. And others believe that the Wild Hunt is more common at certain times of the year, most notably the Summer and Winter Solstices.

In addition to souls and deities, the Wild Hunt is sometimes linked to the fey, or fairy folk. Modern interpretations of the fey tend to be positive, but that's a relatively recent phenomenon. For several centuries, people were absolutely terrified of the fey, and believed their influence on human lives was generally baneful. Seeing the Wild Hunt led by the fairy folk might lead to death or one getting taken to the world of fairy, which was not always a good thing.

Several historical figures have been said to lead the Wild Hunt over the centuries. Charlemagne and Frederick the Great figure in French and German legends, respectively, leading the Hunt, and in parts of England and France, the legendary King Arthur leads the chase.[224] Biblical figures such as Herod the Great, Herodias, and Pontius Pilate have been listed as participants in the Wild Hunt as well. Archangel Gabriel is said to be another huntsman, but for our purposes it's the deities linked to the Hunt who are the most interesting. There's Gwyn ap Nudd, the Welsh Lord of Death, and the previously mentioned Odin and Herne. Goddesses are common, with Diane, Hekate, and Holda being the most referenced.

Today the Wild Hunt is being reimagined by Witches and Pagans for various purposes. I've been to several outdoor Pagan festivals where Wild Hunts are enacted to link individuals to their wilder and more primitive side. Oftentimes Wild Hunts are used as vehicles of transformation, with the participants going through some sort of ordeal that brings them closer to their community, or specific ideas about deities or magickal practice. The Wild Hunt can also serve as a way to connect with one's ancestors or beloved dead. By playing the part of a spectral huntsperson, we can cross over into the realm of the dead to get a taste of what the afterlife might be like. Before

---

224. Fitch, *In Search of Herne the Hunter*, 73.

tarot card readings, Herne (as the leader of the Wild Hunt) can be invoked, with the hope that he'll lend his powers of prophecy to the reading.

The Wild Hunt is one of the most frequently referenced pieces of folklore in Modern Witchcraft. It can be both frightening and enlightening, but it's always transformative when we find ourselves bearing witness to it. At the head of the Wild Hunt, many of us see the face of the Horned God, coming to reunite us with our beloved dead or perhaps sharing a glimpse of the future.

THE GREEN MILE OF THE HORNED GOD

In October of 2014, I took part in a Samhain rite where I played the role of the soon-to-be-sacrificed Horned God. The ritual was written mostly by my "pretty hair twin," Angus McMahan, though I was allowed to make several changes to the dialogue featuring the Horned God and the (soon-to-be) Mother Goddess. It was an otherworldly ritual experience, and one of the ten rituals I'm most proud to have had a role in.

As my inevitable end began to draw closer, I walked around the circle with the Goddess, sharing the story of the Wheel of the Year and just why my death was necessary. I'm using the words *I* and *my* here to describe the Horned God who was walking headlong into his death , because he was most definitely with me that night. The following are most likely the words we spoke that night as we celebrated and lamented the sacrifice of the Horned One. (Since the Horned One was drawn down into me during the ritual, what we said that night might vary from our original script.)

Goddess: *The Wheel turns once more.*

God: *Yes, the Wheel turns, and again we stand here at the end, and the beginning.*

Goddess: *We've shared love and pleasure, grief and joy. It's been a lifetime of feelings and emotions.*

God: *And a lifetime in the span of only a few months.*

Goddess: *At Imbolc we witnessed the earth waking up from her deep sleep and our children sow the year's first seeds.*

God: *Then there were spring flowers, jasmine on the wind, cherry blossoms, life and beauty spread out for all to see.*

Goddess: *There were our days spent playing near the restless ocean …*

God: *Then there were our children, our tribe … all working together, sometimes laughing, and then falling and picking themselves back up so they might try again.*

Goddess: *And then there was the Beltane rite … the Maidens, the promise of summer, the warmth of the sun upon our faces.*

God: *And then there was after the Beltane rite … with its own mysteries.*

Goddess: *Good memories.*

Goddess: *Sun-soaked days at Midsummer, the ocean breeze rippling through the tall redwood trees.*

God: *I was so strong back then and I thought those days might never end, but end they did, like all things. But those nights in your arms under the full moon, those are my favorite memories, and I shall cherish them forever.*

Goddess: *I like that your favorite memories are of me.*

God: *And when I found myself a shadow of my former self at Lughnasadh, it was you who helped me to stand and prepare for the harvest.*

Goddess: *Not only me, but our children, too. As you pour your love out upon the earth, they pour their love out to you, me, us. They have accomplished so much this turn of the Wheel.*

God: *They have, and those victories warm my heart and prepare me for the turning of the Wheel and the changes yet to come.*

Goddess: *The Wheel turns.*

At this point, the Goddess picked a knife up off a table and I adjusted my cloak, pulling up my hood. Symbolically it was like wearing blinders; I knew what was ahead, but I didn't want to see it.

God: *Our children have grown so much this year, and tonight they have taken the biggest step of all.*

Goddess: *A big step—a necessary step—it must be done.*

God: *Is everyone prepared for what is to come this night? Can it all be done?*

Goddess: *Can what?*

God: *The big change, the removal of the final obstacle, all that holds our children back.*

Goddess: *Yes. Oh, yes! We have made them smarter than they know.*

God: *And stronger than they can imagine.*

Goddess: *And we have shown them tonight that they can do the big thing—the hard thing—the ugly, necessary thing that must be done.*

God: *Yes, it all must be done for the Wheel to turn.*

Goddess: *To once more find ourselves in the darktime.*

God: *My bones ache, my antlers must be shed. It has been a long year and I am now so tired.*

Goddess: *Are you, my Love?*

God: *Yes, my Life. What began at Lughnasadh has now overtaken me. I am not the satyr I once was. I am ready.*

Goddess: *No regrets?*

God: *Never. Except being apart from you.*

Goddess: *Never. We are eternal.*

God: *And the weight of that eternity is heavy upon my shoulders.*

At this point, the celebrants began to chant, "Corn and grain, corn and grain, all that falls shall rise again,"[225] and we moved to a stage set up in the middle of our circle. Once there, the Goddess began pleading for one of the celebrants to kill me, because she just couldn't do it, with me as the Horned One resigned to my fate, a fate that only she could bring to its end.

Goddess: *My Love!*

God: *My Life!*

Goddess: *The Wheel turns!*

God: *The Wheel turns!*

Goddess: *[Screams]*

And then the knife was plunged into my side. Many in the audience cried out in anguish and several actually cried. I fell to the floor of the stage, and then the lights went out.

———

The lights going out began a rather awkward sequence in the ritual where I had to put some fake blood on the athame used to stab me (not surprisingly, I cut myself on the athame in the dark during this time) and then set it on our stage. Somewhere in there, I handed our Goddess a kickball to stick under her shirt to make her look pregnant. Immediately after that, I had to crawl under our stage and hide there until the end of the ritual.

I had obviously come back to a semblance of my normal existence after stabbing myself, but as I sat under our stage, I began to cry. After the ritual was officially over, some of those in attendance began to laugh a little bit, a reasonable reaction when being with friends and celebrating a sabbat. However, I didn't find anything about my current predicament as a Dead God

———

225. "Corn and grain" is nearly a universal Pagan chant in the United States and was written by Ian Corrigan. It's generally set to the melody of "We All Come from the Goddess" by Z Budapest.

very funny, and I remember being quite furious for a while because of the laughing (which is also ridiculous and makes me laugh thinking about it).

All in all, it was an incredible experience, and one that still gives me both shivers and intense satisfaction. As a devotee of the Horned One, I've experienced a lot of joy when celebrating his rites. It was eye-opening to be on the other side of the Horned God story.

Chapter Fifteen
JOHN BARLEYCORN RITUAL

THE ENGLISH FOLK SONG "John Barleycorn" is one of the most well-known tunes in the Witchcraft world. The version of John Barleycorn most of us are familiar with today evolved over several hundred years and tells the story of how barley is turned into beer or whisky.[226] The idea of personifying barley as a person comes from fifteenth-century Scotland, while the character of John Barleycorn was created the following century in England. By the mid-eighteenth century, the story of John Barleycorn had been set to music and become a popular English drinking song.[227] The tune sounds rather gruesome until one is let in on the joke, and many recorded versions of the tune seem to take it all far too seriously, especially the well-known version by the band Traffic recorded in 1970.

The song opens with three men from the West vowing that John Barleycorn must die and then putting him into the ground and throwing "clods upon his head." These "murderous" men leave him in the ground until at least the Summer Solstice, where he ripens and grows a "beard," an allusion to the now visible grain at the top of the stalk. John is cut down, bundled, and tied together and allowed to dry for a couple of weeks. He's then taken to a barn, where he is beaten with sticks (threshed), to remove the wheat

---

226. As a Scotch aficionado, I prefer the Scottish spelling of whisky, which drops the Irish *e* between the *k* and the *y*.

227. Wood, "John Barleycorn Revisited: Evolution and Folk Song."

from the chaff. John Barleycorn is then turned into beer or whisky and triumphs over those who have treated him so violently by getting them drunk.

It's an extremely clever tune and has been sung and performed for over five hundred years now. It also expertly tells the story of how grain is gathered each year, which is why it's such a popular tale with Witches and has been a part of thousands of Lammas, Mabon, and Samhain rituals. Traditional pictures of John Barleycorn don't include horns, but as a figure associated with an abundant harvest, the joys of beer and whisky, and the turning of the Wheel, he is often linked to the Horned God and figures like the Green Man by Modern Witches.

Folk-music historians once theorized that the song had origins in medieval Witchcraft, since it so perfectly summarizes the idea of the dying and rising god found in the works of both James Frazer and Margaret Murray.[228] The connection to Witchcraft and the dying and rising god (here called the "Corn King") was even included in popular books on the subject, such as *The Penguin Book of English Folk Songs* in 1958. Witches were so convinced of the song's ancient connection to Witchcraft that it showed up in the Book of Shadows of English Witch (and the founder of the Alexandrian tradition) Alex Sanders (1926–1988) during the 1960s (and most likely the rituals books of hundreds of other Witches as well).[229]

Sanders, who was not media-shy, once let a German TV crew record a Witch ritual based on "John Barleycorn." According to observers, a female coven member mimicked corn in the field being cut down, rising from the ground, and then finally being threshed. The ritual ended with coveners gleefully throwing flour and beer on the Corn Queen. Apparently, it was both "ridiculous" and "wonderful," according to the non-Witches who were a part of the rite.[230]

This ritual doesn't include anything as messy as that, but it does tap into John Barleycorn as a transformational figure and celebrates the end result of his "murder": whisky (or beer or something nonalcoholic, depending on the

---

228. Young, *Electric Eden: Unearthing Britain's Visionary Music*, 127.

229. Young, *Electric Eden: Unearthing Britain's Visionary Music*, 443.

230. Young, *Electric Eden: Unearthing Britain's Visionary Music*, 444.

needs of your coven or group). This is the perfect kind of ritual for Lammas or Mabon or can be done any time in the late summer or early fall. Like the song that inspired it, this rite is not meant to be taken all that seriously. I don't ever want to trivialize the work we do as Witches, but we are also allowed to have fun.

There are dozens of versions of "John Barleycorn," but all of them tell the same story. The only major differences are slight variations in word choice. The version I've chosen here is mainly from *Ancient Poems, Ballads, and Songs of the Peasantry of England*, which was published in 1857 and edited by Robert Bell. The last stanza was taken from *A Bard's Book of Pagan Songs* by Hugin the Bard. Most of the text reflects the original sources, though I changed a few words here and there to make it more gender-inclusive and easier to say. The last stanza is heavily adapted to more accurately reflect the working of the ritual. I suggest simply reading the poem for your ritual. Most versions of the song are too long and too dirge-like for ritual, but do what makes the most sense to you. In addition to the version by Traffic, there are great renditions of the song out there by Jethro Tull and Pagandom's own Damh the Bard.

RITUAL SUPPLIES

For this ritual you will need:

- Your usual altar setup
- Stalks of grain or the leaves from an ear of corn (Wheat sheaves can usually be purchased at craft stores; even better if you pick your own! Alternatively, corn leaves can be used as well.)
- A bottle of beer, whisky, and/or other beverage (Use what your group prefers and be sure to have a nonalcoholic alternative on hand.)
- Rubber bands or twine to secure your sheaves of grain (or leaves) to the bottle (You want the sheaves or leaves to be easy to remove, as people will be pulling them off from around the bottle.)

THE RITUAL

Begin the ritual by setting up your magickal container (casting a circle, calling the quarters, etc.). Once everything has been set up to your specifications, call to the Horned God as John Barleycorn to come and be a part of your ritual.

High Priestess: *On this sacred night of the harvest, we call to the Horned One, the King of the Corn, the God of the Grain, and the Lord of the Harvest as John Barleycorn, the embodiment of the fields and the harvest. Bring to us your powers of transformation as we honor your sacrifice and we remove the chaff from our lives and stand in our circle reborn as children of the harvest. Bless our rite with laughter and joy as we celebrate you and the opportunities given to us. Horned One, be with us tonight in the guise of John Barleycorn, Harvest Lord. Hail and welcome!*

Other deities and powers may be called now if the coven wishes. Once that business has been completed, carry on with the ritual.

High Priestess: *Tonight we honor the harvest and the sacrifice of the Horned God in the form of John Barleycorn. For it is the Horned One's selflessness that brings to us the gifts of the grain: bread, beer, and whisky. The story of the God has been told in the tale of John Barleycorn for hundreds of years, and tonight we share it once more.*

High Priest: *There came three folks out of the West,*
  Their victory to try;
  And they have taken a solemn oath,
  Poor Barleycorn should die.
  They took a plough and ploughed him in,
  And harrowed clods on his head;
  And then they took a solemn oath,
  Poor Barleycorn was dead.
  There he lay sleeping in the ground,
  Till rain from the sky did fall:
  Then Barleycorn sprung up his head,

And so amazed them all.

There he remained till Midsummer,

And looked both pale and wan;

Then Barleycorn, he got a beard,

And so became a man.

Then they sent farm help with scythes so sharp,

To cut him off at knee;

And then poor little Barleycorn,

They served him barbarously.

Then they hired farm help with pitchforks strong

To pierce him through the heart;

And like a dreadful tragedy,

They bound him to a cart.

And then they brought him to a barn,

A prisoner to endure;

And so they fetched him out again,

And laid him on the floor.

Then they set folks with holly clubs,

To beat the flesh from his bones;

But the miller, he served him worse than that,

For they ground him betwixt two stones.

O! Barleycorn is the choicest grain

That ever was sown on land;

It will do more than any grain,

By the turning of your hand.[231]

But little Sir John of the nut-brown bowl

And the brandy in his glass,

Aye, little Sir John of the nut-brown bowl

Proved the strongest man at last.[232]

For John transformed does live on and on

---

231. Stanzas taken from *Ancient Poems, Ballads, and Songs of the Peasantry of England*, edited by Robert Bell, 80–81.

232. Last stanza taken from Hugin the Bard, *A Bard's Book of Pagan Songs*, 120.

By magick born of horn,
And now we Witches shall cast our spells
With the help of John Barleycorn!

At the conclusion of the poem, the High Priestess picks up the John Barleycorn figure (the bottle wrapped with grain) and shows it to the coven.

High Priestess: *The sacrifice of John Barleycorn offers us several paths of transformation. The threshing of the grain removes from it the unwanted chafe. Tonight our Barleycorn offers us an opportunity to remove that which we do not want from our lives. As we pass around our John Barleycorn, place into the wheat whatever it is that no longer serves you. It can be a habit, an attitude, or a relationship. Whatever roadblock is holding you back, place that energy in John Barleycorn. You can even whisper it into the grain, if that works for you. When you feel like what you want to remove is within our Barleycorn, pass him along to the person next to you.*

John Barleycorn is now passed around the circle clockwise (deosil) until everyone has had a moment with him. If there's someone in your circle taking a really long time with John Barleycorn, it's perfectly acceptable to remind them that "the harvest is coming" as a subtle reminder to keep things moving.

High Priestess: *And now we rend skin from bone and cast out what no longer serves us. When John Barleycorn comes to you, pull a sheaf of grain from his body and throw it to the ground. For the sacrifice of the Horned God readies the grain but also takes from us that which no longer serves us. Tonight we Witches work out magick with the help of John Barleycorn. As you pull out your piece of grain from John Barleycorn, say, "The grain from the chaff," and hold it in your hand.*

John Barleycorn is passed around once more, with everyone pulling a piece of grain from him. Once your John Barleycorn has made its way around the circle, the High Priestess should explain the next part of the rite.

High Priestess: *Like the chaff that falls to the threshing room floor, we now throw to the ground that which no longer serves us. John Barleycorn, as Lord of the*

Harvest, we ask that you take from us that which we no longer need! Witches, to work our magick and raise energy, let us repeat the following chant: "From all ills and harms, may we be free. In John Barleycorn's name, so mote it be!" [Repeat until everyone has the chant down.] As we chant, envision that which you wish to be rid of, and see it falling away from you. On my signal, when the energy has reached its peak, we will throw our chaff to the ground!

The High Priestess begins the chant, and if possible, it makes perfect sense to move around here and dance around the circle while the chant goes on. The longer the chant goes on, the more the energy will build. When the energy reaches its peak, the High Priestess should indicate that it's time for everyone to throw their grain to the ground. This can be done by holding up a finger or shouting something like "last time!" before the final round of the chant.

After everyone throws their grain to the ground, the High Priestess should let everyone catch their breath and then continue.

High Priestess: *The God has taken from us that which we no longer want. Horned One, we thank you for your sacrifice! And we know that your sacrifice is not the end. It's simply the start of another transformation, for your fall and harvest leads to many blessings. It gives us bread, beer, and whisky, for we know that behind your death in the fields lie happiness, joy, and the waters of life! For behold, our little John Barleycorn is with us once more!*

The High Priestess holds the John Barleycorn aloft, perhaps removing several more sheaves of grain to reveal the bottle beneath.

High Priestess: *For death is not the end, but a new beginning! Witches, let us drink the gift of the sacrificial god, and as its essence washes over us, let us drink in our new life free from what holds us back from reaching our full potential as Witches!*

The wine or beer can now be poured into a communal cup and passed around, or into individual glasses, depending on the preferences of the coven. As the cup is passed along, everyone can be encouraged to engage in a toast to celebrate the Horned God and the harvest.

When the drinking has finished, be sure to thank John Barleycorn before closing the rest of the circle.

High Priestess: *Harvest Lord, King of the Corn, eternal John Barleycorn, thank you for being with us tonight in our circle. We thank you for your sacrifice this harvest season and for helping us to better our lives. As you make your way to the realms of the dead, we ask you to watch over our beloved dead while you continue to be with us in the forms of your transformation. Hail John Barleycorn! Hail the Horned God! Until next we meet in the circle, we now say hail and farewell!*

The ritual should be concluded as the coven sees fit. Be sure to save some beer or whisky from your bottle to offer as a libation to the Horned One at the end of the rite.

Chapter Sixteen

FROM HORNED GOD TO THE GOD: THE HORNED ONE IN WICCA

WICCAN-WITCHCRAFT'S PRIMARY MALE deity has always been the Horned God. In recent years, I think this has sometimes gotten lost as people talk of "the God" or "the Lord" (with the Goddess being referred to as "the Lady"), instead of "the Horned One." I don't mean to suggest that it's wrong to honor the Sun God or the Sea God or whatever other deity someone wants to place in their circle, but only that at the beginning of Wicca, the God of the Witches was nearly always horned or had attributes that we'd think of as belonging to the Horned God.

While this section is focused mostly on the evolution of the Horned God in texts that most of us would think of as "Wiccan," nearly all of those texts use the word *Witch* exclusively. Because of this, I use Wiccan/Witch and Witchcraft/Wicca as synonyms here, because that's how they are generally used in the books I'm referencing.

In his 1959 *The Meaning of Witchcraft*, Gardner provides perhaps his most thoughtful explanation of the Horned God of the Witches. In just a few sentences, he links his Witch God to life, death, Pan, the King of the Wood, and, perhaps surprising to some, the two-headed Roman god Janus:

> Now, we have seen that Janus or Dianus was a form of the God of the Witches; the two faces depict his dual nature. As the witch ritual says,

"Thou art the Opener of the Doorway of the Womb; and yet, because that which is born must also die, that it may be renewed, therefore art Thou Lord of the Gates of Death." Being the consort of Diana, he was the King of the Wood, and as the Phallic God, he was the renewer of life. It is evident that the bust which Lady Raglan illustrates depicts him as the renewer of life in spring; the green leaves take life from his mouth. Closely akin to him are Faunus and Silvanus, and Pan, who was hailed in Hellas as "Pamphagë, Pangenetor", "All-Devourer, All-Begetter"; and as "Chairë Soter Kosmou", "Beloved Saviour of the World", yet from whose name was derived "panic" as a term of terror. Priapus, too, was the Phallic God and the God of Gardens. The concept of fertility, of eternal, ever-renewing, upspringing life, is the basis of them all.[233]

Here Gardner's God is cosmic and all-encompassing. He's one being, but he's also Pan, Priapus, Janus, the Green Man, the King of the Wood, and the Lord of the Gates of Death. He's the joyous god of the eternal English countryside, but he's also a deity with one foot (or hoof) planted firmly in the afterlife. In *Witchcraft Today*, Gardner wrote that

while the gods wished them [people] well, they [the gods] were not all-powerful, that they needed man's help; that by performing certain rites men gave them power.[234]

Perhaps a phallic renewer of life and Lord of the Gates of Death is not quite all-powerful, but he has to at least come close.

When reading Gardner, I sometimes feel like his Horned God is two separate deities. There's the (Horned) God of the Witches, a rather intimate deity who appeals only to Witches and whose origins are in the green earth and humanity before recorded history. This is the version of the god who is not all-powerful. Next to this figure is one of "the Two Pillars which support the universe," of which every "manifestation of male and female is a manifesta-

---

233. Gardner, *The Meaning of Witchcraft*, 176.
234. Gardner, *Witchcraft Today*, chap. 7.

tion of them."[235] This can be taken to mean that gods such as Yahweh (Jeho-vah) are also a manifestation of the Witch's God.

Though I don't think it was Gardner's intention, these more cosmic mus-ings would have later ramifications and would allow the Horned God to get lost in other manifestations of deity. Instead of him continuing to be the pri-mary (male) god of the Wicca, the door was now open to other possibilities. In later years, the Horned God would be looked at by many as simply one aspect of a much greater whole, the end result being that many began to overlook some of the roles he played in Wicca's earliest published literature.

When discussing the history of any Modern Witchcraft tradition, books are especially important. Until relatively recently, the only way to really learn about a tradition such as Wicca was through direct contact with a Wiccan (hard to find generally) or through the pages of a book. There have been influential Witches over the last fifty years who haven't left much in the way of a written legacy, but the biggest shapers of Witchcraft as a whole have been writers. For many of us, they have been our entryway into Wicca and other forms of Witchcraft. (This is beginning to change with online resources, whether blogs, podcasts, photos, or videos.)

At its beginning, Wiccan-Witchcraft was an initiation-only tradition; to become a Wiccan-Witch required an initiation into an existing coven. That changed over time, but for the first twenty years of Wicca's existence, the only way to obtain Wiccan ritual was to become an initiate or perhaps write one's own, though the aspiring Wiccan would have no way of knowing that their rites were Wiccan, as there was nothing to compare them to. That began to change in 1970 with the publication of Paul Huson's (1942–present) *Mastering Witchcraft: A Practical Guide for Witches, Warlocks & Covens.*

Mastering Witchcraft is a brilliant piece of Witchcraft writing. Many Tradi-tional Witches think of it as a foundational work, and there's certainly a lot in it that is very different from Wiccan-Witchcraft. But there's also a great deal of Wiccan material in its pages, and the book's last chapter, "The Coven and How to Form One," is basically about forming a Wiccan-style coven.

---

235. Gardner, *The Meaning of Witchcraft*, 129.

The Horned One features prominently in Huson's book, but extra attention is also paid to Cernunnos as one of the "so-called Witch deities."[236] Huson's writings on Cernunnos are fascinating because it's a version of Cernunnos that's alien from the deity I know in many respects. Huson explicitly links Cernunnos to Pan, to such an extent that you start to wonder if Cernunnos has goat horns atop his head instead of antlers: ,

> The goat is the age-old representation of lust and debauchery, and Cernunnos himself, for such is his witch name, is frequently represented as possessing the cloven hooves, horns, and erect phallus of his attribute.
>
> His symbolism has much in common with that of the Greek god Pan...
>
> Whenever you wish to perform a spell whose object is to boggle someone's mind with lust, you should invoke holy Cernunnos.[237]

In this passage, Pan and Cernunnos are essentially the same deity, an idea expressed before by Murray, but now they even seem to look alike.

Cernunnos would also feature in Huson's work as a god of vengeance. The god figures prominently in a spell using poppet magick, which utilizes the power of Cernunnos to "vengefully stab the Dagyde[238] into the part of the puppet designated for torment with the words 'So mote it be!'"[239] Later in the same chapter (called "Vengeance and Attack"), the power of Cernunnos is used to call up an electrical storm (but only on Tuesdays during a waning moon).[240]

The use of Cernunnos as Wiccan-Witchcraft's primary or most important male deity would be repeated in other books published in the 1970s. In *Lady Sheba's Book of Shadows* (written, not surprisingly, by Lady Sheba, 1920–

---

236. Huson, *Mastering Witchcraft*, 32.

237. Huson, *Mastering Witchcraft*, 120–121.

238. *Dagyde* are exorcised "needles of the art," in other words, pins or needles that have been blessed and consecrated.

239. Huson, *Mastering Witchcraft*, 196.

240. Huson, *Mastering Witchcraft*, 201. I have always found it amusing just how specific this bit is.

2002), the God and Goddess of the Witches are said to be "Arida and Kernun-nos,"[241] and those names are repeated several times throughout the text. In her Spring Equinox ritual, Sheba calls Cernunnos the "Merciful Son of Cer-ridwen" and states that his "name is Highest of all."[242]

The reason for using an alternate spelling of Cernunnos is worth speculat-ing on. Lady Sheba received much of the information that made up her *Book of Shadows* from an English coven who may or may not have included the name of their coven deity in their book. Not including specific deity names is a common practice among initiatory traditions in order to keep those names secret. It's possible that Sheba was attempting to recreate a name she had simply heard previously and not seen written down. It's also possible that her more phonetic spelling of Cernunnos was one she inherited from the coven she was "initiated" into. (The story of Sheba's initiation is a strange little piece of Witch history. Unlike most initiates, she was initiated remotely, in this case over the phone, by a British coven while she was living in the state of Kentucky. After Sheba received the Book of Shadows she had pledged to keep secret, she promptly sent it to Llewellyn Publications, the publishers of this book.)

Sheba would not be the only Witchcraft writer of the 1970s to use an alternate spelling of Cernunnos as the name of Wicca's Horned God. Doreen Valiente (1922–1999), hailed by many as the Mother of Modern Witchcraft, would call the Horned God *Kernunno* in her 1978 how-to book *Witchcraft for Tomorrow.*[243] In addition to using this specific name, her book also includes the poem "Invocation of the Horned God," focusing on the Horned One as a god of "moonlit meadow, on dusky hill" and "forests wild and woods enchanted."[244] Valiente explained the use of *Kernunno* just over a decade later

---

241. Lady Sheba, *The Grimoire of Lady Sheba*, 119. *Lady Sheba's Book of Shadows* was originally published in 1972, but I'm using the 2001 hardback edition, *The Grimoire of Lady Sheba*, which was released a year after *Lady Sheba's Book of Shadows* and includes the original *Book of Shadows* and additional material.

242. Lady Sheba, *The Grimoire of Lady Sheba*, 205.

243. Valiente, *Witchcraft for Tomorrow*, 168.

244. Valiente, *Witchcraft for Tomorrow*, 190.

in her memoir *The Rebirth of Witchcraft*, stating that it was one of the god names used by the coven she was initiated into by Gerald Gardner.[245]

Contemporary to Sheba, Valiente, and Huson was the English Witch Sybil Leek (1917–1982), who released *The Complete Art of Witchcraft* in 1971. Instead of naming the Horned God Cernunnos (or a variation thereof), she called her Horned God *Faunus*, generally seen as the Roman equivalent of Pan. Her descriptions of Faunus fall in line with other contemporary descriptions of the Horned God. He is "the spirit within the woods, trees, and waters," but she also explicitly links him to the sun. Her Faunus is "the sun, the life-giving force without which there could be no life at all."[246] Leek also gives the names "Sylvester, Crom, Pan, Virnius"[247] for her coven's Horned God, though most of those, much like Faunus, never became very popular outside of the circles she inspired.

Cernunnos is again used as the name of the Wiccan Horned God (and even spelled correctly) in *Eight Sabbats for Witches* (1981) and *The Witches' Way* (1984) by English Witches Janet (1950–present) and Stewart Farrar (1916–2000), with some assistance by Doreen Valiente. Like Lady Sheba, the Farrars utilized a British Book of Shadows in their text, and the two versions of Cernunnos as the Horned One are quite similar. In both works, Cernunnos straddles the worlds of life and death equally and is referred to as the "Dread Lord of Shadows."

Eight Sabbats for Witches and *The Witches' Way* would be some of the last Wiccan books to portray the Horned God as the unquestioned God of the Witches and to include a specific deity name from antiquity. What Gardner hinted at in 1959, "The God" as a manifestation of all male deities, would become the most common way of writing about the God of Wiccan-Witches as the years rolled along. Writers would mention the Horned God, of course, but he became something bigger than a more intimate deity concerned primarily with Witches.

---

245. Valiente, *The Rebirth of Witchcraft*, 52.

246. Leek, *The Complete Art of Witchcraft*, 43.

247. Leek, *The Complete Art of Witchcraft*, 43.

Perhaps the greatest expression of this change can be found in 1979's *The Spiral Dance* by Starhawk, (1951–present). Unlike the previous authors written about in this chapter, Starhawk drew inspiration for her version of Witchcraft from sources far beyond Gardner and British Wiccan traditions. Starhawk's version of Witchcraft was heavily influenced by Wicca, but also second-wave feminism, Dianic Witchcraft, and the work of Victor (1917–2001) and Cora Anderson (1944–2008), the founders of the Feri Tradition.

In *The Spiral Dance*, Starhawk calls the God of the Witches by several different names, including Horned God, the God, Sun Child, Lord of the Winds, and Dying God.[248] Starhawk's Witch God is cosmic and all-encompassing, but beholden to the Goddess. Starhawk writes that the Horned God is "born of a Virgin mother" and that "His power is drawn directly from the Goddess: He participates in her."[249] While the Goddess has always been somewhat predominant in most forms of Wiccan-Witchcraft, the Wicca of Gardner and his descendants generally viewed Goddess and God as equal in terms of power and agency. Here the Horned One is no pushover, but is obviously in a secondary role. Starhawk's conception of the God of the Witches is not one that arose in isolation and was symptomatic of larger trends.

By the end of the 1970s, I think it can be safely said that many within the broader Wiccan community were moving away from the Horned God as the dominant male deity of the tradition and replacing him with a larger concept, "the God." Some of this was most likely intentional, and some of it was probably by accident. Many specific initiatory Wiccan traditions use named gods, such as Sheba's *Kernunnos*, whose names are often not allowed to be said during public ritual. This led to generic titles being used instead, which is why so many early published Wiccan rituals contain exhortations to the "Goddess" and "God" or "Lord" and "Lady." Eventually these placeholder names became names of the deities themselves.

Freeing the Horned God from being specifically Faunus or Cernunnos also opened up what he might be capable of, and what sorts of myths could

---

248. Starhawk, *The Spiral Dance*, 96.
249. Starhawk, *The Spiral Dance*, 97.

be attached to him. He no longer had to be a god with one foot in the realms of the living and the dead; he could now die and be reborn continuously. His life story could be placed on the Wheel of the Year, with the God reborn on Yule as the Sun Child and dying at the Autumn Equinox as John Barleycorn. A more complex Horned God mythology arose, borrowing myths from solar deities and dying and resurrecting gods.

A bigger Witch God who didn't *always* have to wear horns or antlers could also be looked at as "respectability politics." Though we don't think about it very much today, by the late 1970s and into the early 1990s much of the United States was consumed by "Satanic panic." Rumors of Satanic conspiracies focused on murdering and kidnapping children were taken seriously by law enforcement, though there was absolutely no evidence suggesting any of it was true. Child daycare workers went to prison, for decades in some cases, during the panic, and all the hysteria of the period was laid at the feet of a horned devil and his depraved devotes.[250] (And while this all feels very long ago, people were still being held in jail due to these allegations into the 2010s.)

In the most influential texts of the late 1980s and early 1990s, the Horned God had been effectively reduced to "The God" and only "sometimes" wore "horns on His head."[251] This was all quite a change from Gardner's phallic horned deity that originally shaped Wicca. And make no mistake, books like Scott Cunningham's *Wicca: A Guide for the Solitary Practitioner* were widely influential. They made Wicca easy to understand, easy to grasp, and easy to embrace, especially if one was going through Christianity withdrawals and was a little afraid of the Horned God.

When writing specifically about "the Witches' God" in 1989, Janet and Stewart Farrar listed the Horned God as only one aspect of a much more powerful whole. In a short period of time, things had changed from Cernunnos being the God of the Witches to being just one part of him. Now the God was the Time-Measuring God, the Wisdom God, the Vegetation God,

---

250. Selk, "Falsely Accused of Satanic Horrors, A Couple Spent 21 Years in Prison. Now They're Owed Millions."

251. Cunningham, *Wicca: A Guide for the Solitary Practitioner*, 12.

the War God, the Craftsman God, the Monopolist God, and the Underworld God (along with several other names).[252] Silver RavenWolf's (1956–present) *To Ride a Silver Broomstick* (1993) acknowledges that it's hard for many new Witches to "accept the visage of our God," and then makes it easy to do so by encouraging new Witches to pick whatever deity they want as "The God."[253]

I remain a huge fan of RavenWolf, Cunningham, and the work of the Farrars, but by emphasizing "The God" instead of the Horned God, they, to some extent, sidelined Wicca's original male deity. I don't want anyone reading this book to think that the Horned God completely fell out of favor beginning in the late 1970s, but he certainly began to change. He became one possible ritual focus among dozens of choices instead of a primary one. In the process of writing this book and reviewing what has been written about the Horned God in Wiccan-Witchcraft texts, my impression is that the Horned One often comes across as a secret reserved for practitioners. If you know how to look for him, you can find him, but if you are new to all of this Witchcraft stuff, here's a way to get around any negative baggage you or society might have toward him.

(During the writing of this book, I asked my friend and fellow Wiccan-Witch Thorn Mooney if my theory on the transition from "Horned God" to "The God" in Wicca was something that really happened or if I was just projecting my own feelings onto things. In a text message on Monday April 13, 2020, about a month into quarantine for COVID-19, she responded that as a young Witch, she had "confusion about who I'm supposed to be talking to as a Wiccan" and wondered if "the HG (Horned God) is the same as 'the Lord'? Is the God the HG? The difference in terms really confused me." It's good to know that I'm not completely wrong.)

The end result of all of this was that Wicca's Horned God became one part of a much larger God. Sure, that God was often depicted with antlers (he always seems to resemble Cernunnos more than Pan), but they could easily be dismissed or forgotten about, depending on time and circumstances. I

---

252. Farrar and Farrar, *The Witches' God*, from the table of contents.

253. RavenWolf, *To Ride a Silver Broomstick*, 49. I pick on this book a lot in my books, but it remains my favorite "101" book.

think most Wiccan-Witches still associate their primary male deity (or male deities) with horns and antlers, but alternatives now abound. I've always felt Wicca should strive to be as inclusive as possible, and yes, for many people horns and antlers can be a barrier for entry. But by clipping his horns, the Wiccan God loses a bit of his history and mystery.

While the Horned God was slowly folded into a larger representation of deity, Wicca had another problem to overcome: the very denial of the Horned God's true nature, along with the identities of many of his followers. In my experience, Wicca has generally been an accepting and tolerant spiritual practice, but it wasn't always like that. For several decades, many Wiccan coven leaders refused to initiate (or even teach) gay and lesbian Witches. And when those gay and lesbian Witches were allowed into a coven situation, they were often encouraged to "act straight" in circle.

Wicca as originally described by Gerald Gardner and other early Witches had a major emphasis on a male-female polarity, an idea that suggests that magickal operations are stronger when worked in male-female pairings. Within the circle, the Goddess and God were often portrayed as exclusively straight, with no interest in same-sex coupling. If all of my brothers and sisters can be found within the Horned God, then my Horned God has multiple gender identities and an interest in all different kinds of sexual partners. Since gay sex was sacred to Pan, it only makes sense that gay sex (along with all other forms of consensual sexuality) would also be seen as sacred by the Horned God today.

I don't think the Horned God can even be seen as exclusively male. Horned and antlered goddesses can be found throughout history. I have to believe that deity is close to limitless, meaning that it can take whatever form it wishes in order to be better understood and appreciated by devotees. For the most part, Wicca has gotten over its homophobia problems, but the issue still comes up from time to time, often from people who wish to disparage Wicca by focusing on what it once was instead of what it has become.

Chapter Seventeen

THE WITCHFATHER: THE HORNED GOD IN TRADITIONAL WITCHCRAFT

TRADITIONAL WITCHCRAFT (ALSO SOMETIMES called Old Craft or Traditional Craft[254]) is a branch of the Modern Craft that looks to English cunning-craft, folk magick practices, and the witch trials of the late medieval and early modern periods for inspiration. Some practitioners go much further than simply inspiration and insist that their practices represent a surviving Witch tradition much older and more authentic than that of Wiccan-Witchcraft. Many who practice Traditional Witchcraft (especially older generations) have an especially antagonistic attitude toward Wiccan-Witches, derisively describing Wicca as a "neo-Pagan" tradition, while stating that Traditional Witchcraft claims indicate a "pre-modern provenance."[255]

Though my main practice is Wiccan-Witchcraft, I'll admit to also being seduced by the charms of Traditional Witchcraft. The smart Witch uses whatever works, and many of the ritual techniques and ideas from Traditional Witchcraft work! I also see Traditional Witchcraft and Wicca as generally stemming from the same set of ideas and impulses. While Traditional Witchcraft most certainly contains a lot of older folk magick elements, many

---

254. To make all of these terms even more confusing, in the United States, initiatory Wiccan traditions, especially older ones such as Gardnerian and Alexandrian, are often called *BTW* (British Traditional Witchcraft or Wicca).

255. Cochrane, with Jones, *The Robert Cochrane Letters*, 12.

practitioners have also been influenced by modern literary sources such as Robert Graves's *The White Goddess* and James Frazer's *The Golden Bough*. How those elements have been used and interpreted varies, but that's the beauty of Witchcraft! A Craft capable of growth, change, and adaptation is far more desirable to me than one that stands in place.

Unlike Wicca, which often focuses on the Goddess (or goddesses), Traditional Witchcraft tends to emphasize the Horned God. Within Traditional Witchcraft, the Horned God is known by several additional names: Witchfather (or Witch-Father), the Dark Lord of the Mound, and the Witch God, along with additional names and titles, depending on the Traditional Witch one is reading or speaking with. Unlike in Wicca, Traditional Witches often proudly state that their Horned God is "none other than the Devil himself."[256]

AZAZEL AND THE WITCHFATHER

Robert Cochrane is generally credited as being the first public Traditional Witch. Articulating a Witchcraft practice radically different from that of Gerald Gardner, the Witches of Cochrane's tradition worked robed and outdoors and utilized a unique ritual system. Instead of the athame, their primary working tool was (and still is) the *stang*, a pitchfork or walking stick shod with iron and often containing "horns" on top. Cochrane's Witchcraft was heavily influenced by Graves's *The White Goddess* and was the first modern Witchcraft tradition to freely add elements from Christian and Jewish practices.

The theological underpinnings of Cochrane's Witchcraft have always been hard to nail down. Unlike the works of many other Witchcraft architects, much of Cochrane's written legacy is in the form of letters to various individuals, and in those letters Cochrane was often deliberately obtuse. Witchcraft writer Michael Howard (1948–2015) believed that the essence of Cochrane's system was the use of magic and religion to overcome Fate (also the name of a goddess, according to Howard); in other words, Witch-

---

256. Kelden, *The Crooked Path*, 86.

craft was a tool to take control of one's life.[257] Unlike with later Traditional Witches, the Horned God was not always the primary deity in Cochrane's Craft; however, Cochrane did help define modern interpretations of the Horned God in Trad Craft.

Writing to American Witch Joseph Bearwalker Wilson (1942–2004),[258] Cochrane provides a cosmology of deity, ending with the "God of fire, of craft, of lower magic and of fertility and death."[259] Cochrane goes on to write that all the things of this world belong to him, and that he is "the star-crossed serpent." The term *star-crossed serpent* would be used by later Traditional Witchcraft writers and is a reference to Azazel, a former angel and "son of heaven" who fell from grace.

The story of Azazel comes from an apocalyptic Jewish work titled the *Book of the Watchers*.[260] A group of stories most likely collected during the Maccabean Revolt (167 to 160 BCE), the book tells the story of a group of angelic beings known as the "Watchers" who were charged by the Jewish god to look over human beings. (How old the story of the Watchers is in Jewish tradition is an open question, with some scholars suggesting the stories themselves could date back to the third or fourth century BCE.) Upon beginning their duties, the Watchers were consumed with lust for human women and left heaven in order to have sexual relations with them. The union of mortal women and angelic Watchers produced the *Nephilim* ("fallen ones"), a race of giants that brought violence to Earth.[261] When some Traditional Witches talk about "witch blood," they are generally referencing the idea that there are people (witches) descended from the Nephilim and the Watchers.

---

257. Cochrane, with Jones, *The Robert Cochrane Letters*, 22. Edited by Michael Howard. Howard's interpretation is on page 25.

258. Wilson was a true Witchcraft pioneer and helped put together the first Witch newsletter in US history. He's also the founder of the 1734 Tradition, much of which was inspired by letters from Cochrane to Wilson.

259. Cochrane, with Jones, *The Robert Cochrane Letters*, 26.

260. The *Book of the Watchers* was later added to the non-canonical *Book of Enoch*, which includes material from five very different sources.

261. Pagels, *The Origins of Satan*, 49–50.

The *Book of the Watchers* contains two very different stories outlining the fall of the Watchers. In the story above, the angel Semihazah (or Semyaz, depending on the translator) leads the Watchers. A second story gives the name Azazel as the leader of the Watchers, with Azazel's gifts to humanity being more than just carnal. Azazel teaches women magick (Witchcraft) and cosmetology; the "beautifying of the eyelids" is held up as an especially horrible skill to teach human beings.[262] Perhaps even more importantly, it's Azazel who gives humanity the knowledge of the forge, and with it, weapons, introducing violence into the world. Azazel's gift also includes how to manufacture jewelry, which is also condemned. As the story of Azazel progresses, he is credited with introducing all sin into the world.[263] Since Azazel was the architect of so much on earth, it's no wonder that his name most likely translates as "strong god," for strong was Azazel's influence on the world.[264]

The story found in *The Book of the Watchers* was eventually added to another piece of apocalyptic Jewish literature, the *Book of Enoch*. *Enoch* contains material from five very different sources and can be looked at as a document expressing the development of Jewish (and later Christian) ideas about the Devil. Over the course of *Enoch*, the name of the "evil one" changes from Semihazah to Azazel and eventually to Satan. Since they were all added to the same religious "book," the different stories in *Enoch* began to be interpreted as one tale instead of several, with the figures of Semihazah, Azazel, and Satan all becoming one and the same.

While seen as a source of wickedness in Christianity and Judaism, Azazel can be interpreted in other ways. Instead of being an evil force, Azazel is a source of knowledge and human betterment. As a deity of forge and flame, he has parallels with Lucifer, the light bringer. Azazel is a figure who chose to be on Earth and not occupy a place above the natural world. While Yahweh apparently found sex with human females sinful, Azazel believed, like Modern Witches, otherwise. Sex is not some sort of cosmic test; it's something to be enjoyed among consenting adults. Azazel is also the original teacher

---

262. Wray and Mobley, *The Birth of Satan*, 101.

263. Wray and Mobley, *The Birth of Satan*, 101.

264. Wray and Mobley, *The Birth of Satan*, 107.

of magick, certainly an important skill for Modern Witches. Azazel is also intensely human in his longing and desire to be with others physically.

Robert Cochrane called his coven (or *cuveen*) the Clan of Tubal Cain, named after the legendary Hebrew blacksmith Tubal Cain. According to the *Book of the Watchers*, it's Azazel who gave the power of the forge to humanity, so by naming his group after Tubal Cain, Cochrane was linking it to Azazel and the Watchers' gifts of light, knowledge, and magic. Paul Huson, writing in 1970, would later connect Tubal Cain and Azazel to the legends of the goddess Diana and the Babylonian god Shamash.[265] Huson would also retell the tale of Azazel (generally spelled *Azael* by Huson), placing it front and center in the many Witch traditions that would later be inspired by his book *Mastering Witchcraft*.

The star-crossed serpent wasn't Cochrane's only conception of the Horned God and male deity. In other letters, he wrote of the "horned child," an idea most likely inspired by the Maiden-Mother-Crone mythos found in Robert Graves's *The White Goddess*.[266] In another letter, Cochrane calls the Horned God *Carenos* (most likely a misspelling and a reference to Cernunnos) and writes of him in a way that parallels most modern descriptions of the Horned God. Cochrane says that this figure is Lord of the Animals and the god of joy, passion, growth, strength, happiness, fertility, and fruition. He calls him the "wild hunter" and "Ruler of the Woodlands" as well, and compares him to a young Dionysus.[267]

THE HORNED GOD IN LATER TRADITIONAL WITCHCRAFT

If there's any one thing that marks the Witchfather of Traditional Witchcraft as different from the Horned God of Wiccan-Witchcraft, it's the idea that the Witchfather is far more dangerous. Writer Gemma Gary has complained that the Horned God's "darker aspects are ignored" in many Wiccan traditions, and

---

265. Huson, *Mastering Witchcraft*, 9–10.

266. Cochrane, with Jones, *The Robert Cochrane Letters*, 31.

267. Cochrane, with Jones, *The Robert Cochrane Letters*, 165.

that his role has been reduced to something "green and benign."[268] Old Crafter Nigel G. Pearson has written that the Horned God of Traditional Craft is "no, gentle, loving father-figure" and is "the render, the destroyer, the ripper and raper."[269]

Figure 19: A depiction of the Horned God as he often appears in Traditional Witchcraft. One of the most popular images of the Horned God today features the Horned One with the skull of a stag for a face.

While to some this all might sound offensive or needlessly frightening, both writers have a definite point. If the Horned God is the King of the Wildwood, then that wood has to be wild. He's not just the god of gentle summer rains; he's the lord of thunderstorms and earthquakes too. While this book has taken pains to point out that within Wicca the Horned God has tradition-

---

268. Gary, *The Devil's Dozen, Thirteen Craft Rites of the Old One*, 14. If it sounds like I'm being critical, I'm really not. I find Gary to be one of the most lucid and interesting writers in the Traditional Witchcraft world. I highly recommend her work.

269. Pearson, *Treading the Mill*, 21.

ally been associated with death, it's still something that's very uncomfortable to a lot of people, and it's a truth that's often left out of Witchcraft books— which often don't mention the Horned God in anything other than superficial terms to begin with (figure 19).

Life is not always easy, and if the Horned God is a god of life, then he can also be a god of hardship. This is not to suggest that anyone sees the Horned God as purposefully wishing ill on Witches, but only that the world is full of obstacles and adversity that must be overcome. The Horned God then is a part of that adversity, and by working with him and acknowledging this truth, we can grow as people and as Witches. In his book *The Crooked Path*, my friend Kelden writes that the Witchfather is "the wild and untamed natural landscape," and there are few things more powerful and challenging than the raw force of nature.

Most Traditional Witchcraft writers are also very clear that their Horned God has very real links to Christian ideas about the Devil. As mentioned earlier, for many Traditional Witches the Devil and the Horned God are one and the same, and to shy away from such a reckoning is to deny our own impulses and wants as humans.[270] Even though the Devil is freely acknowledged there's still the caveat the Horned Devil of Traditional Witchcraft is not the Christian Satan, architect of all the world's evils. Besides, the evils of Satan were not ever really evils most of the time. As Gemma Gary reminds her readers the Devil is the god of personal freedom and power, sexual satisfaction, dancing, feasting, ecstatic celebrations, and joy.[271]

Many Traditional Witches believe in activities such as cursing and hexing, so it's no wonder that within the tradition, the Horned God is often seen as a source of power.[272] Instead of love and light, the Horned One is capable of bringing all the power of nature to bear on a situation. The idea of the Devil offers a person control over their own situation in life and, much like

---

270. Orapello and Maguire, *Besom Stang & Sword: A Guide to Traditional Witchcraft, the Six-Folk Path & the Hidden Landscape*, 11. Orapello and Maguire are two of the most lucid Trad Witchcraft writers working today. This is a great book.

271. Gary, *The Devil's Dozen*, 10.

272. Gary, *The Devil's Dozen*, 10.

Cochrane's ideas about fate, allows a Witch to control their own life and live as they see fit.[273]

Traditional Witchcraft also acknowledges that Christianity has had a direct impact on the rites of the Witch. While many Witches run screaming from anything having to do with Jesus or the Church, there's a long history of Christians practicing magick in various guises. Because of this, Traditional Witches are generally comfortable embracing all of the folklore associated with the Devil. That folklore is also used to their advantage: people's fear of the Devil lends more power and energy to magick done in his name. Witchcraft has always existed on the margins, and embracing the Horned God as the Devil is a return to Witchcraft's roots and keeps it from being rooted in the passive positivity of New Age thought.[274]

In addition to seeing the Horned God as the Devil and the wild, many Traditional Witches see him as a bearer of light and knowledge, similar to Lucifer.[275] Some Trad Witches go a step further and believe that the Horned One is the "sum and accumulation of all wisdom and knowledge."[276] In order to share that knowledge, some Old Crafters have suggested that the Horned God has physically incarnated on Earth several different times over the centuries, even showing up once as the Christian Jesus.[277] (Just imagine telling Grandma that Jesus and the Devil are the same thing, and that Jesus likely had horns hiding under his hippie hair.)

The exact nature of the Horned God within Traditional Witchcraft varies by practitioner, much like it does in other forms of Witchcraft. For some, he's an amalgamation of countless spirits from across the centuries.[278] Others take the approach that their Horned God has appeared in various roles throughout history, including the familiar Herne and Odin, but also Lucifer,

---

273. Gary, *The Devil's Dozen*, 11.

274. Gary, *The Devil's Dozen*, 14.

275. Kelden, *The Crooked Path*, 86 and 88.

276. Pearson, *Treading the Mill*, 219.

277. Pearson, *Treading the Mill*, 225–266.

278. Kelden, *The Crooked Path*, 86.

the King of Faery, and Azazel as a goat instead of a fallen angel.[279] While the Horned God in most Traditional Craft is generally written about as a deity, some Trad Witches see him primarily as a "spirit of place and a primordial force," despite rituals and practices that suggest a god.[280]

Perhaps my favorite honorific for the Horned God in Traditional Witchcraft is the *King of the Mound*. For me, the phrase brings to mind rot and decay, things generally seen as unwanted by society at large. However, without rot, there is no life. Like the Horned God within Wicca, the Horned One of Traditional Witches is a god of life and death. Traditional Witches just often seem more at ease with the uglier implications of this. The Horned God lives within a decaying carcass just as much as he lives in green forests and bubbling streams.

---

279. Gary, *The Devil's Dozen*, 16.

280. Orapello and Maguire, *Besom Stang & Sword*, 13.

Chapter Eighteen
RITUAL TO MEET THE WITCHFATHER

WHEN I FIRST DISCOVERED Modern Witchcraft, most materials documenting it were focused on the idea of the Great Goddess, along with various female deities. When books mentioned male deity, it was generally in passing and often felt like an afterthought. The idea of the Goddess as central to Witchcraft lies in stark contrast to how Witchcraft has generally been perceived (especially in North America and Europe) over the last seven hundred years. For most of that time, the supreme deity of Witchcraft was a horned god, the Devil.

That Devil was never the menace that the general populace imagined him to be. He was simply a convenient scapegoat for their superstitions, pettiness, and cruelty. That Devil was the repository for everything people didn't understand. He was a source of power, knowledge, and magick, three things that governments and churches have always been terrified of because they know those ideas are beyond the control of their authority.

In many ways, horned deity is largely responsible for Witchcraft as we know it today.[281] Without those images of Witches cavorting with the Devil from five hundred years ago, today's Craft would look very different. While most of us reject the idea that we work with the Christian Satan, the imagery and lore of that period is still intrinsically tied to our modern-day practice. I

---

281. I feel like there are some Hekate followers out there who are going to really disagree with that statement, but I think it's historically accurate.

think there's real power in acknowledging the Horned God as the Witchfather, because in his various guises, the Horned One is truly the father of the Modern Craft. In almost every incarnation of Witchcraft over the last thousand years, the Horned God has been there, sitting comfortably somewhere in the circle, or just outside of it, helping to inspire us once again and give us the tools to grow our personal practices.

When I think of my flesh-and-blood father, I often think of the things he gave me growing up. He put a roof over my head and food in my belly, but he gave me more than just physical stuff. Through him I inherited a love of history and myth, and he taught me how to be a mostly decent human being too. I know that not all of us have this sort of relationship with our father, and for those of you who do not, I feel your pain; my mother left my brother and me when I was in the first grade. But in the Witchfather, we are celebrating the ideal, a figure who makes us a better Witch and imparts to us the wisdom to accomplish our goals in life.

In the Ritual to Meet the Horned God in chapter 3, we gave gifts to the Horned God. Tonight in this ritual, we take gifts given to us freely by the Witchfather. We take all of the wisdom and experiences given to us by the Horned God in his many guises and apply them directly to our Craft. In many ways, this rite is the culmination of everything we've touched on in these pages.

Most Traditional Witchcraft books suggest conducting every ritual in a liminal space, such as a graveyard or a crossroads, but for those of us who live in cities, such things are not just impractical but are often impossible. If you can find such a place, fantastic! But if you can't, an empty room in your home will work just fine. You won't need much in terms of tools and materials for this ritual, but you will need a stang. A stang need not be elaborate; a pitchfork will work (available at most hardware stores), as will a regular walking stick. If both of those are out of reach, a fallen tree branch is also acceptable. If you can't come up with one of those three items, it's best to wait to do this ritual until you obtain one of them.

RITUAL SUPPLIES

For this ritual you will need:

- Ritual tools for setting up your sacred space
- Cakes and ale (both for you and as a libation) and, if indoors, a libation bowl
- A stang, along with a way to place your stang straight up into the air (If you are doing your ritual outside, the ground is the obvious choice here. If you are doing the ritual indoors, I find that a bucket full of rocks works surprisingly well.)
- A small dish of water, if holding your ritual indoors
- 6–8 candles, if your ritual is indoors (Set up your candles in such a way as to indicate a path of some sort. Tealight candles are an easy and safe choice here.)

I suggest performing this ritual in a way that utilizes the techniques found in Traditional Witchcraft. If you are unfamiliar with how Traditional Witches create sacred space, there are numerous examples online as well as several books I personally recommend in the bibliography. (My favorites include those by Gemma Gary, Kelden, and Tara-Love Maguire and Christopher Orapello, as well as my book *Witch's Wheel of the Year*.) If you are uncomfortable with those techniques, you don't have to use them, but I do suggest getting out of your own comfort zone now and then.

If you are doing this ritual indoors, set up your stang and candles before the rite begins. The six to eight candles should be set up in such a way as to symbolize a path. Don't light them when you set them up, but have them on the floor where you want them before the rite starts. If you are doing this ritual outside, this step involving the candles is probably unnecessary, but it can be done if you choose. The stang should be set up in the center of your working space.

THE RITUAL

Start the ritual by leaving your house and going on a walk just after the sun has begun to set. As you walk, breathe in the fresh air and listen to the sounds that surround you. Even in the densest cityscape, there's still a bit of the natural world around, whether it's the chirping of a bird or the touch of the wind. Whatever bit of nature you can sense, take a moment to truly appreciate it.

Your pre-ritual walk does not have to be a major undertaking, but spend some time outdoors thinking about all you've experienced with the Horned God. Imagine him as Pan, wild and free. Picture him as Herne, seeking and finding retribution. Find yourself in the tendrils of the Green Man or experiencing joy in the ecstasy of Dionysus. As your muscles tense and relax as you walk, reflect on Cernunnos running through the woods on the hunt, living in that liminal space between life and death. Finally think about what it is you wish to receive from the Horned God. What else can he give you to make your life more complete and fulfilling as a Witch?

If you are doing your ritual outdoors, reflect on these ideas as you walk to your ritual spot. If you are performing this ritual indoors, light the candles to symbolize your path. As you light the candles, thank the Horned God for the illumination he has provided:

> *These many days and years, I have walked the path of the Witch. Side by side with me has walked the Horned One, lighting my way. Great Horned Lord, show me the way forward so that I might know your greater mysteries and receive your gifts.*

If you are doing this ritual outside, simply be aware of the path you have walked, and say the words above as you approach your ritual space.

Once you have settled into your working area, do whatever setup is required. (This could mean unpacking your cakes and ale, setting up your stang if you are outdoors, and/or cleansing and purifying your ritual space.) Once everything is to your satisfaction, build your sacred space in whatever way works best for you. When that is done, call to the Witchfather to attend your rite:

Great Horned God, tonight I call to you as the Witchfather. I invoke you as the Keeper of Secrets, the Guardian of the Mysteries, and the Father of Witches. Long have I followed you, and tonight I seek your final gifts. Bless me as a Witch so that I might further my Craft and walk where only the bravest tread. May I receive a glimpse of you this night and the blessings that may come only to those who seek you out. So mote it be! Hail and welcome!

In Traditional Witchcraft, the stang is used as an altar and as a way to alter one's consciousness. In this ritual, we are using it to shift our perception so that we might more easily catch a glimpse of the Witchfather. To use the stang in this way, you'll want to stand about five to six feet away from it and begin circling around it in a clockwise direction while chanting, "Io Io Evohe" (pronounced "Yo Yo Eee-voh-hay"). While you move and chant, you should stare directly at the stang while letting your eyes lose focus.

(If you choose to do this ritual with a group, the traditional way to dance around the stang is to form a ring of Witches, with everyone's right hand pointing inward toward the stang. Everyone's left arm should be extended straight out in front of them, with their left hand resting on the left shoulder of the person in front of them. This is one version of a technique known as "treading the mill.")

How long should this part of the ritual last? Ideally until your consciousness has shifted and you catch a glimpse of something holy and sacred. In my experience, you'll probably be dizzy by the time this happens, your dizziness helping to induce a shift in your perception. What will the Witchfather look like when you look upon him? For some, his face appears as a skull, while others see a more traditional Horned God figure. Higher powers appear to us in different ways, providing every Witch with the image that best resonates with them.

After you have seen the Witchfather, end the movement and chanting around the stang and prepare to receive his gifts. Unfortunately, it's unlikely that he's going to stay in your line of sight and walk up to you and present you with a bunch of presents. But you should feel his energy radiating around you, and his presence should be noticeable. In my experience, it often feels like the air around me has gotten thick, even though there's no moisture in the air.

With the Witchfather's energy in your ritual space, reach downward and touch the ground. Feel the heartbeat of the earth, and begin to draw that energy up into your body while saying:

> From the Witchfather I accept this gift of power. May I wield the power of the Witch effectively, forcefully, and for the good of myself and those around me. So mote it be!

As you say these words, you should feel the earth's power radiating through your body, energizing your magickal self.

Look up at the sky and observe the moon. If you are indoors, move to a spot near a window and observe the moon in the night sky. (No windows? Simply look up, project your consciousness upward, and feel the moon's power.) Let the light of the moon shine down upon you, its energy filling up your being. Imagine the light coming into your body and making you glow. The moon's energy is like a flame that stirs within us, making us sure of ourselves and confident in our abilities. Accept this gift of courage by saying:

> From the Witchfather I accept this gift of courage. I shall be true to myself and to my will. I will live as a Witch without fear or shame, embracing my place in this world and my role within it. So mote it be!

If you are outside, touch the grass underneath you. It should be slick with dew. (If you live in an especially dry area of the world, you can do this part of the ritual by simply thinking about the importance of water or bringing a little bit of your own.) Concentrate on the feeling of the water in your hand, and marvel at how it came to be there. If you are indoors, touch the water in the bowl upon your altar and feel it on your palm. Think for a moment of how water shapes the world, carving magnificent spaces such as the Grand Canyon and rearranging the world's shorelines. Water makes changes large and small, depending on the situation, but the change is always there, like a stream slowly carving its way through rock.

See yourself like the water, using your power as a Witch to confront and vanquish all obstacles in your way, even the largest ones. With time, effort, and determination, we can transform our lives and those of the people around us. Feel the power of the water slowly enter your body, and accept this gift of the Witchfather:

> *From the Witchfather I accept this gift of determination. May I let nothing stand in my path that is undesirable. May I accomplish all that I set out to do on this the path of the Witch. Make me steadfast in my loves, my goals, and my magick. So mote it be!*

Stand still for a moment and feel the air around you. Is it still, or is there a subtle breeze blowing? Even indoors you should be able to feel the air move around you, even if that movement is slight. Stand still until you feel it, and let it wash over you. Breathe deeply and notice your breath; feel your lungs expand as they take in air. As you exhale, reflect on your voice and the words that escape your mouth. As Witches, we don't have to play nice all the time, but we should be decent folk, working toward the betterment of the world. Take a deep breath and thank the Witchfather for this last gift:

> *From the Witchfather I accept this gift of decency. With the knowledge granted to me, I shall use my skills and energy for the betterment of this world. May my judgments be sound and my will ever true. So mote it be!*

Feel the energies that you have received from the Witchfather moving through you now. Picture yourself going forward as a strong and powerful Witch, able to overcome anything this life throws at you. That doesn't mean that life will be easy from here on out, but only that you have the ability to overcome those challenges.

Place your hands over your cakes and ale, and ask the Witchfather to bless them:

> *I ask the Witchfather to bless this food and drink. May these gifts remind me of your bounty and the abundance in this world. With thanks, I accept your blessings. So mote it be!*

Eat your cakes and ale and enjoy the energies still resonating in your ritual space.

When you are done eating and drinking, be sure to leave a libation for the Horned One. If you are outdoors, your libations can be poured and placed directly on the earth. If you are indoors, you should place them in your libation bowl and then move them outdoors at the end of your rite. As you share your libation, say goodbye to the Horned God:

> *As you have given unto me, so I give unto you. Witchfather, accept my offering for your gifts this night. Long may we walk with each other. I thank you for your presence at my rite this night and look forward to growing closer to you in the days and years ahead. So mote it be!*

Take down your sacred space in the way that is most comfortable to you. If you are outside, pack up your belongings and visualize the path that brought you to your space. If you are indoors, stand before the candles you have lit symbolizing the road that you have traveled. As you stand in front of the pathway, feel the Witchfather's hand upon your shoulder leading the way. Say:

> *Great Horned God, you have shared with me your light and wisdom, and now I walk forward secure in my path as a Witch. May the blessings of the Witchfather be upon me until the end of my days. This rite has ended, but the journey is only beginning. So mote it be!*

Blow out the candles in front of you and walk through the darkness confident in your abilities as a Witch. If you are outdoors, walk with your stang in front of you confidently into the night.

SOME FINAL THOUGHTS

THE HISTORY OF THE Horned God is not linear. It does not easily move from point A to point B in a traceable and logical manner. Instead, the story of the Horned God jumps around from place to place and era to era, and continues to do so. The Horned God as we understand him today was assembled from a variety of pieces, and I'm not sure those pieces all fit together as securely as we might like, but once they are all assembled, they create something extraordinary.

Modern Witchcraft would not exist today without the Horned One. The writings of Margaret Murray one hundred years ago helped inspire a new generation of Witches, and at the heart of those writings was a deity who loved joy, sex, and the wilds of nature. Those feelings helped fuel the Witchcraft revival that took off in the 1950s, and are still a part of the Craft today. There are sun gods, moon gods, ocean gods, river gods, and sky gods, but the heartbeat of Modern Witchcraft has always worn horns and/or antlers.

One of my mantras in life is *Pan is not Cernunnos*, because history tells us that they are both unique deities separated by both time and geography. But even with that said, it still feels like there might be *something* there connecting the two. Both were gods of hunting, for instance, and both enjoyed the benefits of more urban areas, Pan with his love of wine and Cernunnos with his ever-present torc. One does not make a torc while living in isolation, and crafting wine takes the combined efforts of many people. Cernunnos and

Pan are very different deities, but because of my own experiences, I simply cannot discount the idea that they might be part of a greater whole.

As we've grown as a society, we've come to understand that gender is not simply a matter of "male" and "female," and that there are many identities on the gender spectrum. The fact that Elen of the Ways has emerged and taken her place next to other horned Witch deities during this time can't be a coincidence. The existence of female versions of Pan, Cernunnos, and the Green Man in antiquity suggests that the "Horned God" has always reflected all of humanity. The Horned God represents all different kinds of Witches. There's a way for every Witch to see themselves in the mysteries of the Horned One.

Herne is now a presence in Witch rituals around the globe, all while he still runs wild and free through Windsor Forest. The Green Man looks down at us from old church walls, yet he lives in the bushes and trees just outside our front door. The Dread Lord of Shadows stands at the gates of death and rebirth, yet I also see his fingerprints in my garden and on the branches of the trees that surround my street. The Horned One exists in all of these places simultaneously; he lives between worlds and is a part of our world.

On centuries-old woodcuts, Witches from long ago dance with a shadowy figure that artists have always tried to make look menacing and evil; but instead, that figure nearly always appears joyous and welcoming. Even when people have tried to intentionally distort the significance of the Horned God, they have rarely succeeded. Various forces over the centuries have fought to suppress the light of wisdom and knowledge, but that light always shines through, often carried forward by the Horned One.

We all interact differently with deity. The Horned God that I know may not be exactly the same Horned God that you work with, and that's okay. I've always thought it was the epitome of hubris for any human to think that they alone truly understand the nature of deity. The gods were around before us and will be around after us; they do not operate in the same way that human beings do. In that sense, it's possible that there are many different horned gods, with each of us interacting with the one that's best for us.

My Horned God will always be a combination of many different beings, and our understanding of him has been shaped by multiple writers and artists. My Horned God is a very real being made up of Pan, Cernunnos, Dionysus, Herne, Elen, the Green Man, Lucifer, and dozens more. He is a being with many names and many faces. I honor that being as a collective and as individual parts of a greater whole. I also know that he is all of those things and more, and none of those things and less, depending on who is working with him.

This book is full of history that endeavors to explain the origins of the Horned God as we know him today. There are also rituals, spells, and other activities designed to help build a relationship with that figure. But the Horned God doesn't live in the pages of books; he lives in the woods, in the wild spaces, on our altars, and in our hearts. We can only come to truly know the Horned One by working with him in the ways that make sense to us. So if you truly want to feel the power of the Horned One, mutter a prayer to Faunus, pour a libation to Dionysus, or perform a ritual in honor of Old Hornie, however you see them.

Hail the Horned One, the God of the Witches!

ACKNOWLEDGMENTS

I feel like every book I write these days presents its own unique challenges, but this one in particular was especially difficult. The Horned God is an endless source of historical fascination to me, but the Horned One is also a very real presence in my life. I didn't want to write just a history book or just a book of rituals; I thought it was important to include both of those aspects in this work. I also tried to approach the historical part as honestly as possible, without sounding like I'm an unbeliever.

The Horned God is a fascinating piece of modern mythology yet with very real ties to the ancient world. Hornie has also appeared to Modern Witches in a variety of guises, and I wanted to explore as many of those as possible in three hundred pages. I don't know if I've really succeeded in any of my goals, but I do feel like I gave it my best shot.

This book went through several drafts (which is completely different from my past books), and at one point I scrapped most of it because it was quickly starting to feel less like an approachable book and more like a term paper. If you think this version is long on history and footnotes, the first draft was much worse, and far too clinical. Perhaps more importantly, it completely failed to capture my love for old Horn Head. I'm not sure if this later draft is really that much better, and if you fell asleep on footnote number 212, I'm sincerely apologetic.

This is my seventh book for Llewellyn, and I can't thank the people there enough. Somehow they make my scribblings both presentable and readable. Hats off to my amazing editor Elysia Gallo, who knows exactly when something is lacking and when it's not. Elysia has probably been far too indulgent of me, with my knack for writing long books and my unwillingness to cut anything. (She thought the Krampus section could be shorter. I thought it could be longer!)

This book was months overdue by the time I turned it in, a victim of my difficulty in writing it, an insane travel schedule, and the depression that came about by writing a large chunk of it during COVID-19. But E was already sympathetic, and the extra time I got for this book made it better. Besides, by the time this is published, I'll have released seven books in just six years; it's hard to get blood from a stone. Thank you, E, you are the best at what you do and one of my favorite people to boot.

The name Andrea Neff is not a well-known one in Pagan circles, but she's the genius who edits all of this stuff line by line and removes all of my many typos. She also has to go through all of my footnotes, a thankless and time-consuming job. She has my sympathy and deserves yours too. I've been working with Andrea since *The Witch's Athame* in 2016, and during that time she's come to feel more like a collaborator than an editor. Words cannot express my appreciation.

Bill Krause is the publisher at Llewellyn, and ultimately he decides what gets the go-ahead when it comes to printing stuff. That he has felt the need to print seven books with "Mankey" on the cover is still beyond my wildest dreams. He's also a great guy to hang out with while sharing a dram of Scotch.

My love of the Horned God in the Pagan and Witch communities is not an isolated thing, and I've been inspired by many others. One of the most important of those voices is John Beckett, whose love for Cernunnos feels nearly limitless. John inspires me to be a better Pagan and a better person. Gwion Raven is one of my best friends on the planet, and his devotion to C is so large that it takes up his entire back (it's a tattoo). I love you both, I really do.

I have a really good Pagan writing support group, and a few individuals who need to be named specifically. Astrea Taylor was a major help during the writing of this book just by being generally fantastic and supportive and willing to text or talk on the phone when I found myself plagued with doubt. Laura Tempest Zakroff remains one of my favorite people in the world, and judging by her art (she did the cover!), she knows the Horned God better than I do. That you were the one to do the cover art for this book, Tempest, means more to me than I can put into words. Thank you for the huge impact you've had on my life. I wouldn't be here without you.

When I have questions about the Craft or just feel like I'm wandering lost in the woods, I tend to text Thorn Mooney. Not only is Thorn a great source of moral support, but she's also my go-to when I have questions about Wiccan-Witchcraft. Misha Magdalene's approval of this book means the world to me, and I hope it takes us a step further to a better and more inclusive Witchcraft. Kelden has been my guide to the world of Traditional Witchcraft for the past four years or so. No one writes about the subject with such clarity. We also share nerdy obsessions with much of this stuff. Special thanks to Angus McMahan for instigating the Green Mile of the Horned God, I still get shivers when I read the words from that rite.

I have an extended writing community to thank, too: Heron Michelle, Lilith Dorsey, Phoenix LeFae, Mat Auryn, Devin Hunter, Storm Faerywolf, Martha Kirby Capo, Sorita d'Este, Madame Pamita, Christopher Orapello, Tara-Love Maguire, Patrick Dunn (thank you so much for your gorgeous translation of the Orphic Hymn for Pan!), and the dozens of other people I'm forgetting. Special thanks to those who have helped during my many Horned God rituals over the years, including Kirk Thomas, Utu Witchdoctor, Vicki Vaughn, and Pam Pamdemonium. I know I'm forgetting lots of other people here again, but it's late as I write this, and this book is very much overdue.

Much appreciation to Bali and Geraldine Beskin at the Atlantis Bookshop in London, and Christina Oakley Harrington at Treadwell's also in London. It both blows my mind and makes the world seem so much smaller that I know people in London, and they seem to like me. Book signings at Atlantis have been some of the best moments of my life.

Pat and Paul at Artes & Craft in Michigan don't only make the best incense in the world, but have also been extremely supportive and encouraging the past five years. Thank you both. My first "home bookstore" was Triple Goddess Books in Lansing, Michigan. Dawne and Alan went to Ari and I's wedding. The connections run deep! Closer to home today in California there's Leigh's Favorite Books, run by the amazing Leigh Odum. Leigh's hosted my first-ever book signing. Last but not least, thanks to Susan Diamond and Wolf at Serpent's Kiss in Santa Cruz, California, for throwing the absolute best book launch parties.

There are a lot of great Witch and occult bookstores out there. The ones listed here are among my favorites. I'm a child of books and wouldn't be here without them.

Dad, you continue to be great. There's nothing much else to say. This is my seventh book; can you believe that? I sometimes have to pinch myself.

So many Pagans, so many festivals over the years. To everyone I've met, chatted with, shared a drink with, or most especially talked about the Horned God with at ConVocation, HexFest, Brushwood, Starwood, Earth Warriors, Pagan Unity Festival, Heartland, Mystic South, Pagan Spirit Gathering, Paganicon, Wiccan Fest, PantheaCon, Hexenfest, and all the other festivals I'm forgetting, this book would not exist without you.

Special thanks to Christopher Penczak, who inspired this book way back in 2005. You probably don't remember that, Christopher, but I'm a lot like Pepperidge Farms: I always remember. You are an inspiration to many of us out there.

Back in my Witchling days, I wrote an early version of this book called simply *The Horned God*. It wasn't completely terrible, but it wasn't good either. If you bought a copy of that book, I'm especially appreciative. My friend Sable Aradia (a terrific author herself) gave it a very favorable review a few years ago, leading me to believe she must have ingested several hallucinogens while reading it. Anyway, your kind words inspired me to give a Horned

God book another shot. Thanks to Sable and everyone who had kind words to say to me on my first attempt at writing a book.

As always, I'm most indebted to my beautiful and loving wife, Ari, who puts up with my book writing with patience and grace. As I write these words, her sleep is most likely being plagued by the clickety-clack of my mechanical keyboard as the clock approaches midnight. Why she puts up with me, I'll never know, but I'm grateful she does. I love you, my dear.

While putting the finishing touches on the version of the book that you now hold in your hands, I suddenly remembered that it was being published on the 100th anniversary of Margaret Murray's *The Witch-Cult in Western Europe*. The importance of Murray's work in the Witchcraft revival is often overlooked. I don't think it's an exaggeration to suggest that the Craft many of us love so much in all of its forms would not exist without Dr. Murray's work. I'm often critical of Murray's claims regarding Witches, but her impact on Witchcraft is undeniable, and she had a similar impact on academia. Thank you, Dr. Murray.

This book is dedicated to the memory of Dwayne Arthur Sortor, who was my first ever friend in Pagandom. Dwayne encouraged me to write from the moment we met nearly twenty-five years ago, and his impact on my Craft has been enormous. Dwayne passed far too soon in April of 2020, as I was finishing up this book. You will be missed, my friend.

And finally, thanks to all of you reading these words. These books would not exist without readers, and I remain quite humbled that people are willing to shell out twenty bucks to read the things I write. Thank you for being a part of this journey.

Io Pan!

Jason W. Mankey

April–June 2020 and January 2021

BIBLIOGRAPHY

THERE ARE OVER TWO hundred and seventy citations in this book, which I think is a record for me. I'm sorry in advance, but heck, you've come this far, so what's another 4,500 words? Besides, I've had people tell me they think my bibliographies are rather fun to read because I include my thoughts on many of the sources I use! In addition to the materials cited in this book, my experiences with and understanding of the Horned God have been influenced by dozens of other writers. Witchcraft is very much a religion or practice "of the books," and I'm very much a Witch of those books. There are many drawbacks to our modern age, but access to information and books is not one of them. We are living in a golden age of Witch publishing. Dig in!

Amos, Jonathan. "Ancient Phallus Unearthed in Cave." BBC News, July 25, 2005, http://news.bbc.co.uk/2/hi/science/nature/4713323.stm. I'm guessing my father never dreamed I'd be citing something with the title "Ancient Phallus Unearthed in Cave." I hope he's proud.

Anderson, William. *Green Man: The Archetype of Our Oneness with the Earth.* San Francisco, CA: HarperSanFrancisco, 1990. Though I disagree with some of the history in Anderson's book, it's still wonderful. This book is jam-packed with pictures (many in color) from all over Europe and explores the Green Man mystery inside and out. I will say this often in this bibliography, but I love this book!

Arnold, Matthew. *Complete Poetical Works of Matthew Arnold.* Hastings, East Sussex, UK: Delphi Classics, 2013. In the book I quote the poem "Lines Written in Kensington Gardens." While the works of most poets from the Romantic and Victorian eras can easily be found for free online, citing such poems in a book like this one requires an official source. To read Arnold, one does not have to invest any cash.

Bacon, Francis. *Bacon's Essays & Wisdom of the Ancients.* Boston, MA: Little, Brown, and Co., 1884. The relevant part here is *Wisdom of the Ancients,* and not so much the essays. I feel so literary that Francis Bacon is in my bibliography!

Balter, Michael. *The Goddess and the Bull: Çatalhöyük: An Archaeological Journey to the Dawn of Civilization.* New York: Free Press, 2005. If you're looking for an extensive look into Çatalhöyük, then you might be disappointed in this book. The focus here is mostly (but not completely) on the excavations that have taken place there. Those looking for their biases to be confirmed, especially ones pertaining to matriarchal prehistory, will be disillusioned and angry, but for those of you who enjoy a good archaeological yarn (and who doesn't?), this book is recommended. I'm sure this book is out in paperback; I own the hardcover.

Barrett, Clive. *The Egyptian Gods & Goddesses.* London: Diamond Books, 1996. I purchased this in Ann Arbor, Michigan, sometime in the late 1990s. Just commenting because I've owned this book for a couple of decades now, and also because Ann Arbor is a very cool city, despite it being the home of the Michigan Wolverines. (Go Green! Go White!)

Bell, Robert, ed. *Ancient Poems, Ballads, and Songs of the Peasantry of England.* London: J. W. Parker & Son, 1857. There are probably hundreds of rituals that could be built around the songs in this collection.

Boardman, John. *The Great God Pan: The Survival of an Image.* New York: Thames & Hudson, 1996. This is an adorable little book and covers over 2,500 years of Pan imagery.

Bober, Phyllis Fray. "Cernunnos: Origin and Transformation of a Celtic Divinity." *American Journal of Archaeology* vol. 55, no. 1 (January 1951): 13–51. https://www.jstor.org/stable/501179. This is a fantastic paper dedicated to all things Cernunnos. It also contains a lot of pictures, so you can see the other Cernunnos imagery not included in this book.

Borgeaud, Philippe. *The Cult of Pan in Ancient Greece.* Translated by Kathleen Atlass and James Redfield. Chicago, IL: University of Chicago Press, 1988. There are so many footnotes referencing this book in the Pan chapter that I feel kind of guilty about it, but there's nothing else like this book. For whatever reason, Pan just isn't on the radar of many scholars, leading me to have to go this route. It's a terrific book, though, and easy enough to read for an academic text if you want more info on Pan—and I know you want more info on Pan.

Bowler, Gerry. *Santa Claus: A Biography.* Toronto: McClelland & Stewart, 2005. Bowler is a one-man Christmas cottage industry, having written nearly half a dozen books on the subject. I don't agree with all of his thoughts on Santa, but we can't have everything. I wrote my own book on Yule, *Llewellyn's Little Book of Yule*, in 2020. I realize that's not really relevant, but I couldn't pass up the opportunity for a plug. If you've read this deep into the book, you probably like my work. I also cite Bowler's *The World Encyclopedia of Christmas* in the Krampus section. That book was also published by McClelland and Stewart back in 2004.

Boys-Stones, George. *L. Annaeus Cornutus: Greek Theology, Fragments, and Testimonia.* Atlanta, GA: SBL Press, 2018. Cornutus has even more to say about Pan in his work than what I quoted in this book. Boys-Stones translation is also revelatory, and a bit different from previous ones.

Burkert, Walter. *Greek Religion: Archaic and Classical.* Translated by John Raffan. Oxford: Wiley-Blackwell, 1991. This is probably *the* standard textbook for armchair historians interested in Greek religion. There's so much in this book, every time I go back to it, I tend to find something I've missed previously.

Cochrane, Robert, with Evan John Jones. *The Robert Cochrane Letters: An Insight into Modern Traditional Witchcraft.* Edited by Michael Howard. Milverton, Somerset, UK: Capall Bann, 2002. Most of Cochrane's letters can be easily found online, but there's something nice about having them in printed form with notes from Michael Howard.

————. *The Roebuck in the Thicket: An Anthology of the Robert Cochrane Witchcraft Tradition.* Milverton, Somerset, UK: Capall Bann, 2001. This one features more of Evan John Jones than Cochrane, but I'm probably an even bigger fan of Jones's work!

Congail, Mac. "Cernunnos and the Ram-Headed Serpent." BalkanCelts. 2015 and 2019. https://balkancelts.wordpress.com/2015/07/04/cernunnos -and-the-ram-headed-serpent/.

Conway, D. J. *Lord of Light and Shadow: The Many Faces of the God.* St. Paul, MN: Llewellyn, 1997. This book is very much a product of its time, which means a lot of the information in it is not very good. It's worth pointing out, though, that no one in the Witch community was ever intentionally trying to mislead anyone on matters of history; we just simply didn't know better back then. That being said, this book is still a wonderful introduction to how people view the God of Wicca.

Crowley, Aleister. *The Equinox: Volume 3, Number 1* (most commonly known as *The Blue Equinox,* due to its cover being blue), 1919, and *Liber Liberi vel Lapidis Lazuli* (more commonly known as *Liber VII*), 1904. The latter can be found on the O.T.O.'s online library: https://lib.oto-usa.org/libri/liber0007.html. Tracking down specific Crowley material can be a frustrating task. That will most likely improve in the coming years, as Crowley's material is now in the public domain in the United States. Prior to that, much of it was illegally bootlegged, though the O.T.O. has released several fine collections of Crowleyana over the years, generally through the publisher Samuel Weiser. The bits from Crowley included in this book can easily be read online, though I'm hopeful someone will put together a handsome and well-edited edition of Crowley's poetry over the next few years. Crowley's influence on Modern Witchcraft cannot be overstated.

Cunningham, Scott. *Wicca: A Guide for the Solitary Practitioner.* St. Paul, MN: Llewellyn, 1989. Cunningham's *Wicca* has been widely influential and is a well-written and easily accessible introduction to Wicca, but I think a lot of it doesn't hold up very well in 2021. This was one of the first books to ever include *Wicca* in the title, and the first book to use that word that attracted a large audience. Over twenty-five years after Cunningham's passing, his influence is bigger and stronger than ever.

Curtis, Gregory. *The Cave Painters: Probing the Mysteries of the World's First Artists.* New York: Oxford University Press, 2009. Since this book was released, a lot of new information has come to light about the painted caves in France, Spain, and Portugal, and they keep finding new ones, many of which are older than the previously discovered ones.

Dalrymple, William. *Nine Lives: In Search of the Sacred in Modern India.* London: Bloomsbury, 2013. I picked up this book on a lark at Heathrow Airport while heading home from London, and finished it while flying over Greenland. If you are wondering what true polytheistic culture might look like, this book is a great place to start. Captivating.

Daniélou, Alain. *The Phallus: Sacred Symbol of Male Creative Power.* Rochester, VT: Inner Traditions, 1995. This book is focused primarily on phallus imagery in India and Asia, so it didn't really apply to this work, but for those wanting a little more phallus mythology, it's worth picking up. This book might be even more valuable for its images than its text. There are some absolutely beautiful pictures here, most in full color.

D'Aulaire, Ingri, and Edgar Parin D'Aulaire. *D'Aulaires' Book of Greek Myths.* Garden City, NY: Doubleday, 1962. Did you own a copy of this book as a kid? I did not, but I checked it out from my elementary school library two dozen times. I still enjoy reading it, even if some of it is now humorous to me.

Deo Mercurio. "Kapnonoy: to Carnonos." http://www.deomercurio.be/en /cernunnos.html#carnonon. This website is dedicated to all religious things Gaulish. The page there on Cernunnos is quite satisfying.

Doniger, Wendy. *The Hindus: An Alternative History.* New York: Penguin Press, 2009. Highly recommended if you want to know about Hinduism or gods such as Shiva. While written for a general audience, this is still a challenging book, and you might want to take notes to keep things from getting confusing as you go through the different eras of Indian history.

Don's Maps: Resources for the Study of Paleolithic/Paleolithic European, Russian and Australian Archaeology/Archeology. https://www.donsmaps .com. Do you like ancient shit? You'll love Don's Maps. There's just a treasure trove of information to be found there. In particular, see "Tools from the Stone Age," https://www.donsmaps.com/tools.html.

Dunn, Patrick. *The Orphic Hymns: A New Translation for the Occult Practitioner.* Woodbury, MN: Llewellyn, 2018. This is a terrific book, and includes not only Dunn's wonderful translations but also some history on the Orphic Hymns, along with suggestions for using them in magickal ritual. It also includes the original English translations by Thomas Taylor from 1792.

Ehrman, Bart D. *Did Jesus Exist?* New York: Harper Collins, 2012. For those interested in Jesus and ancient religions, I can't recommend Ehrman enough. He's easily understood, not an Evangelical, and yet acknowledges that the historical Jesus was most likely a real person. In the Pagan community, there's a tendency to dismiss the historicity of Jesus, a view that is not supported by most scholars of the New Testament.

Elliot, Ben, Becky Knight, and Aimée Little. "Antler Frontlets." In *Star Carr, Volume 2: Studies in Technology, Subsistence and Environment*, edited by Nicky Milner, Chantal Conneller, and Barry Taylor, 297–333. York: White Rose University Press, 2018. https://doi.org/10.22599/book2.l.

Farrar, Janet, and Stewart Farrar. *The Witches' God.* Custer, WA: Phoenix, 1989. Please don't think I'm picking on the Farrars because of my citation in the text. I love the Farrars! *A Witches' Bible* remains a big favorite of mine, and this book, along with its companion volume, *The Witches' Goddess*, were hugely influential in my life. *Eight Sabbats for Witches* was published in 1981 and *The Witches' Way* in 1984, with the two books later republished in one volume as *A Witches' Bible* in 1996.

Fitch, Eric. *In Search of Herne the Hunter.* Chieveley, UK: Capall Bann, 1994. This is one of the best books ever produced on the Horned God. Since Fitch's book is focused squarely on Herne, it covers a lot of ground I didn't get to in this book, specifically some really strange ghost stories from around the Windsor Forest that may involve Herne. Highly recommended! I love this book wholeheartedly. The co-founder of Capall Bann Publishing, Jon Day, passed away in 2015, and with him Capall Bann, so everything from them is quickly becoming a collector's item.

Flecker, James Elroy. *The Collected Poems of James Elroy Flecker.* Edited by J. C. Squire. New York: Doubleday, Page & Co., 1916. I quote the poem "Oak and Olive" in this book.

Frazer, James G. *The Golden Bough: The Roots of Religion and Folklore.* New York: Gramercy, 1993. This particular edition features the abridged version from 1922. I know some Witches find Frazer to be a bore to read, I'm not one of them. I think his prose is poetic and illuminating, but only if you are really interested in a particular topic Frazer is writing about. Frazer is very much a product of his time, which is a nice way of saying that much of the text comes across as racist.

Gardner, Gerald. *Witchcraft Today.* London: Rider and Company, 1954. I wish I had the Rider edition of this book. What I have is a 1999 edition from I-H-O Books that has incorrect page numbers; though, according to Amazon, copies are selling for two hundred bucks today, this edition is not worth five bucks, let alone two hundred. Luckily, *Witchcraft Today* is available for free online, as is Gardner's 1959 *The Meaning of Witchcraft*, which was originally published by Aquarian Press in London. Despite its availability online, I still have a hard copy of *Meaning* from 1991 published by Magickal

Childe out of New York City. Magickal Childe was the publishing house of the bookstore of the same name owned by Herman Slater. There are many Witches who think Gardner is required reading; I'm not one of them. For every five interesting things he says, there are four dozen pieces of poorly regurgitated Margaret Murray.

Gargett, Robert H., et al. "Grave Shortcomings: The Evidence for Neandertal Burial [and Comments and Reply]." *Current Anthropology* vol. 30, no. 2 (1989): 157–190. www.jstor.org/stable/2743544. The only benefit that came from writing this book during the Covid-19 quarantine of 2020 was that a great many scholarly journals offered free access during that period of time. That allowed me to sift through some academic journals, such as this one.

Gary, Gemma. *The Devil's Dozen: Thirteen Craft Rites of the Old One.* London: Troy Books, 2015. Looking for more Traditional Witchcraft rites involving the Horned God? This is the book for you. Gemma Gary is one of the most influential authors writing today about Traditional Witchcraft, and that influence is well deserved. Her books are terrific.

Godwin, Joscelyn. *The Pagan Dream of the Renaissance.* York Beach, ME: Weiser Books, 2005. I'm a huge fan of Godwin's various works. He once wrote a history of esoteric religions confined to Western New York, and it was illuminating! If you like seeing Pagan deities outside of the contexts we generally see them in, meaning the ancient world and the present, this book can't be beat!

Gokhale, Namita. *The Book of Shiva.* New Delhi: Viking, 2001. I chose to leave Shiva out of this work, but he appeared in my first attempt at a Horned God book many years ago. This book is not cited in the text but is included here for those looking for more information on my favorite Indian deity.

Grahame, Kenneth. *The Wind in the Willows.* New York: Charles Scribner's Sons, 1913. I probably read at least parts of *Willows* in elementary school, but I have no real memories of meeting the Piper at the Gates of Dawn back then. Instead, my first real read of *Willows* occurred in my mid-twenties, after embracing Witchcraft and Paganism. When I do workshops on the Horned God, I often end with the Grahame passages quoted in this book, and it's not an exaggeration to say that reading it generally makes me cry. If someone were to ask me to sum up the Horned God in under five hundred words, I'd just quote that bit from Grahame.

Graves, Robert. *The White Goddess: A Historical Grammar of Poetic Myth.* New York: Farrar, Straus, and Giroux, 2001. This book was first published in 1948. My edition was published in 2001. I find Graves difficult reading, but his work had a tremendous impact on Modern Witchcraft, inspiring practitioners like Robert Cochrane and others.

Guiley, Rosemary Ellen. *The Encyclopedia of Witches and Witchcraft.* 2nd ed. New York: Facts on File, 1999. I'm always amazed by the sheer amount of information in this book; it really lives up to its title. Rosemary passed suddenly in 2019, but I was lucky enough to meet her at the HexFest gathering in New Orleans in 2018. I'm thankful to Christian Day and Brian Cain, the organizers of HexFest, for affording me that opportunity.

Hayden, Brian. *Shamans, Sorcerers, and Saints.* Washington, DC: Smithsonian Books, 2003. There are a lot of things wrong with this book, the biggest one being that Hayden seems to be working from a twenty-year-old playbook when it comes to his interpretations of things. However, there's a lot of information in this book, and it's lavishly illustrated for what is essentially a textbook. I like it because of the amount of stuff in it, which provides a great starting point, and from there you can sort of draw your own conclusions.

Hirst, K. Kris. "Qafzeh Cave, Israel: Evidence for Middle Paleolithic Burials." ThoughtCo. Updated November 18, 2019. https://www.thoughtco.com /qafzeh-cave-israel-middle-paleolithic-burials-172284. This is not my usual go-to website when it comes to history, but the information was accurate, and it contained a lot of links.

Hughes, Virginia. "Were the First Artists Mostly Women?" National Geographic. October 9, 2013. https://www.nationalgeographic.com/news/2013

/10/131008-women-handprints-oldest-neolithic-cave-art/. Were the first artists mostly women? The answer seems to be yes!

Hugin the Bard. *A Bard's Book of Pagan Songs: Stories and Music from the Celtic World.* St. Paul, MN: Llewellyn, 1996. When this was originally released, it came with a CD of Hugin singing all the songs in the book. The copy of the CD is long gone at the Mankey household. If you have a copy of it, shoot me an email, because I've never heard it!

Huson, Paul. *Mastering Witchcraft: A Practical Guide for Witches, Warlocks & Covens.* New York: Perigee Books, 1980. Originally published in 1970. Huson's book has had an extraordinary impact on Witchcraft, and fifty years after its initial publication, there's still nothing else like it.

Hutton, Ronald. *The Triumph of the Moon: A History of Modern Pagan Witchcraft.* Oxford, UK: Oxford University Press, 1999. Ronald Hutton released an updated version of this seminal work in 2019 as I was in the process of writing this book. If you find yourself intrigued by the rebirth of Pan in the nineteenth century, Hutton's summary of that information is far more detailed than what is in this book. I'll also admit that I've read this book so many times that I sometimes quote directly from it without a second thought.

———. *Pagan Britain.* Oxford: Oxford University Press, 2014. In many ways, this is an updated version of Hutton's earlier *Pagan Religions of the British Isles* but with more depth and the latest in research. If you say you like Celtic stuff, you owe it to yourself to read this book.

———. *The Stations of the Sun: A History of the Ritual Year in Britain.* New York: Oxford University Press, 1996. An exhaustive and illuminating journey through the holidays celebrated in Great Britain and often beyond.

———. *The Witch: A History of Fear, from Ancient Times to the Present.* New Haven, CT: Yale University Press, 2017. I remember this particular Hutton book as being difficult early on but a great read after the first few chapters. There are some really interesting things in this book that suggest some fascinating Pagan survivals, specifically spectral female visitors who come in the night, which might have played a role in the development of the Wild Hunt.

————. *Witches, Druids, and King Arthur.* London: Hambledon & London, 2003.

Isidore of Seville. *The Etymologies of Isidore of Seville.* Edited and translated by Stephen A. Barney, W. J. Lewis, J. A. Beach, and Oliver Berghof. New York: Cambridge University Press, 2006.

Jackson, Nigel. *The Masks of Misrule: The Horned God & His Cult in Europe.* Chieveley, UK: Capall Bann, 1996. Not that this book is crazy old, but it's old enough that Capall Bann changed addresses between when this was published and some of their later titles. I didn't quote *Masks* in this book, but if you're looking for a history of the Horned God more grounded in mythology and connected to just about everything over the last two thousand years, you'll love this book.

Kaczynski, Richard. *Perdurabo: The Life of Aleister Crowley.* Tempe, AZ: New Falcon Press, 2002. There are many biographies about Crowley that have been written. This one is my favorite.

Keats, John. *The Poetical Works and Other Writings of John Keats.* Edited by Harry Buxton Forman. London: Reeves & Turner, 1889. Keats's "Hymn to Pan" is a part of the much longer *Endymion*. The Pan stuff is fabulous. I want to stage an entire ritual using it in my backyard.

Kelden. *The Crooked Path: An Introduction to Traditional Witchcraft.* Woodbury, MN: Llewellyn, 2020. I don't think anyone writes about Traditional Witchcraft more clearly than Kelden. If you find yourself confused about what Traditional Witches actually do and how to set up a ritual, Kelden is your best bet!

Kerenyi, Carl. *Dionysos: Archetypal Image of Indestructible Life.* Princeton, NJ: Princeton University Press, 1976. I prefer Otto's work, but this is great too, and has more in the way of illustrations. Highly recommended if you like looking at ancient Greek pottery.

Lady Sheba. *The Grimoire of Lady Sheba.* St. Paul, MN: Llewellyn, 2001. Hardcover edition. Sheba's original *Lady Sheba's Book of Shadows* was released in 1971, and an extended version was issued the following year as *The Grimoire of Lady Sheba.* If you're interested in a Sheba book, pick up *Grimoire,* because it has more stuff in it.

Leek, Sybil. *The Complete Art of Witchcraft.* New York: Signet, 1973. The hardcover edition of this book was published in 1971 by the World Publishing Company. For a period of nearly twenty-five years, Sybil Leek was one of the most influential Witches living in the US (and before that England). She released perhaps over a hundred books in her lifetime (most of them about astrology) and was even on a TV game show back in the mid-1960s (you can find this on YouTube). Her written work hasn't aged very well but is still worth picking up for its historical value. All of Leek's work is now sadly out of print, and used copies of her mass-market paperback output often begin at thirty bucks. Dear publishers who might be reading this, I'm down to edit a Sybil Leek anthology if you can figure out the thorny copyright issues.

Leins, Ian. *Celts: Art and Identity.* London: British Museum Press, 2015. This book was released to coincide with *The Celts* exhibition hosted first by the British Museum in London and then the National Museum of Scotland in Edinburgh, where we caught the exhibit. The night before visiting, I caught a pretty nasty head cold on our trip, but nothing was going to keep me from seeing the Gundestrup cauldron. Post-museum trip, I went to bed and slept for the next eighteen hours. Useless information like me having a cold in Scotland is why some people enjoy reading my bibliographies.

Leland, Charles Godfrey. *Aradia, or the Gospel of the Witches,* 1899. There are lots of versions of *Aradia* out there, and many of them can be found (legally) online. My favorite is the Mario and Dina Pazzaglini edition that came out in 1998 through Phoenix Publishing, though I just yanked what I used in this book off the Sacred Texts website (https://www.sacred-texts.com/pag/aradia/index.htm). The Pazzaglini edition includes the original text, a new translation based on Leland's notes (sadly, his original sources are nowhere to be found), and several informative essays.

Link, Luther. *The Devil: The Archfiend in Art from the Sixth to the Sixteenth Century.* New York: Harry N. Abrams, 1996. This book more than lives up to its title. Not only is it full of art, but it's full of history and explanation too. I weirdly own way too many books about the Christian Devil.

Livingstone, Josephine. "The Remarkable Persistence of the Green Man." *The New Yorker*, March 7, 2016. https://www.newyorker.com/books/page -turner/the-remarkable-persistence-of-the-green-man. One of the most interesting things about this short article is that it's really more of a book review than a history of the Green Man, yet Livingstone includes several very informative paragraphs about the history of the Green Man that are mostly absent from other sources.

Lloyd, Michael G. *Bull of Heaven: The Mythic Life of Eddie Buczynski and the Rise of the New York Pagan.* Hubbardston, MA: Asphodel Press, 2012. Though I didn't cite this book in the text, I was reading it while writing much of this book in the spring of 2020, and during that time I found myself appalled at the level of homophobia that was once a part of the Pagan community. I've always found my Wiccan-Witchcraft very LGBTQ+ inclusive, but that wasn't always the case in certain circles and covens. This book is highly rec-ommended for anyone wanting to know about our homophobic past. Don't be put off by the title; while this is nominally a book on the life of New York Witch Ed Buczynski, it's more a greater history of the New York Pagan scene in the 1970s, a history that has a very real overlap with the gay rights movement sparked by the Stonewall riots in 1969. Sorry for the long note here, but if you're a history person, you should pick up this book. It's well worth the investment in money and time.

Malotki, Ekkehart. *Kokopelli: The Making of an Icon.* Lincoln, NE: University of Nebraska Press, 2004. There are lots of books about Kokopelli, and while most of them have very little to say, that's not the case here. Malotki explores the popular Kokopelli petroglyph, and the Hopi kachina Kookopölö, who is directly related to the image most of us are familiar with today. Kokopelli showed up in my first attempt at this book many years ago, and if you want to learn more about him, this is the place to start.

Mankey, Jason, and Laura Tempest Zakroff. *The Witch's Altar: The Craft, Lore & Magick of Sacred Space.* Woodbury, MN: Llewellyn, 2018. Since this book was released just two months before my *Transformative Witchcraft* and Tempest's wonderful *Weaving the Liminal*, we sometimes think of it as our "forgotten" book-baby, but we shouldn't. This is a really fun book, if I do say so myself. Writing a book with Tempest was great. The only downside is that every once in a while, someone thinks we're married as a result. (Tempest is married to Nathaniel and Jason is married to Ari.) There is also at least one footnote in this text referencing *Transformative Witchcraft: The Greater Mysteries*, which was published in January of 2019 by Llewellyn.

Maugham, W. Somerset. *Cakes and Ale; or, The Skeleton in the Cupboard.* London: William Heinemann, 1930. I love that this book is titled *Cakes and Ale*! It's like this book was created for Witches or something. It wasn't really, but I still like that it has a great Pan quote and a phrase that's common in Witch circles.

Merivale, Patricia. *Pan the Goat-God: His Myth in Modern Times.* Cambridge, MA: Harvard University Press, 1969. This is the only book of its kind, I do believe, and it's pretty exhaustive if you're interested in the Pan revival of the nineteenth century. This book was out of print for several decades, with copies routinely going for over a hundred dollars back in the early 2000s; however, I'm happy to report that's no longer the case, as Harvard University Press now publishes the book on demand as part of their Studies in Comparative Literature series. There's even an e-book version of it now too, if that's your preference.

Murray, Margaret Alice. *The Witch-Cult in Western Europe* and *The God of the Witches*, published in 1921 and 1931, respectively. Both of these books are available for free online. Whatever relatives Murray had were simply not interested in her keeping the copyright of her books alive. Out of the two, I think *God of the Witches* is the more informative read. It's also the easiest to digest, as she was writing for a nonacademic audience. Murray's ideas have not held up particularly well from a scholarly standpoint, but as pieces of modern myth, they are extraordinary.

Oates, Shani. *Tubelo's Green Fire.* Oxford: Mandrake of Oxford, 2010. There are several editions of this book. Apparently the hardcover now runs over eight hundred dollars used. This book is not worth eight hundred dollars, but it's interesting. Oates is a former Magister of the Clan of Tubal Cain, making her the heir of Robert Cochrane in a way. I contend that Oates's version of Cochrane's Craft is different from that of the original, but that's just me.

Orapello, Christopher, and Tara-Love Maguire. *Besom, Stang & Sword: A Guide to Traditional Witchcraft, the Six-Fold Path & the Hidden Landscape.* Newburyport, MA: Weiser Books, 2018. This is simply one of the best Traditional Witchcraft books on the market. A lot of Traditional Witchcraft books are intentionally difficult to read, but not so with this book. Highly recommended.

Otto, Walter F. *Dionysus: Myth and Cult.* Dallas, TX: Spring Publications, 1986. First published in 1965. Books specific to the great god Pan are hard to find, that's not the case with Dionysus. I'm not going to tell you that there are dozens and dozens of them, but there are a number of titles full of solid academic information out there. This is one of them and probably my favorite.

Pagels, Elaine. *The Origin of Satan.* New York: Vintage Books, 1995. Pagels is not only a good read, but she's also one of the most influential New Testament scholars of the past forty years.

Parfrey, Adam, and Craig Heimbichner. *Ritual America: Secret Brotherhoods and Their Influence on American Society: A Visual Guide.* Port Townsend, WA: Feral House, 2012. An absolutely beautiful book full of fascinating pictures of histories of American fraternal orders. While the cover features a giant esoteric eye, the contents are rather straightforward.

Pearson, Nigel G. *Treading the Mill: Workings in Traditional Witchcraft.* London: Troy Books, 2017. An earlier edition of this was printed by Capall Bann in 2007. While this book doesn't have much on the subject of treading the mill, it's a really great look at Traditional Witchcraft. Along with Gemma Gary's *The Devil's Dozen*, it features one of the best descriptions of the Horned God in Traditional Witchcraft.

Perkins, Sid. "An Early Start for Some of Europe's Oldest Cave Art." American Association for the Advancement of Science, April 11, 2016. https://www .sciencemag.org/news/2016/04/early-start-some-europe-s-oldest-cave-art.

Pike, Albert. *Morals and Dogma*. Richmond, VA: L. H. Jenkins, 1946. First published in 1871. One of the great things about Pike being dead for over a hundred years now is that his book is available for free online if it's something you want to read. Because of its use in Masonry, it also shows up with some frequency in garage and estate sales.

RavenWolf, Silver. *To Ride a Silver Broomstick*. St. Paul, MN: Llewellyn, 1993. Along with Cunningham's *Wicca*, this is probably *the* Generation X Witchcraft book, though some of my millennial friends argue that it's their book. Since I read this book while wearing flannel and listening to Nine Inch Nails, I'm pretty sure I'm right.

Riel-Salvatore, Julien, and Geoffrey A. Clark. "Grave Markers: Middle and Early Upper Paleolithic Burials and the Use of Chronotypology in Contemporary Paleolithic Research." *Current Anthropology* vol. 42, no. 4 (August/October 2001): 449–479. More academic journals, yay.

Rott, Nathan. "Decline in Hunters Threatens How U.S. Pays for Conservation." National Public Radio, March 20, 2018. https://www.npr.org/2018/03 /20/593001800/decline-in-hunters-threatens-how-u-s-pays-for-conservation.

Selk, Avi. "Falsely Accused of Satanic Horrors, A Couple Spent 21 Years in Prison. Now They're Owed Millions." *Washington Post*, August 25, 2017. https: //www.washingtonpost.com/news/acts-of-faith/wp/2017/08/24/accused -of-satanism-they-spent-21-years-in-prison-they-were-just-declared-innocent-and-were-paid-millions/. We tend to think of the innocent victims of Satanic panic as ancient history, but there were still people in prison for phantom crimes into the 2000s! It pays to be ever vigilant.

Serith, Ceisiwr. "Cernunnos: Looking a Different Way." Ceisiwr Serith's Homepage. http://www.ceisiwrserith.com/therest/Cernunnos/cernunnos paper.htm. In the Pagan community, and probably even outside of it, no one knows more about Cernunnos than Serith. Due to space and time considerations, I've only scratched the surface of Cernunnos in this book. If you want to learn more about the antlered god of Gaul, you should start here.

Shakespeare, William. *The Merry Wives of Windsor.* In *The Yale Shakespeare: The Complete Works.* Edited by Wilbur L. Cross and Tucker Brooke. New York: Barnes & Noble Books, 1993. At over a foot tall, this is the largest book in my wife and I's library. It also weighs several pounds, which makes looking up citations in it rather tedious. While the name for the author included here is "William Shakespeare," I'm a rather committed Oxfordian and believe that the 17th Earl of Oxford, Edward de Vere, is the actual author of the plays. My wife was horrified when I wore a T-shirt to the Globe Theatre in London with a picture of de Vere on it and the words "Team Edward."

Shelley, Percy Bysshe. *The Complete Poetical Works of Percy Bysshe Shelley, Vol. 1.* Edited by Thomas Hutchinson. New York: Oxford University Press, 1914. It's not a surprise that I quote from the *Hymn of Pan* in this book. I was mostly an indifferent student in high school, but I vividly remember studying the Romantic era poets during my senior year. I was a fan of Shelley and Keats long before I was a Pagan.

———. *The Letters of Percy Bysshe Shelley: Vol. 2, Shelley in Italy.* Edited by Frederick L. Jones. Oxford: Clarendon Press, 1964. I find it so easy to get lost in the Pagan-longings of Shelley and those in his orbit.

Smith, Jonathan Z. "Dying and Rising Gods." In vol. 4, *Encyclopedia of Religion,* edited by Mircea Eliade. New York, Macmillan, 1987.

Starhawk. *The Spiral Dance: A Rebirth of the Ancient Religion of the Goddess.* San Francisco, CA: Harper & Row, 1979. I originally owned the second edition of this book that came out in 1989, but someone stole it from me! (I guess they needed it more than I did.) Several years later, I purchased the original edition because I'm a history nerd. Anyway, this is one of the most important books in the Witchcraft revival, and if you don't agree with Starhawk's fusing of spirituality and politics, you should still read it because it's been so wildly influential.

Stavish, Mark. *Freemasonry: Rituals, Symbols & History of the Secret Society.* Woodbury, MN: Llewellyn, 2007. A useful and easy-to-read history of Masonry, including its more esoteric parts. Stavish is much nicer to Albert Pike than I am.

Stewart, R. J. *Celtic Gods, Celtic Goddesses.* London: Cassell, 1990. There's stuff I agree with in this book and stuff I don't. I think much of Stewart's take on Cernunnos is rather fanciful, but at the same time, isn't that how a lot of Modern Witches perceive Cernunnos? Should I tell them they are all wrong? I don't think so. It's also worth noting that the illustrations in this book are absolutely gorgeous, so it's worth picking up for the art alone.

Storl, Wolf-Dieter. *Shiva: The Wild God of Power and Ecstasy.* Rochester, VT: Inner Traditions, 2004. There are issues with this book, and times when Wolf-Dieter simply gets history wrong, but there's still a lot of Shiva information here, and it's often contrasted with other gods from around the world.

Swinburne, Algernon Charles. *Selected Poems.* Edited by L. M. Findlay. Manchester: Carcanet Press, 1982. In chapter 11 of this book, I quote two stanzas from "A Nympholept," which was first published in 1894 as part of the collection *Astrophel and Other Poems*, but there's much more to Swinburne's work worth reading than that one poem. In fact, Swinburne is my favorite poet quoted in this book. Be sure to look up "Hertha," another forgotten Swinburne masterpiece that you'll want to throw into a ritual.

Teagasc: The Agriculture and Food Development Authority. "Harvest." Accessed February 11, 2021. https://www.teagasc.ie/crops/crops/cereal-crops/spring-cereals/harvests/.

Thompson, R. Lowe. *The History of the Devil, the Horned God of the West: Magic and Worship.* Home Farm Books, 2013. Originally published in 1929. While finishing up this book, I came across Thompson's *History of the Devil* and became worried that it would require me to rewrite a few chapters in the book you now hold in your hands. I erroneously saw the original publication date as 1919 instead of 1929, which might have made Thompson, and not Margaret Murray, one of the most influential people in the development of the Horned God. Most of what's in Thompson's book is a deep dive into the ideas of Murray as found in *The Witch-Cult in Western Europe*, but it's notable because of its use of the term *Horned God* (note the capital letters) throughout the text and its attempts to link Cernunnos to the Christian Devil. It's even possible that Thompson's ideas on the subject of the Horned God influenced Murray's 1931 *The God of the Witches*, but she doesn't cite his work, and given how long it takes to get a book written and published, it's unlikely (though again, not impossible).

Valiente, Doreen. *Witchcraft for Tomorrow.* London: Robert Hale, 1978. No Witchcraft book is complete without some Doreen in the bibliography! She is one of the five most influential Witches ever. *Witchcraft for Tomorrow* was one of the first how-to books, though it's often overlooked today, most likely because Valiente's books never got as much distribution in the United States as they deserved.

———. *The Rebirth of Witchcraft.* Custer, WA: Phoenix Publishing, 1989. *Rebirth* is Valiente's memoir, and it's aptly titled, as she was there for many of Witchcraft's most important moments throughout the 1950s, 1960s, 1970s, and into the 1990s. A biography of Valiente was released a few years ago by historian Philip Heselton, and it's great, but Valiente's writing is so vivid in this book that it mostly felt redundant. This is an essential piece of Craft history. Also, I point this out in every book I write: Doreen and I share a birth date—January 4!

West, M. L. *Indo-European Poetry and Myth.* Oxford: Oxford University Press, 2007. As we near the end of this bibliography, I'm reminded of how many times I've said "I really love this book," but every time I do, it's true! I promise, I do really love this book.

Wise, Caroline. "Elen of the Ways, Parts 1 & 2." AndrewCollins.Com. 2007. Accessed February 2, 2021. https://www.andrewcollins.com/page/articles

/elen_1.htm and https://www.andrewcollins.com/page/articles/elen_2.htm. In addition to these articles, Wise released a book in 2015 titled *Finding Elen: The Quest for Elen of the Ways* through CreateSpace. In addition, there are several other small books about Elen that have been released over the last ten years by devotees and worshippers.

Wood, Pete. "John Barleycorn Revisited: Evolution and Folk Song." November 2, 2010. http://www.mustrad.org.uk/articles/j_barley.htm#top. There's a lot more that could be written about John Barleycorn than what's included in this book. Wood's essay, parts of which were first published in a 2004 edition of *Folk Music Journal*, is a great place to start.

Wordsworth, William. *The Complete Works of William Wordsworth.* Edited by Alexander Balloch Grosart. Amazon Services, 2014. Wordsworth is a true and deserving giant of English literature.

Wray, T. J., and Gregory Mobley. *The Birth of Satan: Tracing the Devil's Biblical Roots.* New York: Palgrave Macmillan, 2005. If you want an easy to read yet scholarly examination of how "the obstacle" became Satan, the Prince of Darkness, you'll enjoy this book.

Young, Rob. *Electric Eden: Unearthing Britain's Visionary Music.* New York: Farrar, Straus, and Giroux, 2011. It's weird just how much music and Paganism interact, and there are few books that illustrate this connection better than *Electric Eden*. If you're looking for some Pagan music for your next sabbat celebration or get-together, you'll find something in this book.

ART CREDITS

1. Bison-Man: Illustration of Homme masque en Bison jouant de la flute from the Wellcome Collection
2. The Sorcerer: from the Wellcome Collection
3. Pan: from the Wellcome Collection
4. A sacrifice for Pan: "Sacrifice to the God Pan" by Jean Jacques Lagrenée (ca. 1760–63) from the Yale University Art Gallery
5. "Attic Black-Figure Column Krater," Artist/Maker: Painter of Munich 1736 (Greek (Attic), active about 520 BC). Digital image courtesy of the Getty's Open Content Program
6. Val Camonica rock drawing by Laura Tempest Zakroff
7. Gundestrup cauldron: photographer: Lennart Larsen, from the Ancient Denmark, National Museum
8. Gundestrup cauldron detail, from the Ancient Denmark, National Museum
9. The Reims stela: Cernunnos. Autel de Cernunnos, Reims, Musée Saint-Remi (inv. 978.20189). Photo: © Devleeschauwer Christian
10. A Green Man drawing by Laura Tempest Zakroff
11. Herne the Hunter drawing by Laura Tempest Zakroff
12. Elen of the Ways drawing by Laura Tempest Zakroff
13. Lucifer: GettyImages/476658332/THEPALMER

14. A Delightful Devil: The History of Witches and Wizards, 1720, from the Wellcome Collection
15. Robin Goodfellow drawing by Laura Tempest Zakroff
16. Baphomet drawing by Tim Foley
17. Krampus: Getty / 462374357 / xochicalco
18. Dread Lord of Shadows: GettyImages / 1134256597 / Daniel Eskridge
19. Horned God: GettyImages / 451166349 / xochicalco

INDEX

TO WRITE TO THE AUTHOR

If you wish to contact the author or would like more information about this book, please write to the author in care of Llewellyn Worldwide Ltd. and we will forward your request. Both the author and the publisher appreciate hearing from you and learning of your enjoyment of this book and how it has helped you. Llewellyn Worldwide Ltd. cannot guarantee that every letter written to the author can be answered, but all will be forwarded. Please write to:

Jason Mankey
℅ Llewellyn Worldwide
2143 Wooddale Drive
Woodbury, MN 55125-2989

Please enclose a self-addressed stamped envelope for reply, or $1.00 to cover costs. If outside the U.S.A., enclose an international postal reply coupon.

Many of Llewellyn's authors have websites with additional information and resources. For more information, please visit our website at http://www.llewellyn.com.